LIFE SKILLS 4 AND TEST PREP

Wendy Pratt Long Dawn Furushima
Garnet Templin-Imel

Life Skills and Test Prep 4

Pearson Education, 10 Bank Street, White Plains, NY 10606

Acknowledgments: The authors wish to acknowledge with gratitude the following reviewers, who helped shape the content and approach of the *Life Skills and Test Prep* series: Dr. Maria H. Koonce, Broward County Schools, Ft. Lauderdale, FL • Dr. G. Santos, The English Center, Miami, FL • Edith Uber, Santa Clara Adult Education, Santa Clara, CA • Merari L. Weber, Metropolitan Skills Center, Glendale Community College, Los Angeles, CA • Theresa Warren, East Side Union High School District, San Jose, CA.

Staff credits: The people who made up the *Life Skills and Test Prep 4* team, representing editorial, production, design, and manufacturing, are Tracey Cataldo, Dave Dickey, Christine Edmonds, Irene Frankel, Katherine Keyes, Susan Lanzano and Jane Townsend.

Cover Image: José Ortega c/o theispot.com
Text composition: ElectraGraphics, Inc.
Text font: 11 pt Minion
Illustrations: Steve Attoe: pp. 2, 29, 51, 64, 94, 109, 112, 113; Gary Torrisi: pp. 22, 24, 34, 62, 67, 118, 122, 123, 133.
Technical art: Tinge Design Studio

Library of Congress Cataloging-in-Publication Data
Furushima, Dawn.
Life skills and test prep 4 / Dawn Furushima, Wendy Long, Garnet Templin-Imel.
p. cm.
Includes bibliographical references.
ISBN 978-0-13-208573-1 (student bk.)—ISBN 978-0-13-208575-5
(student bk. audio cd 4)—ISBN 978-0-13-208574-8 (teacher's manual 4)
1. English language—Textbooks for foreign speakers. 2. English
language—Examinations—Study guides. 3. Life skills—Problems,
exercises, etc. I. Long, Wendy. II. Templin-Imel, Garnet. III. Title.
IV. Title: Life skills and test prep four.
PE1128.F87 2009
428.2'4—dc22

2008039969

ISBN-13: 978-0-13-208573-1
ISBN-10: 0-13-208573-9

Printed in the United States of America

9 17

Contents

Correlations

Unit 1: Talk about the Past, Plan for the Future	CASAS*	LAUSD**	Florida***
Lesson 1: Personal and Work History	0.1.2, 0.1.4, 0.1.5, 0.2.1, 4.1.5, 4.1.6	IH/A-1b, 34, 36 IH/B-1a, 31a, 31b	5.03.02
Lesson 2: Indentifying Interests and Skills	0.2.2, 4.1.9, 7.1.4, 7.2.6, 7.5.1	IH/A-1b IH/B-3	5.01.03
Lesson 3: Educational Opportunities	2.1.8, 2.5.5, 2.8.1, 2.8.2, 2.8.6, 4.1.4, 4.1.8, 7.1.1, 7.2.1, 7.7.3, 7.7.5	IH/A-11b, 11c IH/B-10b, 10c	5.03.05, 5.03.12
Lesson 4: Setting Goals	0.1.2, 0.1.5, 2.8.7, 4.1.8,.4.1.9, 4.4.5, 7.1.1, 7.1.2, 7.1.3, 7.1.4, 7.2.2, 7.2.7	IH/A-42 IH/B-35	5.03.13
Unit 2: Community Life	**CASAS***	**LAUSD****	**Florida*****
Lesson 1: Community Events	1.1.3, 2.5.8, 2.6.1, 2.6.2, 7.2.2, 7.2.4	IH/A-18 IH/B-12, 13	5.02.02
Lesson 2: Directions	0.1.5, 0.1.7, 1.1.3, 1.9.4, 2.2.1, 2.2.5, 6.6.5, 7.4.8	IH/A-16a, 44 IH/B-40	5.02.05
Lesson 3: Recycling	2.5.8, 5.6.4, 5.7.1, 7.2.1, 7.4.4	IH/A-43 IH/B-12, 21	5.02.06
Lesson 4: Postal Services	0.1.2, 0.1.5, 0.1.7, 2.4.2, 2.4.3, 7.2.2	IH/A-17a, 17b, 43, 44 IH/B-12, 40	

*CASAS: Comprehensive Adult Student Assessment Systems Competency List
**LAUSD: Los Angeles Unified School District (ESL Intermediate High A (IH/A) Intermediate High B (IH/B) content standards)
***Florida: Adult ESOL High Intermediate Course Standards

Unit 3: Getting a Job	CASAS*	LAUSD**	Florida***
Lesson 1: Looking for a Job	0.1.5, 4.1.3, 4.1.6	IH/A-34, 44 IH/B-29, 40	5.03.02
Lesson 2: Resumes	0.1.2, 4.1.2, 4.1.6, 7.7.3	IH/A-1a, 37, 44 IH/B-30, 40	5.03.03
Lesson 3: Cover Letters	4.1.2, 4.1.3, 4.1.7,.4.1.8	IH/A-4b, 34 IH/B-4, 29	5.03.03
Lesson 4: Job Applications	0.2.2, 4.1.2, 4.1.6	IH/A-3 IH/B-3	5.03.02
Lesson 5: Job Interviews	0.1.1, 0.1.5, 4.1.4, 4.1.5, 4.1.7, 7.5.6, 8.1.1, 8.1.2, 8.1.4	IH/A-35a, 35b, 35c, 36 IH/B-31a, 31b, 31c	5.01.01, 5.03.04
Lesson 6: Thank-You Notes	0.2.3, 7.5.6	IH/A-43 IH/B-4	5.03.03

Unit 4: Safety and Emergency Planning	CASAS*	LAUSD**	Florida***
Lesson 1: Fire Safety	0.1.7, 1.4.1, 1.4.8, 2.1.2, 2.5.1, 3.4.2, 3.4.7, 3.4.8, 7.2.2, 7.3.2	IH/A-32	5.07.01
Lesson 2: Reporting an Emergency	0.l.5, 0.1.8, 2.1.2, 2.2.1, 2.5.1, 5.3.8, 7.2.2, 7.2.3, 7.2.4, 7.3.4	IH/A-12, 16a IH/B-24a, 42a	5.01.06, 5.07.01
Lesson 3: Emergency Evacuations	0.1.2, 2.5.1, 3.4.7, 3.4.8, 7.2.2, 7.2.5, 7.3.2, 7.3.4, 7.7.3	IH/A-32 IH/B-28	5.02.07

Unit 5: Smart Shopping	CASAS*	LAUSD**	Florida***
Lesson 1: Researching Before You Buy	0.1.2, 0.15, 1.2.1, 1.2.2, 1.2.5, 1.6.5, 7.2.3	IH/A-43 IH/B-17	5.04.03, 5.04.06
Lesson 2: Advertising Techniques	0.1.5, 1.2.1, 1.2.2, 1.2.3, 1.6.1, 1.6.5, 6.4.1, 6.5.1, 7.2.5	IH/A-43 IH/B-18	5.04.03
Lesson 3: Returns and Exchanges	0.1.5, 1.3.3, 1.6.3, 7.3.1, 7.3.2, 7.3.3, 7.3.4, 7.4.5	IH/A-21a, 44 IH/B-40	5.04.02
Lesson 4: Warranties	0.1.5, 1.2.2, 1.2.5, 1.7.1, 7.2.3	IH/A-21a, 44 IH/B-17, 40	5.04.02

Unit 6: Cars	CASAS*	LAUSD**	Florida***
Lesson 1: Buying a Car	1.3.1, 1.8.4, 1.8.6, 1.9.5, 6.0.3, 6.1.4, 6.2.4, 6.5.1, 7.2.3	IH/A-20a, 43, 44 IH/B-14, 17, 40	5.04.01, 5.04.07
Lesson 2: Car Problems and Maintenance	0.1.5, 1.1.1, 1.7.4, 1.7.5, 1.9.6, 7.2.2, 7.2.5	IH/A-43, 44 IH/B-16, 40	5.06.04
Lesson 3: Reporting a Car Accident	0.1.5, 1.9.7, 1.9.8, 7.2.1	IH/A-25a, 25b IH/B-24a	5.06.02

Unit 7: Parenting	CASAS*	LAUSD**	Florida***
Lesson 1: Enrolling a Child in School	2.8.1, 2.8.6, 2.8.7, 7.7.1	IH/A-10a, 11a IH/B-10a	5.01.06, 5.02.08
Lesson 2: Calling to Report an Absence	0.1.5, 2.1.8, 2.8.4, 2.8.6	IH/A-14, 43	5.01.06, 5.02.08
Lesson 3: Interpreting a Child's Report Card or Progress Report	0.1.2, 0.1.5, 2.8.2, 2.8.4, 2.8.6, 2.8.7, 7.3.2, 7.7.3	IH/A-11a, 41, 43 IH/B-10a, 11	5.02.08
Lesson 4: Making Your Home Safe for Children	0.1.3, 0.1.5, 3.4.2, 3.6.5, 3.6.9, 7.2.3	IH/A-32	

Unit 8: On the Job	CASAS*	LAUSD**	Florida***
Lesson 1: Giving and Following Instructions	0.1.2, 0.1.6, 0.1.7, 4.6.1, 7.7.2, 7.7.6	IH/A-38b, 38c IH/B-33a	
Lesson 2: Correction at Work	0.1.5, 0.1.6, 4.4.4, 4.6.1, 7.5.3	IH/A-38a, 44 IH/B-33b, 34a, 40	5.01.03
Lesson 3: Workplace Safety	0.1.2, 0.1.5, 4.3.1, 4.3.2, 4.3.3, 4.3.4, 4.6.2, 4.6.3, 7.2.2, 7.2.5	IH/A-32, 33, 40c IH/B-32	5.03.08, 5.03.15, 5.07.01
Lesson 4: Getting Paid	0.1.5, 4.2.1	IH/A-40a, 44 IH/B-40	5.03.09

Unit 9: Managing Your Money	CASAS*	LAUSD**	Florida***
Lesson 1: Personal Expenses	0.1.5, 1.1.6, 1.5.1, 6.1.1, 7.3.4	IH/A-19, 43, 44 IH/B-40	5.04.01, 5.04.08
Lesson 2: Preparing a Monthly Budget	0.1.5, 1.1.6, 1.5.1, 6.1.1, 6.1.2, 6.1.4, 7.3.4	IH/A-19, 43 IH/B-19	5.04.01, 5.04.08
Lesson 3: Banking	0.1.5, 1.8.1, 1.8.2, 1.8.3, 7.2.3, 7.3.4	IH/A-20b, 43	5.04.03
Lesson 4: Applying for an Educational Loan	1.8.4, 1.8.6, 2.8.7, 4.9.3, 6.0.3, 7.4.4	IH/A-20a, 43, 44 IH/B-40	5.04.07

Unit 10: Health and Wellness	CASAS*	LAUSD**	Florida***
Lesson 1: Good-Health Basics	0.1.5, 0.2.4, 3.5.9, 7.2.2, 7.5.4	IH/A-28, 43 IH/B-27	
Lesson 2: Food and Nutrition	1.2.8, 3.5.2, 3.5.3, 3.5.9, 7.2.2, 7.2.3	IH/A-28, 43 IH/B-27	5.05.06
Lesson 3: Food Safety	0.1.5, 1.2.8, 3.5.3, 3.5.5, 7.2.2	IH/A-28, 43 IH/B-27	
Lesson 4: Finding Health Care Providers	0.1.5, 3.1.3, 3.1.6, 3.5.6, 3.6.9, 7.4.4	IH/A-29a, 29b, 43 IH/B-27	5.05.01
Lesson 5: Communicating with Your Doctor	0.1.5, 3.6.3, 3.6.4	IH/A-30a, 30b IH/B-42a	5.05.01
Lesson 6: Medical History Forms	0.1.5, 0.2.2, 3.2.1	IH/A-30c, 43 IH/B-26	5.05.03
Lesson 7: Drug Labels	0.1.5, 3.3.1, 3.3.2, 3.3.3, 3.3.4	IH/A-31, 43	5.05.04

Unit 11: Housing and Utilities	CASAS*	LAUSD**	Florida***
Lesson 1: Rental Leases	0.1.5, 1.4.3, 1.4.5, 7.2.3	IH/A-24, 43, 44 IH/B-20, 40	5.04.04, 5.04.05
Lesson 2: Fair Housing Laws	0.1.2, 1.4.5, 2.5.8, 7.4.4	IH/B-20	5.04.05
Lesson 3: Utility Bills	0.1.5, 1.4.4, 1.5.3, 7.2.2	IH/A-22b, 43, 44 IH/B-19, 40	5.04.01
Lesson 4: Communicating with Utility Companies	0.1.2, 0.1.5, 0.1.7, 1.4.4, 1.5.3, 2.1.4, 2.1.7, 2.1.8	IH/A-15a, 22c IH/B-19	5.01.06, 5.01.08

Unit 12: Getting Ahead at Work	CASAS*	LAUSD**	Florida***
Lesson 1: Reporting Progress	0.1.5, 4.4.1, 4.4.6, 4.6.4, 4.8.1, 4.8.4, 4.8.5, 4.9.1, 7.3.1, 7.3.2, 7.3.4	IH/A-38b, 38c, 39a, 43, 44 IH/B-33b, 40	5.03.06, 5.03.07
Lesson 2: Job Evaluations	0.1.5, 4.1.6, 4.1.9, 4.4.1, 4.4.3, 4.4.4, 4.4.5, 4.4.6, 4.6.1, 4.9.1, 7.2.5	IH/A-39c, 41, 43, 44 IH/B-33b, 34a, 40	5.03.11, 5.03.13
Lesson 3: Job Promotions	4.1.8, 4.1.9, 4.4.1, 4.4.2, 4.4.4, 4.4.5, 4.4.6, 4.4.8, 4.6.4, 4.8.1, 4.8.5, 4.9.1, 4.9.2, 7.4.4	IH/A-41, 43, 44 IH/B-33b, 34b, 40	5.03.12, 5.03.13

To the Teacher

Course Overview

Life Skills and Test Prep 4 is a competency-based, four-skills course for adult ESL students at the high-intermediate level. It is designed to help students acquire the language and life skills competencies they need in all their roles—at home, at work, in school, and in their communities. The course also includes listening and reading tests to give students invaluable practice in taking standardized tests, motivating them to achieve their benchmarks and persist in their learning goals.

Unit Organization

There are twelve units, organized thematically. Units contain from three to seven lessons, each one focusing on a specific competency, such as writing a resume, planning for an emergency evacuation, or using an automated phone system. The first page of the unit lists the lessons in the unit, along with the goal(s) for each lesson.

At the end of each unit, there is a unit test with both a listening and a reading section. This unit test is a multiple-choice test, much like the CASAS test or other standardized tests. Students must bubble in their answers on a separate answer sheet, found in the back of the book. The answer sheet is perforated so students can easily remove it.

Lesson Organization

Lessons are composed of the following sections as appropriate for the competency being presented:

- Learn
- Practice
- Make It Yours
- Listen
- Note
- Bonus

CD1 TRACK 1 *Note:* Listening activities occur throughout the lesson. The icon before the direction line indicates the CD number and track.

Learn

Each lesson begins with a section called Learn, where the target competency is introduced. Some competencies focus on speaking and listening, while others focus on reading and writing. However, all four skills are integrated within the lesson.

Practice

In the Practice section, students apply what they have just learned. Practice exercises vary in type, depending on the competency. Practice sections often present model conversations, such as someone calling about renting an apartment. Here are the steps for most model conversations:

1. Students first listen to the conversation.
2. They practice the conversation in pairs.
3. They reverse roles and practice the conversation again.
4. They practice the conversation again, substituting other information provided.

Make It Yours

This section allows students to personalize the material. These activities range from controlled role plays to more open-ended discussions.

Listen

In addition to the listening exercises built into the other sections of the lesson, every unit includes at least one Listen section that focuses on listening discrimination. The Listen section further reinforces the material in the lesson.

Note

Notes on language and culture appear in the lesson as needed. Additional notes give practical information related to the life skill competency. For example, a note in a lesson about postal services explains the rules for mailing liquid, fragile, perishable, or hazardous items in the United States.

Bonus

The Bonus section that occurs at the end of some lessons presents optional activities that go beyond the competency, giving students additional speaking and writing practice.

Unit Tests

Unit tests appear after every unit and contain both a listening and a reading section.

Listening

The listening section includes a variety of item types and is divided into two parts. In the first part, students listen to the questions. They hear and read the answer choices on the test page. The second part of the listening section is all on the audio CD. The answer choices are not on the test page. The directions, which vary unit by unit, include:

- Listen to the first part of the conversation. What should the person say next: A, B, or C?
- You will hear a conversation. Then you will hear three sentences. Which sentence is true: A, B, or C?
- You will hear a conversation. Then you will hear a question about the conversation. What is the correct answer: A, B, or C?
- Listen to the question or statement. What is the correct answer: A, B, or C?
- Listen to the sentence. Which of the following means the same as the sentence you heard: A, B, or C?

Each question in the listening sections is on a separate track on the audio CD. We recommend that you *play each track twice*, pausing for 10 to 20 seconds between each play. This will approximate how listening is presented on standardized tests.

Reading

The reading section tests students' ability to read and answer questions about a variety of print material, such as signs, forms, schedules, and paragraphs.

Answer Sheets

Each unit test is formatted like a standardized test. Students fill in (bubble in) their answers on the perforated answer sheets included in the back of the book. The answer sheets are printed on both sides of the page in case you want the students to take a test twice or to have additional practice completing the required personal information.

Answer Keys

The answer keys and audioscripts for the tests are found in the *Life Skills and Test Prep 4 Teacher's Manual*. Each answer key can be used as a scoring mask to make tests easy to grade. It also serves as a diagnostic tool; each test item is labeled with its corresponding objective, giving you a clear picture of which competencies the student has not yet acquired.

Life Skills and Test Prep 4 Teacher's Manual

In addition to the answer keys described above, the *Life Skills and Test Prep 4 Teacher's Manual* includes a section to prepare students for the tests in the book and for standardized tests. It helps students use an answer sheet, understand the directions in a test, and learn important test-taking strategies. We recommend that you go through this section of the manual with students before they take the Unit 1 Test or before they take the post-test on a standardized test.

The manual also includes a Classroom Methodology section, with general information for using the *Life Skills and Test Prep 4* material. This section suggests ways for doing pair and group work activities, presenting vocabulary, checking answers, and correcting students' language production.

Please ask your Pearson Longman rep about this manual if you do not already have it.

Built-in Flexibility

Life Skills and Test Prep 4 provides 80 to 100 hours of class instruction. All the material is aimed at high-intermediate students. As such, the lessons do not have to be taught in a specific order, and lessons may be skipped. If you do not want to use all the lessons, here are some ideas for how to select which ones to use:

- Ask your students which topics they are interested in and teach only those lessons.
- Give the unit test as a pre-test to find out how students perform. Use the diagnostic information in the *Life Skills and Test Prep 4 Teacher's Manual* to guide you to which lessons students need.
- If you are using *Life Skills and Test Prep 4* along with *Center Stage 4*, use the information in the *Center Stage 4 Teacher's Edition* to direct you to specific lessons.

To the Student

Life Skills and Test Prep 4 will help you improve your scores on ESL tests like the CASAS test. It will help you prepare for these tests in several ways:

- You will learn the English skills you need for the test.
- You will learn about tests and test-taking strategies.
- You will take a test after each unit, which will give you practice in taking tests and using answer sheets.

Preparing to Take a Test

Here are some things you can do to prepare for a test.

- [ ] Get a lot of sleep the night before the test.
- [ ] Eat a meal or snack before the test.
- [ ] Bring two sharpened #2 pencils.
- [ ] Bring a pencil eraser.
- [ ] Bring a ruler or a blank piece of paper.
- [ ] Arrive early at the testing room.
- [ ] Make sure you can easily see and hear the tester.
- [ ] Turn off your cell phone.
- [ ] Try to relax and do your best! Good luck!

Talk about the Past, Plan for the Future

Lesson 1 Personal and Work History
- Ask and answer questions about self and work history

Lesson 2 Identifying Interests and Skills
- Understand the importance of self-assessment in career planning
- Identify personal interests and skills

Lesson 3 Educational Opportunities
- Identify and investigate educational opportunities

Lesson 4 Setting Goals
- Set educational and professional goals
- Plan steps for reaching educational and professional goals

Lesson 1 Personal and Work History

Learn

One way to get help looking for a job is to visit a career center. Many adult schools as well as some public libraries have career centers. Some community colleges also offer career services to members of the community even if they're not students there. At a career center a career counselor will ask you questions about your personal and job history.

CD1 TRACK 8 **Ana Silva is talking to a career counselor. Listen and read.**

Counselor: Hi, I'm Rachel Carter.
Ana: Hi, I'm Ana Silva. It's nice to meet you.
Counselor: You, too. So, tell me a little about yourself, Ana. Where are you from, and how long have you been in the United States?
Ana: Well, I'm from Brazil, and I came to the United States two years ago.
Counselor: I see. Tell me about your education.
Ana: I graduated from high school in Brazil. And right now I'm taking English classes two nights a week.
Counselor: OK. Tell me about your present job. What do you do?
Ana: I'm a salesperson at a health food store.
Counselor: I see. And what are your job responsibilities?
Ana: I answer customers' questions about products, and I help them find items they're looking for. I organize items on shelves and make sure the store always looks good. I also use a cash register.
Counselor: All right. Tell me about your work history. Have you had other jobs in the past?
Ana: Yes. Before my present job, I worked as a delivery person for a drugstore. I was at that job for about a year. And in Brazil I worked in an office. I was an administrative assistant.
Counselor: What skills do you have?
Ana: I'm responsible and very organized. I'm hardworking and efficient. I speak Portuguese and Spanish. Also, I can use a computer and other office equipment.
Counselor: That's great. Now I'm going to ask you to fill out a few forms. . . .

Practice

Read the conversation again. Then read the sentences. Circle *T* for *True* or *F* for *False*.

1. Ana has lived in the United States for two years. (T) F
2. Ana goes to school. T F
3. Ana works as a delivery person now. T F
4. Ana's last job was in an office. T F
5. Ana doesn't have any skills. T F
6. Ana knows how to use a computer. T F

Listen

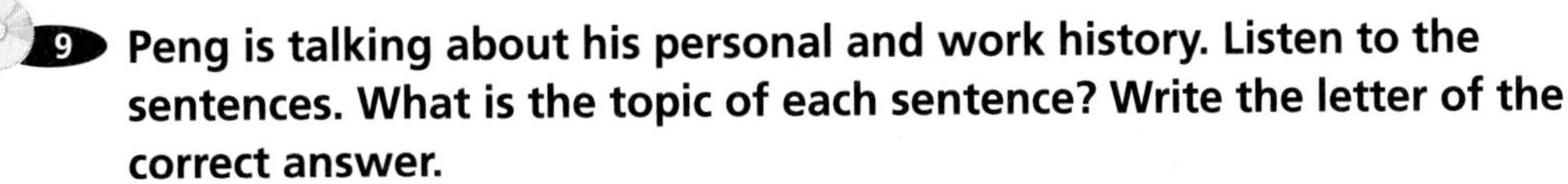

Peng is talking about his personal and work history. Listen to the sentences. What is the topic of each sentence? Write the letter of the correct answer.

____ 1.	a. Peng's past job
____ 2.	b. Peng's skills
____ 3.	c. Peng's present job
____ 4.	d. Peng's education
____ 5.	e. Peng's job responsibilities

Make It Yours

A **Answer the questions on another piece of paper. Use your own information.**

1. Where are you from?
2. How long have you been in the United States?
3. Tell me about your education.
4. What do you do now?
5. What are your job responsibilities?
6. Tell me about your work history.
7. What skills do you have?

B ***PAIRS. ROLE PLAY.* Practice the conversation on page 2 again. Use your own information. Switch roles.**

BONUS

***CLASS.* Introduce your partner from Make It Yours, Exercise B. Tell the class two things you learned about your partner.**

Lesson 2 Identifying Interests and Skills

Learn

PAIRS. **Which words do you know? Write each word from the box next to its meaning.**

consult	self-assessment	strength	survey	weakness

__self-assessment__ 1. process of getting information about yourself

__________ 2. a set of questions asked to find out a person's opinions

__________ 3. something you're good at

__________ 4. something you're not good at

__________ 5. ask for information or advice from someone

B **Read the article. Then read the two sentences on page 5. Check the sentence that is true.**

Choosing a Career

The First Step

Whether you're starting your first career or making a career change, choosing a career is a big decision. The first step in planning your career should involve self-assessment, or discovering some things about yourself. This means you should think about the things you like and don't like to do, what you're good at, and what is important to you.

One good way to identify these things is to take an interests survey. You can ask for information about this kind of survey at a public library or career center. You can also do interests surveys online. Go to a search engine website, such as www.google.com or www.yahoo.com. Type in keywords *interests survey*, *interests assessment*, or *work interests quiz*. You have to pay to take some surveys, but many of them are free.

When you take an interests survey, think carefully about your answers to the questions. Answer honestly. Self-assessment is important because it can help you make a good decision about a career that's good for *you*.

Be Careful

Interests surveys can be useful, but they won't instantly tell you your dream job. Interests surveys can help you identify your strengths, weaknesses, likes, and dislikes. They might also lead you to consider some career choices you hadn't thought of. But don't depend on self-assessments alone to choose a career. It's a good idea to consult a career counselor about the results of your survey.

- ☐ After you take an interests survey, you'll probably know what career you want.
- ☐ After you take an interests survey, you'll probably know more about the things that are important to you.

Practice

Read the article again. Answer the questions. Circle *a* or *b*.

1. What should a person do before choosing a career?
   a. find a job
   (**b.**) learn about him or herself
2. What is an example of self-assessment?
   a. an interests survey
   b. a search engine
3. Why is self-assessment a good idea?
   a. It can help you choose a career you like.
   b. It can help you find a good career counselor.
4. What can an interests survey help you do?
   a. identify things you're good at
   b. find a work interests quiz
5. What should you do after you take an interests survey?
   a. look for your dream job
   b. talk about the results with a career counselor

Make It Yours

PAIRS. **Talk about answers to these questions.**

1. Have you ever taken an interests survey? Where? What were the results?
2. Why do you think it's important to answer questions honestly on an interests survey?

Learn

Look at part of an interests survey. Match the sentences in the survey with their meanings below. Write the letter of each sentence next to the numbers below.

	Always	Sometimes	Never
a. I like to be in charge.			
b. I like motivating people.			
c. I like to do things my own way.			
d. I like to work with my hands.			
e. I like to work independently.			
f. I like to take care of people.			
g. I'm a good communicator.			
h. I'm good at decision making.			
i. I'm good with people.			
j. I'm a good mediator.			
k. I'm good at time management.			
l. I'm good at handling details.			
m. I have good problem-solving skills.			

__c__ 1. I like to do things without a lot of instruction from others.

____ 2. I'm good at helping end disagreements between people.

____ 3. I'm good at paying attention to small things.

____ 4. I like to work alone.

____ 5. I listen carefully and express myself well.

____ 6. I enjoy making things with my hands.

____ 7. I like taking responsibility for things.

____ 8. I'm good at finding solutions to problems.

____ 9. I enjoy being around people, and people feel comfortable with me.

____ 10. I enjoy getting people excited about and interested in things.

____ 11. I can make good decisions quickly.

____ 12. I'm good at planning and using my time well.

____ 13. I enjoy caring for people.

Practice

A **Look at the interests survey again. This time, complete the survey with information that's true for you. Check *always*, *sometimes*, or *never* for each sentence.**

B ***PAIRS.* Share your answers with a partner.**

Make It Yours

Here are some questions that can help you think about your future career. Answer them with your own, true information.

1. What are my interests? (Think about everything you're interested in, for example, reading, talking to people, sewing.)

   ____

   ____

2. What am I good at? (Think about your skills and talents, for example, taking care of your children, organizing your family's schedule, preparing the family budget.)

   ____

   ____

3. What's important to me? (Think about all the things you value, for example, taking care of your family, helping the community, feeling proud of your work.)

   ____

   ____

4. How do I feel about getting more education?

   ____

5. What kind of work schedule do I want to have?

   ____

6. How much money do I want to make?

   ____

7. What things do I like about my present or past jobs? (Consider job responsibilities, schedule, pay, location, relationships with bosses and co-workers, etc.)

   ____

   ____

8. What things do I *dislike* about my present or past jobs? (Consider job responsibilities, schedule, pay, location, relationships with bosses and co-workers, etc.)

   ____

   ____

***PAIRS.* Share your answers with your partner.**

Lesson 3 Educational Opportunities

Learn

Read the information about different educational opportunities. Then complete the sentences. Use the words in the box.

SCCC South City Community Center

Many jobs require at least a high school diploma. If you haven't graduated from high school, you can take the GED (General Education Development) exam. When you pass the test, you get your GED certificate, which is generally recognized as equivalent to a high school diploma. Call 302-555-0202 and improve your reading, writing, and math skills to prepare for the GED exam.

Nostra College

Nostra College offers options for every student. Study full-time and get your associate degree in just two years or your bachelor's degree in four. Or, study part-time and take our night, weekend, or online classes.
Think college is too expensive?
Financial aid is available.
Apply online or call to request an application.
Prerequisite: Students must have a high school diploma or GED certificate to apply.

Cedar Community College:
Non-credit Courses

We offer over 100 non-credit classes for personal and professional development, such as introduction to computers, web development, computer network systems, ESOL (all levels), business writing, yoga, and many more. Look at our course selection and enroll online at www.cedarcommunitycollege.edu.

VOT Tech offers technical education programs in the areas of construction, health care, computers, childcare, electronics, and many others. For most programs, you can complete your education, get a certificate, and start your career in less than one year. Receive training from expert teachers, including hands-on experiences that will prepare you for your career and your future. Call 1-800-555-TECH for more information.

certificate	degree	diploma

1. When you graduate from high school, you get a ____________________.
2. When you pass the GED test or graduate from a technical program, you get a ____________________.
3. When you graduate from college, you get a ____________________.

B **Read the information about educational opportunities again. Complete the sentences below. Use the words in the box.**

apply	bachelor's	enroll	hands-on	prerequisite
associate	development	financial aid	non-credit	training

1. It takes two years to get an ___associate___ degree if you study full-time. This kind of degree is focused on a specific area of study.
2. It takes four years to get a ____________ degree if you study full-time. For this kind of degree, students take classes in a larger number of subjects.
3. You have to ____________, or make a formal request to enter, before you can study at a university.
4. Money that is given or lent to students to pay for their education is ____________.
5. A ____________ is something you have to do or have before you can do a certain thing.
6. A ____________ course doesn't count toward a degree or certificate.
7. ____________ is the process of becoming better or more advanced at something.
8. When you ____________ in a class, you register, or sign up for it.
9. A ____________ experience is when you learn something by doing it, not just studying it.
10. When you receive ____________, someone teaches you the skills for a particular job or activity.

C **Read the information about educational opportunities again. Complete the sentences. Circle the correct words or phrases.**

1. **A non-credit course / College** is good for someone who wants to take a class to learn a little more about something.
2. **A technical program / GED preparation** is good for someone who wants to study for a specific career and start work quickly.
3. If you don't have a high school diploma, you can get a **college degree / GED certificate** instead.
4. You can get a degree at a **technical school / college**.
5. It can take one year or less to **get a college degree / finish a technical education program**.

Practice

A  **10 A person is calling to get more information about an educational program. Listen and read.**

A: Meyers Technical Institute.
B: Hi. I'd like more information about the hotel and restaurant management program.
A: Sure. What would you like to know?
B: How long does the program last?
A: It's a 10-month program.
B: Are there any prerequisites?
A: Yes. You must be at least 16 years old, and you have to pass an English skills test.
B: And when could I start?
A: A new program starts each term—January, May, and September.

B ***PAIRS.*** **Practice the conversation. Switch roles.**

C ***PAIRS.*** **Practice the conversation again. Use the information below. Switch roles.**

Morgan Learning Center

Improve your skills and increase your job opportunities with our General Computer Training course.

In this 12-week course, you'll get hands-on experience in our computer lab.
You'll learn all the basics of using a computer.
New courses begin each month.
Students must be 18 or older to enroll.

NEW!

Aviation Maintenance Certificate Program

Get your certificate in just 12 months.
Programs begin in January and June.
Must pass basic math and English skills tests. Must be 18 years or older.

BONUS

Get information about a class or program you might be interested in. Call, go online, or visit the school to get the information. Find out any prerequisites for the class or program, its length, and start date. Also ask about the cost. Report your information back to the class.

Lesson 4 Setting Goals

Note

A goal is something you hope to do or achieve in the future. Setting a goal involves making a plan for the steps to take to reach it. The first steps you take are your short-term goals, and the next ones are medium-term goals. After you reach those, you're ready to achieve your long-term goal.

Learn

A **Badal wanted a new career. He went to his school's career center to get more information on choosing a career. A career counselor talked to him and helped him make a chart to organize his goals. Look at the chart.**

	How I'll Achieve the Goals	When I'll Achieve the Goals
Short-term Goals		
identify interests	• take interests survey at career center	take survey by June 15
identify possible careers	• talk to career counselor about results of interests survey • choose three jobs to investigate	talk to counselor by June 30
Medium-term Goals		
get information about possible careers, including education needed	• Saturday mornings from 9:00–12:00 use computer at library to find information online • go to career center to get more information	finish getting information by end of July
Long-term Goals		
choose a career	• talk to career counselor about information found • list advantages and disadvantages of each career	identify a career I want by August 2009

B **Look at the chart again. Put the steps in order. Write *1*, *2*, *3*, or *4* next to each step.**

_____ Badal will look for information about careers at the library.

_____ Badal will take an interests survey.

_____ Badal will write the good and bad things about each job.

_____ Badal will choose three jobs he wants to learn more about.

Practice

After his research, Badal decided that he wanted to be a dental assistant. With his career counselor's help, Badal made another chart to help him plan how to reach his educational goals. Look at the chart. Then answer the questions below.

	How I'll Achieve the Goals	When I'll Achieve the Goals
Short-term Goals		
improve reading and writing in English	• take ESOL class at community college • go to language lab twice a week after class • join reading group at public library	finish semester in Dec. 2009
Medium-term Goals		
pass Sims Technical School English skills test	make appointment to take test at Sims Tech	take test in Jan. 2010
enroll in dental assistant program at Sims Tech	fill out registration forms	complete registration forms by Feb. 2010
apply for financial aid	fill out financial aid forms	finish forms by Mar. 2010
complete dental assistant training	take classes full-time from May 2010 to Jan. 2011	finish program in Jan. 2011
Long-term Goals		
get job as dental assistant	• write resume and cover letters* • learn and practice interview skills* • apply for jobs	find new job by June 2011

*See Unit 3 for more information on resumes, cover letters, and interview skills.

1. What three things will Badal do to improve his English?

   ____

   ____

2. Why does Badal need to improve his English?

   ____

3. When is Badal planning to begin classes at Sims Tech?

   ____

4. What is Badal's long-term goal?

   ____

Listen

Listen to each conversation. Answer the questions. Circle *a*, *b*, or *c*.

1. What is the woman's long-term goal?
   a. get accepted to college **b.** get a bachelor's degree **c.** get a job as a teacher
2. What is the man's short-term goal?
   a. finish high school **b.** get a part-time job **c.** finish college
3. What does the woman have to do before she reaches her long-term goal?
   a. get a job **b.** get a degree **c.** get a certificate
4. What does James want to do in the future?
   a. get a high school diploma **b.** get a GED certificate **c.** study at a technical school

Make It Yours

Think of a goal you have. You can think about educational goals (such as what you want to learn in this class or a specific program or degree you want to study) or career goals (such as choosing a career or finding a job). What steps do you need to take to reach that goal? Make those your short- and medium-term goals. Use the chart below.

	How I'll Achieve the Goal	When I'll Achieve the Goal
Short-term Goals		
Medium-term Goals		
Long-term Goals		

B ***PAIRS.*** **Talk about your long-term goal. Explain what steps you will take to achieve your goal (your short-term and medium-term goals) and when.**

Unit 1 Test

Before you take the test

ⒶⒷⒸⒹ Use the answer sheet for Unit 1 on page 205.

1. Print your name.
2. Print your teacher's name.
3. Write your student identification number, and bubble in the information below the boxes.
4. Write the test date and bubble in the information.
5. Write your class number and bubble in the information.

CD1 Listening I [Track 12]

Listen to the first part of the conversation. What should the person say next: A, B, or C?

1. A. My goal is to get my GED.
B. I want to be a teacher.
C. I'm going to take an English class.

2. A. After I finish high school.
B. When I finish the class I'm taking to prepare for it.
C. After I get my degree.

3. A. Yes, I'm going to college now.
B. Yes, I want to go to a four-year college and get a degree.
C. Yes, I graduated from high school.

CD1 Listening II [Track 13]

Listen. Test items 4, 5, 6, and 7 are on the audio CD.

Reading

Read. What is the correct answer: A, B, C, or D?

Davis Tech offers technical education programs in many areas, including automotive repair, electronics, computers, hotel and restaurant management, health care, and construction.

Most students complete our programs, receive a certificate, and start a career in less than one year.

We offer expert training and hands-on experiences.

Financial aid is available.

Prerequisite: Students must have a high school diploma or GED certificate.

Call **1-800-555-DTEC**

for more information or to request an application.

---

8. What do all students need to do before they can study at Davis Tech?

A. complete a technical program

B. get expert training

C. get financial aid

D. get a high school diploma or a GED certificate

9. Which sentence is true?

A. Students can get help with the cost of classes.

B. Students will receive a diploma when they finish the program.

C. Most students study at Davis Tech for two years.

D. Students can prepare for the GED exam at Davis Tech.

Maribel's Goals

	How will I achieve the goal?	When will I achieve the goal?
Short-term goal		
improve English to prepare for GED course	take ESL course at Lakeview Learning Center	finish in May
Medium-term goal		
prepare for GED exam	take GED course at Valley Adult School	finish in August
Long-term goal		
get GED credential	take exam	will take exam by end of September

10. What is Maribel going to do before she takes the GED course?

A. take an exam

B. take a class at Lakeview Learning Center

C. take a class at Valley Adult School

D. get her GED certificate

11. What is Maribel's short-term goal?

A. to prepare for the GED exam

B. to get her GED credential

C. to improve her English

D. to finish in August

12. When does Maribel plan to reach her short-term goal?

A. in May

B. in August

C. by the end of September

D. after she reaches her medium-term goal

13. How will Maribel meet her medium-term goal?

A. She'll study English.

B. She'll take a class.

C. She'll take an exam.

D. She'll get her GED certificate.

	Always	Sometimes	Never
I like to work independently.	✓		
I like to be in charge.	✓		
I like motivating people.		✓	
I'm good at decision-making.			✓
I'm good with people.		✓	
I like to handle details.	✓		
I like to do things my own way.	✓		
I have good problem-solving skills.	✓		
I'm good at time management.		✓	
I'm a good mediator.			✓
I'm a good communicator.	✓		
I like to take care of people.			✓
I like to work with my hands.		✓	

14. Which sentence is true?

A. The person doesn't like to work alone.

B. The person likes to take responsibility for things.

C. The person isn't good at solving problems.

D. The person is good at helping end disagreements between people.

15. What does the person enjoy doing?

A. working with a lot of other people

B. paying attention to small things

C. working with a lot of instruction from another person

D. caring for people

Cong Tran grew up in Vietnam. After he finished high school, he came to the United States. He got a job as a clerk in a supermarket. Two years ago, he started to work as a waiter in a restaurant.

Cong is ready for a new career. He went to the career center at his community library. A career counselor at the center told Cong to take an interests survey.

After he took the survey, Cong talked to the counselor about the results. Then Cong investigated different careers. He learned about different jobs and the education required for each one. Cong compared all the information, and he decided that he wants to become an automotive technician.

Now Cong is investigating the automotive technician programs at different technical schools in his area. He's looking for a school that offers classes part-time so he can continue to work at the restaurant. He also wants to find a school that offers financial aid to help him pay for his classes.

16. What is Cong doing now?

A. looking for a job

B. looking for a new career counselor

C. looking for a technical school

D. taking classes part-time

17. Which information is *not* given in the story?

A. Cong's work history

B. Cong's education

C. Cong's skills

D. Cong's career goal

Unit 2 Community Life

Lesson 1 **Community Events**
- Discuss community events
- Find information about community events

Lesson 2 **Directions**
- Ask for and give directions to places in the community
- Follow directions to places in the community

Lesson 3 **Recycling**
- Understand the importance of recycling
- Understand recycling regulations

Lesson 4 **Postal Services**
- Use different postal services

Lesson 1 Community Events

Learn

Note *There are many ways to find out about events in your community. Look for information at your public library, your local community center, schools, or online. You can also check the entertainment, lifestyle, or metro section of your local newspaper.*

A **Look at the information about weekend events in a local newspaper. Then read the question. Check the correct answer.**

There's a lot going on in our community.

Join us this weekend!

Event	Day and Time	Location	Other Information
Yoga class for seniors	Friday, 6:00–7:00 P.M.	Crandon Community Center	Start the weekend with a healthy mind and body. Cost of class is $5.00. (ages 60 and over)
Movie in the park	Friday, 9:00 P.M.	Bayfront Park	Bring a blanket and enjoy a free movie under the stars. This week's movie is *Happy Ending*.
Community Clean-up Day	Saturday, 8:00 A.M.	locations throughout the community	Help make our community beautiful! Call 378-555-0022 to join a trash pick-up group in your neighborhood.
Baseball game: Crandon Cougars vs. Altown Giants	Saturday, 1:10 P.M.	Crandon Ball Park	Cheer for the Crandon team! Tickets are $12. Children 4–12 pay just $8. Children 3 and under enter for free.
Crandon Arts Festival	Saturday and Sunday, noon–9:00 P.M.	McArthur Convention Center	See the work of local artists. Fun for the whole family! Free admission.
Mac Derby's Jazz Night	Saturday, music starts at 9:00 P.M.	Café Loli (2424 Leon Avenue)	Enjoy the music of the Mac Derby Jazz Trio live. ($5 cover charge)
Group walk	Sunday 7:30 A.M.	Meet at the entrance of Grover Park	Join us for a 4-mile walk around the park. Get some exercise, and make new friends!
Readers' club	Sunday 5:00–6:30 P.M.	Crandon Public Library	Help us choose this month's new book. Read, discuss, and meet new people.

Who is this information for?

☐ people in the community ☐ organizers of the events

B **Look at the events information again. Answer the questions.**

1. Who can go to the yoga class? ____seniors____
2. What's the cost of the movie in the park? ________
3. What should you do if you want to join in the community clean-up?

   ____
4. How many days does the arts festival last? ________
5. Which night can you go to a music event? ________
6. What day and time does the readers' club start? ________

Listen

CD1 TRACK 14 **Listen. Match the topics to the conversations.**

____ 1.	a. a description of the event
____ 2.	b. the day and time of the event
____ 3.	c. the price of the event
____ 4.	d. the location of the event

Practice

A CD1 TRACK 15 **Two friends are talking about their weekend plans. Listen and read.**

A: What are you doing this weekend?
B: Well, on Friday, I'm going to a yoga class for seniors.
A: Oh, really? Where is it?
B: The Crandon Community Center. It starts at 6:00.

B ***PAIRS.*** **Practice the conversation.**

C ***PAIRS. ROLE PLAY.*** **Make new conversations. Ask and answer questions about the events on page 20. Switch roles.**

BONUS

GROUPS OF 4. **Find out about a future event in your community, including the name of the event and the date, time, and place. Get any other information you can, such as the cost or a description of the event. Share the information with your group.**

Lesson 2 Directions

Learn

A *PAIRS.* **Which words do you know? Match the words with their meanings.**

____ 1. block
____ 2. cross street
____ 3. intersection
____ 4. legend

a. a place where two roads cross each other
b. a street that crosses another street
c. part of a map that explains the symbols, or pictures, on it
d. the distance along a city street from where one street crosses it to the next

B **Look at the map. Answer the questions on page 23.**

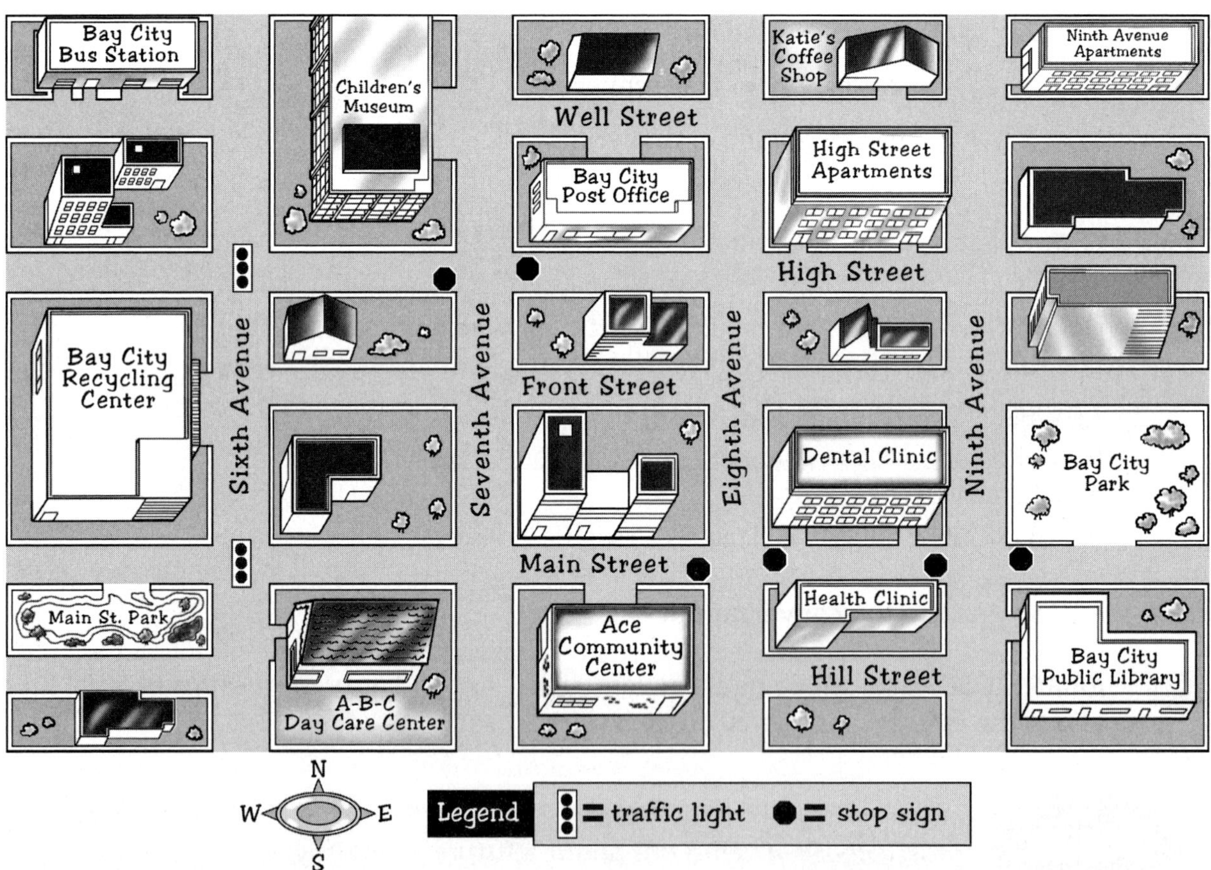

1. Luke is on Ninth Avenue going from the Ninth Avenue Apartments to the Bay City Public Library. Which direction is he going? ___south___
2. Emma is leaving the Children's Museum. She is going south on Seventh Avenue. What is the first cross street? ______
3. What is the nearest park to the High Street Apartments? ______
4. Pablo just left the Health Clinic and he is walking north on Eighth Avenue. How many blocks is it from Main Street to Well Street? ______
5. The library is at the intersection of which two streets? ______
6. Ida is walking on Main Street from Bay City Park to the Ace Community Center. Will the community center be on her left or her right? ______
7. Is there a stop sign at the intersection of Main and Sixth? ______
8. Roni is leaving the Ace Community Center. She wants to go to the Bay City Bus Station. She's walking west on Main Street. Which direction should she go on Sixth Avenue? ______

Practice

Look at the map again. Complete the conversations. Use *north, south, east, west, left,* or *right*.

1. **A:** How do I get from the A-B-C Day Care Center to the Children's Museum?

   B: Go ___north___ on Sixth Avenue, then turn ______ on High Street. Make a ______ onto Seventh Avenue.

2. **A:** Can you tell me how to get from the High Street Apartments to the Bay City Recycling Center?

   B: Sure. Head ______ on High Street, then turn ______ on Sixth Avenue. It's the building on your right.

3. **A:** Excuse me. Could you give me directions from Main Street Park to the Bay City Bus Station?

   B: Sure. Go ______ on Main Street, then make a ______ onto Sixth Avenue. Go ______ until you get to Well Street. Make a ______ onto Well. It's on your ______.

Make It Yours

***PAIRS.* Make new conversations like the ones in Practice. Take turns asking for and giving directions to different places. Use the map in Learn.**

Listen

Look at the map. Listen. Answer the questions. Circle *a*, *b*, or *c*.

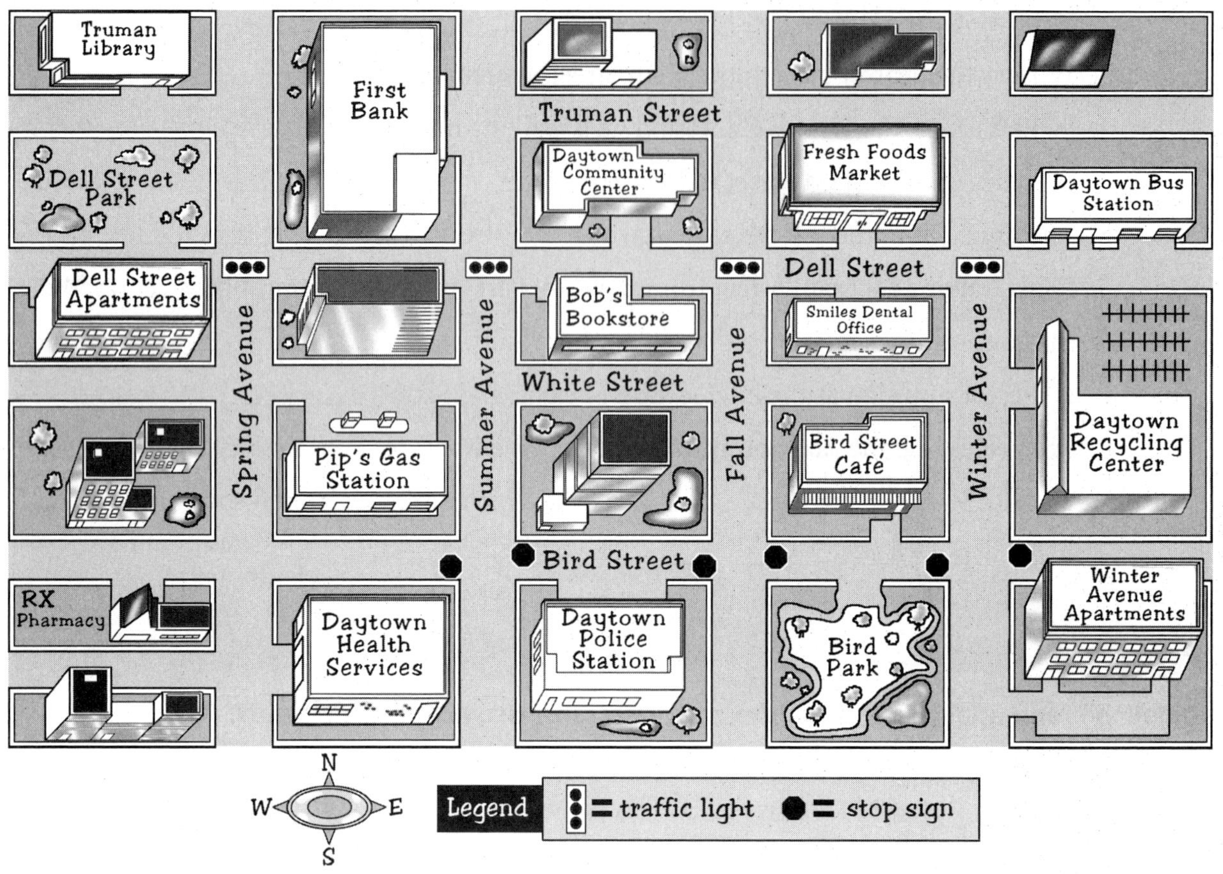

1. Start at the Daytown Police Station. Listen and follow the directions. Where are you?

   a. Truman Library **b.** Dell Street Apartments **c.** Bob's Bookstore

2. Start at First Bank. Listen and follow the directions. Where are you?

   a. Bird Street Café **b.** Bird Park **c.** Dayton Police Station

3. Start at the Winter Avenue Apartments. Listen and follow the directions. Where are you?

   a. Bob's Bookstore **b.** Daytown Health Services **c.** Pip's Gas Station

4. Start at the Daytown Bus Station. Listen and follow the directions. Where are you?

   a. Daytown Health Services **b.** Daytown Police Station **c.** Bird Park

Make It Yours

PAIRS. **Student A, choose two places on the map. Tell your partner to start at one of the places. Give directions to the other place. Student B, follow Student A's directions. Are you in the correct place? Switch roles.**

Lesson 3 Recycling

Learn

A **Find out how much you know about recycling. Read the sentences. Then circle *T* for *True* or *F* for *False*. If you don't know an answer, you can guess.**

How much do you know about recycling?

Take this quiz and find out!

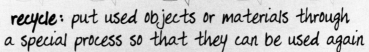

recycle: put used objects or materials through a special process so that they can be used again

1. The average American produces more than 4 pounds of trash each day. T F
2. The average American uses more than 650 pounds of paper each year. T F
3. Every Sunday 500,000 trees could be saved if everyone recycled their newspapers. T F
4. A glass bottle you throw away today will still exist in a million years. T F
5. Every year Americans throw away more than 270 million glass bottles. T F
6. Recycling one aluminum can saves enough energy to run a TV for three hours. T F
7. Twenty recycled aluminum cans can be made with the energy it takes to make one new aluminum can. T F
8. More than 75 percent of the trash we throw away could actually be recycled. T F
9. Americans produce 30 percent of the world's garbage. T F

Now check your answers.

All the sentences are true.

How did you do?

7–9 correct: Congratulations! You know a lot about recycling. Share what you know with others.

4–6 correct: You're on the right track, but there are still some things you could learn.

0–3 correct: It's time to get "green." Learn the facts about recycling.

Note

Most Americans live in communities with recycling programs. In some communities, residents put their recyclable items in a bin, or large container, near the street in front of their house. The items are collected and taken to a place to be recycled. In other communities, recyclable items aren't collected. Residents must take these items to a specific place where they can be recycled.

B **Read the information about one community's recycling program.**

The city of Wilmington recycles!

Recyclable items are collected every Friday.
Follow these guidelines.

Newspapers, magazines, and catalogs are accepted.

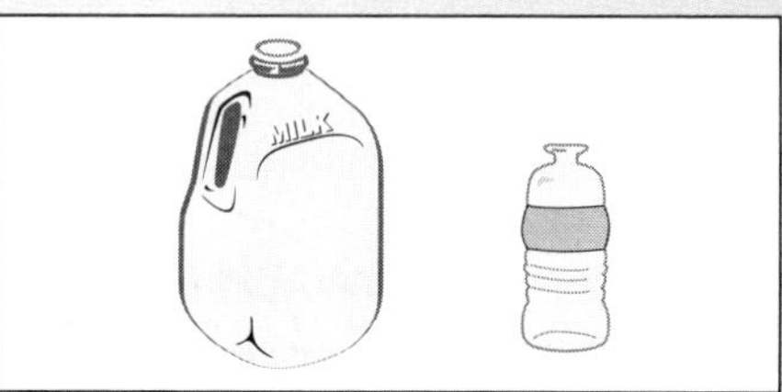

Plastic containers with the numbers ♳ and ♴ are accepted.

All clear, brown, and green glass containers are accepted.

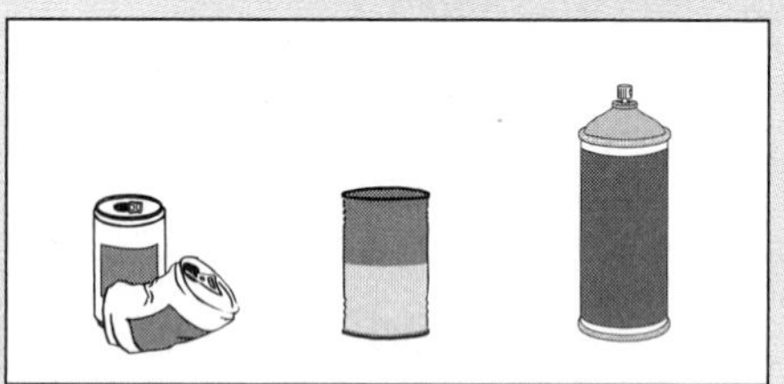

Aluminum, steel, and tin cans are accepted. Empty aerosol cans are also accepted.

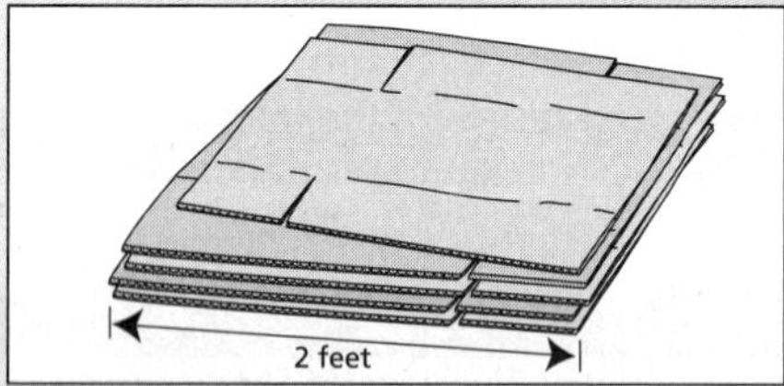

Corrugated cardboard is accepted. Cardboard boxes must be flattened and cut or folded to a size of 2 × 2 × 2 ft. or smaller.

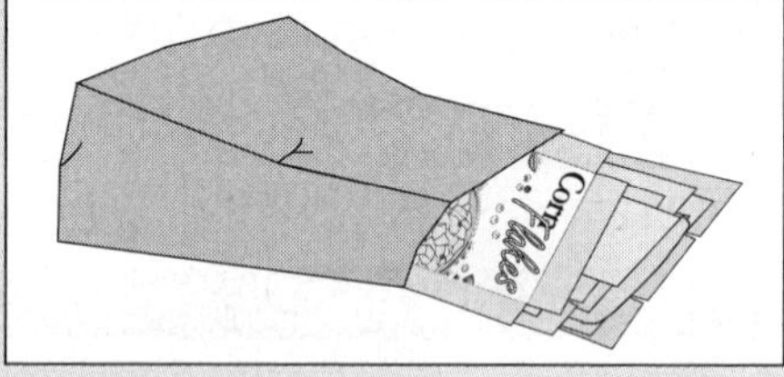

Tissue boxes, shoe boxes, cereal boxes, and almost all other food boxes are accepted. Remove any plastic inner bags, flatten the boxes and put them into a larger box or a brown paper bag.

Rinse out all containers before recycling.

Do not include caps or lids.   

Labels are OK.

C **Look at the recycling information again. Then complete the sentences. Circle the correct words.**

1. Guidelines are **ideas** / **instructions**.
2. Aluminum, tin, and steel are types of **soda** / **metal**.
3. When you flatten something, you make it **flat** / **bigger**.
4. When you rinse something, you **throw it away** / **wash it quickly**.
5. You have to cut or fold big pieces of **newspaper** / **corrugated cardboard**.
6. A cap goes on the **top** / **bottom** of a bottle or container.

Practice

Look at the information about the community's recycling program again. Answer the questions. Circle *a*, *b*, or *c*.

1. What can you recycle in Wilmington?
   a. magazines **b.** all plastic containers **c.** bottle caps
2. What kinds of plastic containers can you recycle?
   a. containers with numbers 1 and 2 **b.** clear plastic containers **c.** all plastic containers
3. What should you do to cans before you recycle them?
   a. Take off the caps. **b.** Take off the labels. **c.** Rinse them.
4. What should you do to food boxes before you recycle them?
   a. Make them flat. **b.** Cut them. **c.** Put them in plastic bags.
5. What *can't* you recycle in Wilmington?
   a. glass **b.** plastic bags **c.** aerosol cans

BONUS

Answer the questions below. If you don't know the answers, you can ask your neighbors, call your local Department of Public Works (look in the Blue Pages of the phone book for the number), or look online (type the name of your city + *recycle* in a search engine).

- **Does your community have a recycling program?**
- **If yes, are recyclable items collected or do you have to take the items somewhere?**
- **If yes, what are three things that you can recycle in your community?**

Lesson 4 Postal Services

Learn

***PAIRS.* Which words do you know? Complete the sentences. Use the words in the box.**

fragile	potentially hazardous	secure
perishable	replace	value

1. Something that is easily broken or damaged is ____fragile____.
2. Food that is ________________ can become bad quickly.
3. Something that is ________________ might be dangerous or cause problems.
4. The ________________ of something is the amount of money it's worth.
5. When something gets lost or stolen, sometimes you ________________ it, or get a new one.
6. Something that is ________________ is safe.

Read the information about some of the services offered by the post office.

Certified Mail™

- You get a receipt that shows the time and date you mailed the item.
- You can check online or by phone to see when the item was delivered.

Insured Mail

- When you purchase insurance, you tell the post office the value of the item you're sending. If the item gets lost or damaged in the mail, the post office will pay you up to $5,000 to replace the item.

Registered Mail™

- This is the safest, most secure post office service. Each step of the item's journey is recorded until it is delivered.
- You get a receipt that shows the time and date you mailed the item.
- You can check online or by phone to see when the item was delivered.
- Insurance for items with a value up to $25,000 is included in the cost.

Return Receipt

- When your package is delivered, you are sent a postcard or an e-mail that tells you the person received it.

C **Look at the information about post office services again. Read the situations. Which service should each person use?**

1. Sarah is sending an item worth $100. She wants to get money back if something happens to it. She doesn't need to show when she mailed the package or know when it arrives. ____________
2. Dennis is mailing something that isn't valuable, but he wants a receipt to show the day he mailed it. ____________
3. Ricardo wants to be notified when the person receives the package he's sending. He doesn't need insurance. ____________
4. Teresa is mailing something very important and very valuable. She wants it to be very safe. ____________

Note

When you mail a package through the United States Post Office, the clerk will ask you if it contains anything liquid, fragile, perishable, or potentially hazardous. You must answer the question truthfully. There are special rules for mailing these things. Some items require a label on the outside of the box, and some items can't be mailed through the post office. If you're not sure whether you're allowed to mail something, you can ask at the post office, check online at www.usps.com, or call 1-800-USPS (8777).

Practice

A post office clerk is talking to a customer. Listen and read.

Clerk: Hi, how can I help you?
Customer: I need to mail this package.
Clerk: OK. Does it contain anything liquid, fragile, perishable, or potentially hazardous?
Customer: No. But the item I'm sending was very expensive.
Clerk: OK. You should use insured mail. You need to fill out this form. . . .

Make It Yours

PAIRS. **Practice the conversation again. Use the information below.**

1. **Student A:** You're sending a package, and you need to show you mailed it today.
   Student B: You're the post office clerk. Recommend a service.
2. **Student B:** You're sending a package, and you want to be notified when the person receives it.
   Student A: You're the post office clerk. Recommend a service.

Unit 2 Test

Before you take the test

Ⓐ Ⓑ Ⓒ Ⓓ Use the answer sheet for Unit 2 on page 207.

1. Print your name.
2. Print your teacher's name.
3. Write your student identification number, and bubble in the information below the boxes.
4. Write the test date and bubble in the information.
5. Write your class number and bubble in the information.

Listening I [Track 18]

CD1

You will hear a conversation. Then you will hear three sentences. Which sentence is true: A, B, or C?

1. A. The woman is at Green Park.
B. The woman should walk north.
C. The woman should turn left first.

2. A. The man is going to play tennis in the park.
B. There's a concert in the park.
C. The man is going to see a movie.

3. A. The man wants to buy insurance.
B. The man wants to return the package.
C. The man wants to know when the person receives the package.

4. A. Newspapers aren't recycled.
B. Glass is recycled.
C. All plastic is recycled.

Listening II [Track 19]

CD1

Listen. Test items 5, 6, and 7 are on the audio CD.

Reading

Read. What is the correct answer: *A*, *B*, *C*, or *D*?

Recyclable items are collected every Tuesday. Please follow these guidelines.

- Newspapers and papers, ads, or coupons inside newspapers are accepted. Do not include the plastic bags papers are delivered in.
- Notebook and computer paper, magazines, catalogs, and phone books are accepted.
- Paper boxes (cereal boxes, shoe boxes, tissue boxes, etc.) and corrugated cardboard (no larger than 2 feet × 2 feet) are accepted.
- All metal cans are accepted. Do not include lids.
- Plastic containers with the numbers 1, 2, 3, and 4 are accepted. Do not include lids. Containers with numbers 5, 6, or 7 are not accepted at this time. Plastic bags are not accepted.
- Brown, green, and clear glass are accepted. Broken glass, glass from windows, and drinking glasses are not accepted.
- Rinse out all containers before recycling. It's not necessary to remove labels from metal, glass, or plastic containers.

8. Which of the following sentences is true about recycling glass in Port City?

A. You have to take off the label.

B. You have to rinse out the container.

C. You have to put it in a bag.

D. You have to break it.

9. Which of the following is accepted for recycling in Port City?

A. plastic lids

B. all plastic containers

C. plastic bags

D. plastic containers with the number 2 on them

10. What do you have to do before you recycle a newspaper?

A. Take out the coupons, ads, and papers that are inside.

B. Take it out of the plastic bag.

C. Cut it so the size is 2 feet by 2 feet.

D. Remove the labels.

Bellview Community Weekend Calendar

Event	Day and Time	Location	Other Information
Family Storytime	Saturday, 10:00–10:30 A.M.	Bellview Library	This event is for children ages 3–8 and their families. The whole family can join in stories, songs, and other activities.
Community Cultural Day	Saturday, 12:00–10:00 P.M.	Finnigan Park	Free admission. Come and enjoy the different cultures of our community members. Try different foods, see traditional art and dance, and hear music from around the globe.
Community Health Fair for Seniors	Saturday, 2:00–4:00 P.M.	Bellview Community Center	All residents ages 65 and up: Memorial Hospital is offering free medical tests and information on nutrition, exercise, and health services available in the community.
Concert in the Park	Saturday, 8:00 P.M	Edison Park	Bring a blanket and enjoy a free concert in the open air. This week hear the music of Latin singer Celia Lopez.

11. Who is the Community Health Fair for?

A. children

B. families

C. families from different cultures

D. people age 65 and older

12. Where and when can you listen to music?

A. Saturday at 10:00 A.M. at Finnigan Park

B. Saturday at 12:00 P.M. at Edison Park

C. Saturday at 2:00 P.M. at the Bellview Community Center

D. Saturday at 8:00 P.M. at Edison Park

13. When can you get health information?

A. Saturday at 12:00 P.M.

B. Saturday at 1:30 P.M.

C. Saturday at 3:00 P.M.

D. Saturday at 4:30 P.M.

You must tell the clerk if your package contains anything liquid, fragile, perishable, or potentially hazardous.

You can add extra services when you mail a package.

Return Receipt
- Receive a postcard or an email that tells you when the person receives your package.

Certified Mail™
- Get a receipt that shows the date and time you mailed the package.
- Check online or by phone to see when the package was delivered.

Insured Mail
- When you buy insurance, tell the clerk the value of the item you're sending. If the item gets lost or damaged in the mail, the post office will pay you up to $5,000.

Registered Mail™
- Use the safest, most secure post office service. We record each step of the package's journey until it is delivered.
- Get a receipt that shows the date and time you mailed the package.
- Check online or by phone to see when the package was delivered.
- Get insurance for items with a value of up to $25,000.

---

14. You have to tell the clerk if your package contains which of the following?

A. something valuable

B. something that could be dangerous

C. money

D. a receipt

15. Which service should you use if you want the post office to let you know when your package is received?

A. Return Receipt

B. Certified Mail

C. Insured Mail

D. Registered Mail

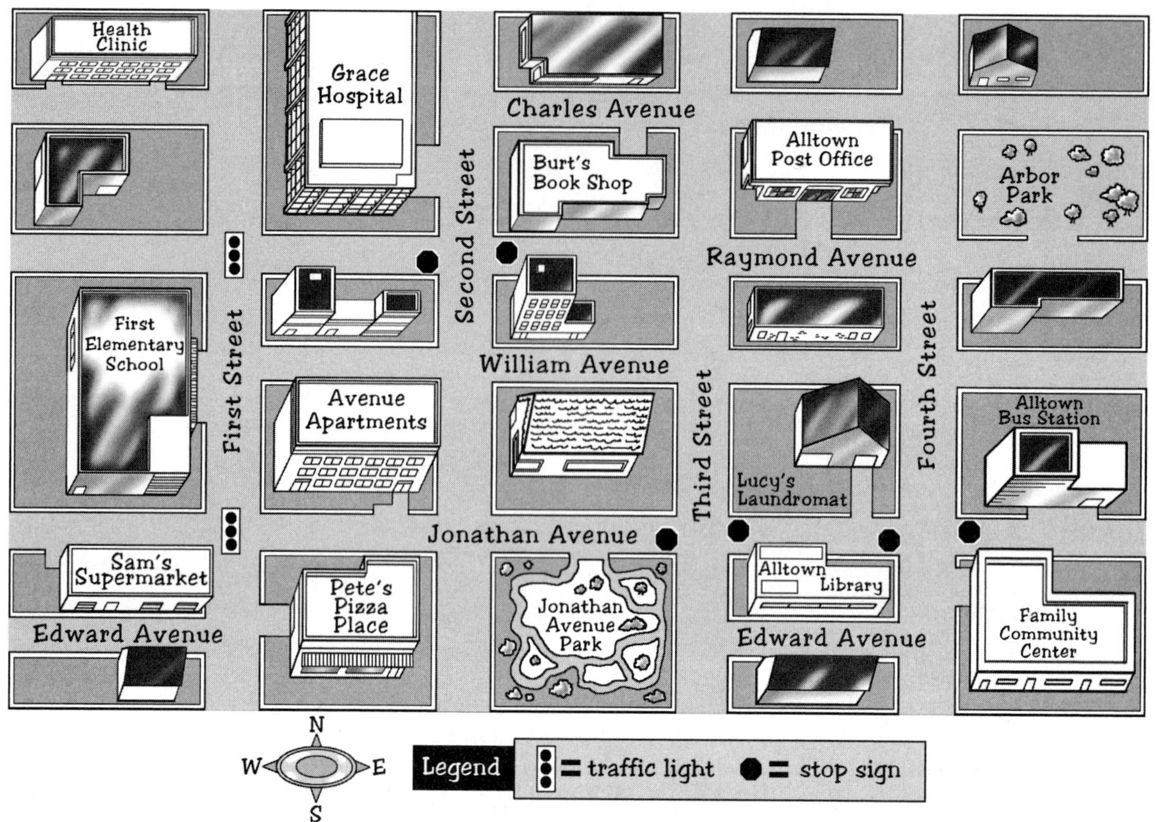

16. Where is the Family Community Center?

    A. It's two blocks west of Jonathan Avenue Park.

    B. It's at the intersection of Jonathan and Fourth.

    C. It's two blocks north of Arbor Park.

    D. It's east of the Alltown Bus Station.

17. Rosa wants to walk from First Elementary School to the Health Clinic. What should she do first?

    A. Go north on First Street.

    B. Turn right on First Street.

    C. Go east on Jonathan Avenue.

    D. Go west on William Avenue.

18. Start at the intersection of Raymond and Third. Head west for one block and turn left at the stop sign. Go south for two blocks, and make a right and head west on Jonathan. Which building is on your right?

    A. Jonathan Avenue Park

    B. Sam's Supermarket

    C. Avenue Apartments

    D. Pete's Pizza Place

Unit 3 Getting a Job

Looking for a Job

Learn

A *PAIRS.* **The words below are often used in job ads. Which words do you know? Match words 1–8 with meanings a–h. Match words 9–15 with meanings i–o.**

_e_ 1. hire	a. smallest number it's possible or OK to have
____ 2. full-time	b. one of the periods each day when someone is at work
____ 3. shift	c. necessary
____ 4. overtime	d. working for the number of hours that people usually work (In the United States this is usually 35–40 hours a week.)
____ 5. required	e. employ someone to work for you
____ 6. benefits	f. knowledge or skills you get from doing a job
____ 7. minimum	g. time that you work at your job, usually for extra pay, in addition to your usual working hours
____ 8. experience	h. advantages you get from your job, such as health insurance, training, vacation days, and paid sick days

____ 9. reference	i. go somewhere yourself to do something instead of calling or sending an e-mail
____ 10. apply	j. good, but not necessary
____ 11. bilingual	k. a person who recommends you for a job
____ 12. preferred	l. officially ask to be considered for a job opening
____ 13. part-time	m. able to speak two languages
____ 14. position	n. working for only part of each day or week
____ 15. in person	o. a job

B **You will see abbreviations of many of the words in Exercise A in the job ads below. Read the ads. Then read the words on the next page. Write the abbreviation for each word.**

NOW HIRING
Welder
FT, 2nd shift, Mon–Fri,
some OT req.
$16/hr., exc. bens.
min. 1 yr. exp. or certificate
in welding technology
refs. req.
Call Shawn Stark
at 623-555-9999
for information or to apply.

STYLISTS WANTED
FT and PT positions avail.
min. 2–3 yrs. exp.
biling. pref.
exc. refs. req.
Apply in prsn. at The Hair Shop.
Ask for mgr. No appt. nec.

1. full-time	FT		10. references	
2. overtime			11. part-time	
3. required			12. available	
4. hour			13. bilingual	
5. excellent			14. preferred	
6. benefits			15. in person	
7. minimum			16. manager	
8. year			17. appointment	
9. experience			18. necessary	

Practice

Look at the job ads again. Read the sentences. Check *Welder*, *Stylist*, or *Both*.

	Welder	Stylist	Both
1. Sometimes you need to work extra hours at this job.	☑	☐	☐
2. You can work part-time for this job.	☐	☐	☐
3. You don't have to have experience for this job.	☐	☐	☐
4. The company is looking for more than one worker.	☐	☐	☐
5. You have to go to the place of business to apply for this job.	☐	☐	☐
6. You need references for this job.	☐	☐	☐

Listen

Listen. Then read the sentences. Which is correct? Circle *a*, *b*, or *c*.

1. **a.** Go in person to apply for the job.
   b. Call the manager to apply for the job.
   c. Make an appointment to apply for the job.

2. **a.** The man works the first shift.
   b. The man works part-time.
   c. The man works overtime.

3. **a.** Experience is necessary.
   b. They prefer a person with experience.
   c. They prefer a person without experience.

4. **a.** Call Bob to apply for the job.
   b. Go to the store to apply for the job.
   c. Call the store manager to apply for the job.

Make It Yours

A Create an ad for the job you have or a job you want. Include information about the schedule, pay, benefits, and requirements. Give instructions on how to apply for the job. Use abbreviations. You can use made-up information.

B *PAIRS.* Explain your ad to your partner. Tell about the job.

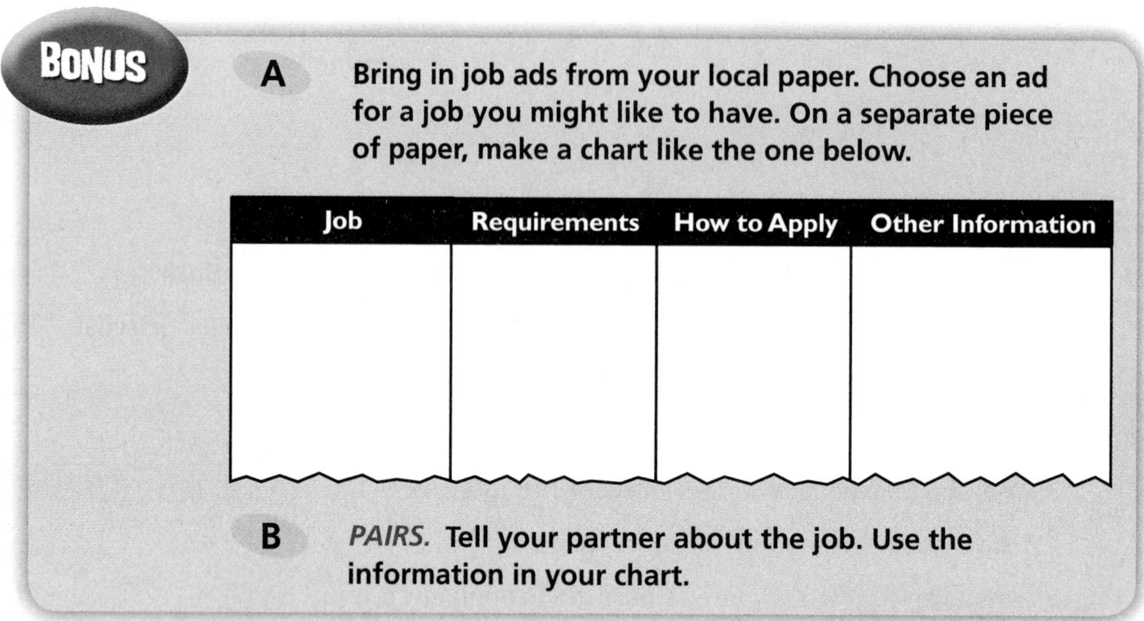

BONUS

A Bring in job ads from your local paper. Choose an ad for a job you might like to have. On a separate piece of paper, make a chart like the one below.

Job	Requirements	How to Apply	Other Information

B *PAIRS.* Tell your partner about the job. Use the information in your chart.

Learn

A *PAIRS.* Which words do you know? Write each word from the box next to its meaning.

eventually	expand	field	job offer	network

____expand____ 1. make something larger

__________ 2. subject that people study or the type of work they're involved in

__________ 3. (v.) meet and talk to other people in order to help each other, share information, etc.; (n.) a group of people who are connected or work together

__________ 4. after a long time

__________ 5. statement saying you're willing to give someone a job

B **Read the article about another way to look for a job. Then answer the question. Check the correct answers.**

Creating, Expanding, and Using Your Network

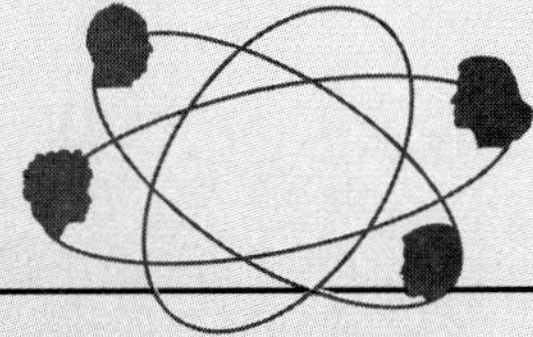

Answering job ads can be a good way to find a job. But some career experts say that the most common and most successful way to find a job is by networking.

Networking is talking to people. When you're looking for a job, let people know. Tell your friends, family, and neighbors. Talk to your classmates, teachers, counselors, and co-workers. Try to talk to people who already work in the field you're interested in. Talk to as many people as you can—you never know who might be able to help you.

When you network, you can ask people about job openings, but you should also ask for their help and suggestions. Ask if they know anyone in the field you're interested in or if they know how you might learn more about the job you want. Get the name and phone number of anyone they think might be able to help. Then call that person and ask for some information. You can say, for example, "I'm looking for a job as a computer support specialist. Lucy Bower gave me your name. I'm interested in any advice or suggestions you can offer."

In this way, you might not immediately get a job offer, but you might meet a person who can eventually help you get a job. Remember, every time you talk to someone, your network gets bigger, and you increase your chances of finding a job.

Which two of the following are examples of networking?

- ☐ looking at job ads in the newspaper
- ☐ asking a career counselor for help with looking for a job
- ☐ talking to someone who has a job similar to the job you want

Practice

Read the article again. Then complete the sentences. Write *should* or *shouldn't*.

When you network, you . . .

1. ______should______ talk to a lot of people.
2. ____________________ only talk to people who you think can help you find a job.
3. ____________________ ask for people's advice, ideas, and suggestions.
4. ____________________ try to learn more about the job you want.
5. ____________________ expect to find a job immediately.

Lesson 2 Resumes

Learn

Note

When you apply for certain jobs, you need to send a resume. A resume is a short (usually one page) document that states your job objective, that is, the type of job you want, and lists your job experience, skills, and education. People often tailor, or individualize, their resumes for specific jobs so that employers can see how their experience and abilities would make them good candidates for those particular positions.

A ***PAIRS.*** **It's important to use descriptive words on a resume. Look at the action verbs below. Which words do you know? Match the words with their meanings.**

Action verbs

__j__ 1. obtain		a. show others how to do something
____ 2. achieve		b. make something continue in the same way as before
____ 3. train		c. give
____ 4. manage		d. successfully complete something or get a good result
____ 5. maintain		e. make a process or activity easier to happen
____ 6. provide		f. do something, especially something difficult or useful
____ 7. handle		g. direct or control employees in a business department
____ 8. perform		h. use and control a machine or equipment
____ 9. demonstrate		i. take care of a situation or problem
____ 10. ensure		j. get something that you want
____ 11. facilitate		k. make sure something happens
____ 12. operate		l. teach someone particular skills

Words to describe workers

____ 13. capable		a. putting a lot of energy into work
____ 14. detail-oriented		b. having a strong desire to do well at something
____ 15. effective		c. well-trained and skilled at working in a particular field
____ 16. hard-working		d. good at paying attention to small things
____ 17. motivated		e. producing the result that is wanted
____ 18. professional		f. having the power, skill, or other qualities that are needed to do something

Words to describe a workplace environment

____ 19. fast-paced
____ 20. high-energy

a. with a lot of different things happening
b. moving at a quick speed

Words to describe levels of employment

____ 21. crew member
____ 22. entry-level position
____ 23. manager

a. someone who directs, or is in charge of, a business or organization
b. someone who works with a group of people to do a job
c. beginning-level job

Words to describe things people work with

____ 24. records
____ 25. orders
____ 26. supplies

a. requests by customers for a company to supply goods
b. things that are necessary for a particular purpose
c. documents, either written or stored on a computer, which contain information that can be looked at in the future

B **Answer the questions. Circle *a* or *b*.**

1. Are you good at paying attention to small things?
   a. Yes, I'm detail-oriented. **b.** Yes, I'm motivated.
2. Tell me about your work environment.
   a. It's an entry-level position. **b.** It's fast-paced.
3. What kind of job do you want?
   a. I want to obtain an entry-level position. **b.** I want to perform my job well.
4. What is one of your job responsibilities?
   a. I maintain records. **b.** I'm a crew member.
5. Do you work with customers at your job?
   a. Yes, I manage a crew of five people. **b.** Yes, I handle customer complaints.

Practice

Read the job ad and the resume.

Our mid-size company is looking for a capable, hard-working, and motivated individual to join our team. The ideal candidate communicates effectively, can handle customer service complaints professionally, has experience with training others, and is organized and detail-oriented.

MIGUEL RAMOS

14224 N. 51st Ave., Apt. 2B, Glendale, AZ 85306

623-555-0192 • miguelramos@wow.com

JOB OBJECTIVE

To obtain an entry-level position as a computer support specialist

WORK EXPERIENCE

Manager/Crew member Jan. 2008–present

Harry's Hamburger House, Glendale, AZ

- achieved promotion from crew member to manager in less than one year
- manage crew of seven people in high-energy environment
- train new employees
- organize and maintain records of orders and supplies
- provide excellent customer service, including handling customer complaints

Baggage Handler May 2006–Jan. 2008

Sky Harbor Airport, Phoenix, AZ

- performed physical labor in fast-paced environment
- demonstrated effective communication skills, including reading and following directions
- ensured correct location of bags with great attention to detail
- facilitated smooth operations through cooperation and team work
- operated luggage cart, scissor-lift truck, and forklift

EDUCATION

Computer Support Specialist Certificate Jan. 2008–June 2009

Top Technical School, Phoenix, AZ

OTHER SKILLS

- Knowledge of Windows 2003, Exchange 2000/2003, and Office 2003
- Fluent in Spanish

B **Look at the resume again. Answer the questions.**

1. What job does Miguel want? ______________________________
2. Where does Miguel work now? ______________________________
3. Where did Miguel work before? ______________________________

C **Look at the resume again. Then read the sentences. Circle *T* for *True* or *F* for *False*.**

1. Miguel uses organizational skills in his job.	(T)	F
2. Miguel has experience with customer service.	T	F
3. Miguel can use a forklift.	T	F
4. Miguel has worked as a computer support specialist before.	T	F
5. Miguel studied to be a computer support specialist.	T	F
6. Miguel speaks Spanish.	T	F

D **Look at the resume again. Answer the questions. Check *Harry's Hamburger House* or *Sky Harbor Airport*.**

At which job does/did Miguel . . .	Harry's Hamburger House	Sky Harbor Airport
1. get a promotion?	☑	☐
2. have to work quickly?	☐	☐
3. show he was detail-oriented?	☐	☐
4. teach other people how to do things?	☐	☐
5. direct and supervise other workers?	☐	☐

E ***PAIRS.* Explain to your partner how you got your answers for Exercises B, C, and D. If the answers are in the resume, underline the words and show them to your partner.**

F **Look at the resume again. Answer the question.**

What are Miguel's job duties (things he has to do as part of his job) at Harry's Hamburger House?

1. ______________________________
2. ______________________________
3. ______________________________
4. ______________________________

Learn

Read the information about writing a resume.

RESUME RULES

Your resume should have the following parts:

- **Your contact information.** Give you name, address, phone number, and e-mail address.
- **Your job objective.** State the specific job you want. (This should be the same as the job you are applying for.)
- **Your work experience.** List your present or most recent job first. For each job:
  - give your job title or position, the name of the employer, the city and state, and your start date and end date.
  - list two or more details about each job. You can include your job duties, skills you learned, things you achieved, ways that you helped your employer, or awards you received.
- **Your education.** List your most recent training first. For each degree, certificate, or diploma, specify your area of study, the name of the school, the city and state, and your start date and end date. List only high school if that is your highest level of education. Do not list elementary or middle school.
- **Other skills.** This section is optional. List any other skills you want the employer to know about. For example, you can include computer skills, languages you speak, or other specific knowledge that you have.

Here are some important tips for writing your resume:

- Your resume should be very easy to read. Make it look formal and professional. Use a computer or typewriter. Print on white or off-white paper (no colors).
- Give short, descriptive pieces of information. Don't write sentences.
- Include only honest information that is related to your job objective. Never lie.
- Check it very carefully. Make sure there are no mistakes in spelling, capitalization, punctuation, or grammar. Ask at least two other people to check it.
- Do not give any personal information, such as your height, weight, age, marital status, etc., on your resume. Do not include a photo when you send a resume.

Note >>>>>

A career center can be an excellent place to get help with your resume. Counselors can provide you with information about resume-writing and sample resumes. They can look at your resume, help you find mistakes, and make suggestions for improvement.

Practice

Look at the article again. What should be included on your resume? Read the information below. Circle *Y* for *Yes* or *N* for *No*.

1. the job you want	(Y)	N
2. the company where you work now	Y	N
3. the duties of your present job	Y	N
4. reason for leaving your last job	Y	N
5. skills you want the employer to know about	Y	N
6. personal information	Y	N
7. the name of the college or last school you attended	Y	N
8. your birth date	Y	N

Note >>>>>

You can find many examples of resumes on the Internet for free. It's good to look at these to get different ideas for your own resume. But, you must never copy another person's resume or include any information on your resume that is not true.

BONUS

Follow these steps to write a resume. Use a separate piece of paper.

- **Write your job objective. Remember, this should be the job that you are applying for.**
- **List your work experience, starting with your present or most recent job. Make a list of all your duties and responsibilities at each job. Then look at your lists. Which duties are related to the job you want? Make sure to include those on your resume. Try to use action words, like the ones in Exercise A on page 40. These words are descriptive and make your resume more interesting to an employer.**
- **List any schools after high school you've gone to. (Include high school if that was the last school you attended.) Name the schools you graduated from and specify what kind of certificate, diploma, or degree you received.**
- **Have at least two other people check your resume for mistakes. If you have a career center available to you, make an appointment with a counselor to go over your resume with you before you send it out.**
- **Use a computer or typewriter to make a final version of your resume.**

Lesson 3 Cover Letters

Learn

Note

When you send a resume to an employer, you must send a cover letter also. This is a short letter in which you introduce yourself, express your interest in the position, and explain your qualifications, or reasons why you would be a good person for the job. Your qualifications can include skills, experience, and education, as well as personal qualities. The letter should be typed and follow business-letter form as shown below.

Read the cover letter. Then read the sentences on page 47. Circle *T* for *True* or *F* for *False*.

14224 N. 51st Ave., Apt. 2B
Glendale, AZ 85306
623-555-0192
miguelramos@wow.com] **return address**

July 14, 2009] **date**

Vivian White
Carlson Communications
204 South Central Ave.
Phoenix, AZ 85001] **inside address**

Dear Ms. White,] **salutation**

body of letter

① I am writing to express my interest in the position of computer support specialist advertised in the *Arizona Republic* on July 12, 2009. I have recently completed my education at Top Technical School, where I received a computer support specialist certificate.

② My training, skills, and experience make me an excellent candidate for the position. I am organized, hard-working, and good with people. I have developed strong customer service skills in my current job as a restaurant manager.

③ My resume is enclosed for your review. Next week I will call your office to request a time when we may meet to discuss my qualifications and your company's needs. Thank you for your time and consideration.

Sincerely,] **closing**

Miguel Ramos] **signature**

Miguel Ramos] **typed name**

1. Carlson Communications is located at 204 South Central Ave. (T) F
2. Miguel gives Ms. White his e-mail address. T F
3. Miguel wants to work for the *Arizona Republic.* T F
4. Miguel has experience in customer service. T F
5. Miguel will call Ms. White to ask for an interview. T F

Practice

A **Read the cover letter again. Answer the questions. Write *1, 2,* or *3*.**

In which paragraph does Miguel . . .

1. mention some of his skills? ____
2. explain how he found out about the job? ____
3. thank the person? ____
4. state the position he is interested in? ____

B **Read the cover letter again. Answer the questions.**

What words does Miguel use in his letter to . . .

1. explain the purpose of the letter? I am writing to express my interest in the position of computer support specialist. . . .
2. tell about his education? ____________________
3. tell about his skills and personal qualities? ____________________
4. tell about his experience? ____________________
5. request an interview? ____________________

Note >>>>> *Begin a cover letter with* Dear Mr./Ms. ________. *If you don't know the name of the person in charge of hiring, try to find out. Call the company and ask for the name of the hiring manager. End the letter with* Sincerely. *Then sign and type your name.*

Make It Yours

Imagine you saw this ad in your local newspaper. Fill in the blank with a job you're interested in. Use the information in the ad and your own information to write a cover letter for the job.

New company needs
hard-working and
motivated ______.
Excellent ref. req.
Experience preferred.
Apply to Mr. Derrick James,
ACC Inc., 1001 First Ave.,
Phoenix, AZ 85005.

Lesson 4 Job Applications

Learn

 Read the job application.

EMPLOYMENT APPLICATION

Personal Information

Name: ______________________ Phone: ______________ Email: ______________

Address: ____

Availability

Desired position: ______________________ Available starting date: ______________

Are you available: _____ full-time _____ part-time _____ overtime

_____ days _____ nights _____ weekends

Are you eligible to work in the United States? _____ Yes _____ No

Employment (Begin with present or last job.)

Employer: ______________________ Position: ______________________

Address: ______________________________ Phone: ______________

Duties: ______________________ Supervisor's Name: ______________

From (Month/Year): ______________ To (Month/Year): ______________

Reason for Leaving: ____

Employer: ______________________ Position: ______________________

Address: ______________________________ Phone: ______________

Duties: ______________________ Supervisor's Name: ______________

From (Month/Year): ______________ To (Month/Year): ______________

Reason for Leaving: ____

Education (Give only your highest level of education.)

School name: ____

School address: ____

From: ____________ To: ____________ Did you graduate? _____ Yes _____ No

Other Skills (languages, training, equipment, machines, etc.)

____

References (no family members)

Name	Phone number	Relationship	Years known

I certify that this information is true and complete.

Signature: ______________________ **Date:** ______________________

Some employers may ask you to fill out an application instead of giving a resume. Some employers may ask you to do both.

Look at the application again. Write each word in the box next to its meaning.

certify	desired position	eligible	present	supervisor

desired position 1. the job you want

__________ 2. able or allowed to do something

__________ 3. happening or existing now

__________ 4. a person who is in charge of something or someone; a boss

__________ 5. state that something is correct or true

Practice

Look at the application again. Name the section of the application where you would provide information about each of these things.

Other Skills 1. things you can do well

__________ 2. people who can recommend you for the job

__________ 3. your home address

__________ 4. schools you've attended

__________ 5. your job experience

__________ 6. the schedule you can work

Make It Yours

Answer the questions.

1. Use the *Other Skills* section of a job application to tell the employer about abilities you have, such as languages you speak, training you've received, or equipment or machines you can use. Write at least one skill you have below.

____

2. Past or present bosses, co-workers, and teachers can be good references. But make sure you choose people who will say good things about you and your work. Write the names of three people you could use as references.

__________ __________ __________

B **Think of a job you'd like to have. Imagine you're applying for that job. Complete the application on page 48 with your own information.**

Lesson 5 Job Interviews

Learn

Read the article. Then answer the questions below. Circle *Y* for *Yes* or *N* for *No*.

Ace Your Interview

Did you know . . . ? Studies show that less than half of communication is spoken. The rest of the message you send comes from your appearance (the way you look) and behavior (the things you do). This is very important when going to a job interview. An interviewer will quickly form an opinion about you based on how you look and act. Here are some tips to help you send the right message.

- ✓ Choose clothing that is appropriate for the job you're interviewing for, and not too casual. For example, it's usually better for men to wear a button-down shirt, slacks, and shoes instead of a T-shirt, jeans, and sneakers. Your clothes should always be clean, pressed, and in good condition.
- ✓ Make sure your hair is neat and clean.
- ✓ Make sure your fingernails are short, neat, and clean.
- ✓ Use little or no perfume or cologne. Women should wear light makeup.
- ✓ Wear little or no jewelry.

Once you get to the interview, here are a few things to keep in mind:

- ✓ Throw away your gum and any drinks or food before you meet the interviewer.
- ✓ In the United States, men *and* women shake hands. With each person you meet at an interview, give a firm handshake, smile, and look the person in the eye. Introduce yourself.

Try to remember these things during the interview:

- ✓ Sit up straight. Keep both feet on the floor and your hands in your lap.
- ✓ Don't move around a lot. Don't tap your fingers or feet.
- ✓ Make eye contact with the person.
- ✓ Nod your head as the interviewer talks to show you're interested.
- ✓ Speak clearly. Don't talk too fast.

Should you . . .

1. wear jeans and sneakers? Y (N)
2. have a neat, clean appearance? Y N
3. chew gum? Y N
4. give a strong handshake? Y N
5. look the interviewer in the eye when you're talking? Y N

Note >>>>>> *Some employers will ask you to fill out a job application at your interview. Take with you the names, addresses, and dates of your past jobs and schools, as well as names and phone numbers of your references, so you can complete the application if necessary. If the job requires a resume, take several copies with you.*

Practice

A **Look at the pictures. Write two positive things and three negative things about each candidate's appearance or behavior.**

Michael Parks

Positive

1. ______________________________

2. ______________________________

Negative

1. ______________________________

2. ______________________________

3. ______________________________

Angela Hudson

Positive

1. ______________________________

2. ______________________________

Negative

1. ______________________________

2. ______________________________

3. ______________________________

B *PAIRS.* **Compare your answers.**

Make It Yours

CLASS. **Walk around the room and introduce yourself to at least five classmates. Give a strong handshake, make eye contact, and smile.**

Learn

It's a good idea to practice answering some common interview questions before you go on an interview. Read these questions and the advice on how to answer them.

Question	How to answer
Tell me about yourself.	Unless the interviewer asks for personal information, talk only about your work experiences or your education. Tell about jobs you have had and things you have done that relate to the position you're interviewing for. ***Example:*** *I just graduated from Top Technical School with a computer support specialist certificate. I'm also working part-time as a restaurant manager. My duties include keeping records of orders and managing others. I work with people a lot, including giving excellent customer service. Before that, I was a baggage handler. At that job I had to make sure that each bag got to the correct destination. That required a lot of attention to detail.*
What is your greatest strength?	List a few things, such as your problem-solving skills, your ability to make decisions quickly, or your positive attitude. ***Example:*** *I'm very good with people. I'm patient, and I work well in a team.*
What do you dislike about your present (or last) job?	Don't say anything negative. Focus on the positive things that you want from your next job, such as more challenges (things that test your skills and abilities), the chance to move up (or get a higher position) in the company, or the opportunity to work in a certain field. ***Example:*** *I enjoy my present job. But I'm looking for more challenge—a position where I can use the technical knowledge from my education as well as my other skills and abilities.*

Make It Yours

A **Read the questions in the chart again. On a separate piece of paper, write your own answers to the questions. Always give honest answers, so use only the ideas that are true for you.**

B ***PAIRS. ROLE PLAY.*** **Practice an interview. Student A, you're interviewing for the job. Introduce yourself and shake hands. Then answer the interviewer's questions. Remember to make eye contact and show other good interview behavior. Student B, you're the interviewer. Ask the questions in the chart. Switch roles.**

BONUS **Look on the Internet for other common interview questions. Practice answering them. Then role-play an interview: Have someone else ask you the questions, and you answer them.**

Learn

Read the article.

The Most Important Question

One of the most important questions at a job interview may come at the end. Before the interview is done, the interviewer will probably ask if you have any questions. What's your answer? Yes! Career experts say that it's very important to ask questions at an interview to show you're interested in the job.

Also, this is a chance for you to interview the employer. Ask questions to find out if this is the right job for you and if this a place you want to work.

It's fine to have your questions written down when you go on an interview. Here are a few questions you might ask:

- **What are the responsibilities of the position?**
- **What are the biggest challenges of the position?**
- **How would you describe a typical work day for an employee in this position?**
- **What is the schedule for a typical work week? Is overtime required?**
- **How do employees advance in the company?**

Here are a few things you *shouldn't* ask in an interview:

- **What does the company do?**
  (You should find this out before you go to the interview.)
- **How much would I get paid?**
  (Wait until you are offered the job to talk about pay and benefits.)
- **Did I get the job?**
  (It's unusual for an employer to offer a job at the time of the interview. They'll let you know later.)

Practice

Look at the article again. Read the sentences. Circle *T* for *True* or *F* for *False*.

1. When you ask questions, you show your interest in the job. T F
2. You can take some questions written down with you to a job interview. T F
3. It's OK to ask about job responsibilities at a job interview. T F
4. It's OK to ask about money at a job interview. T F

Make It Yours

Make a list of five questions you could ask at a job interview. You can use the ones on this page, or you can look on the Internet for more suggestions.

Thank-You Notes

Learn

Read the article. Then complete the sentences. Circle the correct words or phrases.

Don't Forget to Say *Thank You*

**So, you've finished your interview—congratulations!
Now you can relax, right? Not quite yet.
There's one more thing you need to do: Write a thank-you note.**

Why? There are several reasons why you should send a thank-you note.

- It's polite, and it shows respect for the person's time.
- It shows you really want the job.
- It gives you the chance to remind the employer why you're the best candidate for the job.
- It can help you stand out from other people who also want the job.

In your note you should thank the interviewer for his or her time. Refer to the position you interviewed for, and briefly remind the interviewer why he or she should hire you.

You should send the note the day of the interview or the next day at the latest. Notes typed on a computer look formal and are fine. Handwritten notes are more personal, and they're OK, too. You may send thank-you notes by regular mail or by e-mail. If you interviewed with more than one person, send a note to each of them.

As with any written communication, check your spelling and grammar carefully before you send your note. If you're not sure of an interviewer's correct name or how to spell it, call the office to check.

1. You should include **how much you want to make / the position you interviewed for** in your thank-you note.
2. Use a thank-you note to **remind the interviewer of your skills / ask if you got the job**.
3. You should send a thank-you note about a **day / week** after an interview.
4. You should send a thank-you note to **everyone / the most important person** that you interviewed with.
5. Make sure you spell **the interviewer's name / everything** correctly in your note.

Practice

Read the thank-you note. Then answer the questions.

14224 N. 51st Ave., Apt. 2B
Glendale, AZ 85306
623-555-0192
miguelramos@wow.com

August 7, 2009

Vivian White
Carlson Communications
204 South Central Ave.
Phoenix, AZ 85001

Dear Ms. White,

Thank you for meeting with me today to discuss the computer support specialist position. Based on our conversation, I believe my skills, education, and experience are a good match for the job.

My training as a computer support specialist as well as my work experience have prepared me well for this position. I have developed strong customer service skills in my current job as a restaurant manager. I am organized, hard-working, and good with people. If hired, I would bring to this position excellent work habits and a positive attitude. I would appreciate the opportunity to provide excellent service to Carlson Communications' customers.

I look forward to hearing from you. Again, thank you for your time and consideration.

Sincerely,

Miguel Ramos

Miguel Ramos

1. What two things have prepared Miguel for the job? ____________________ and ____________________

2. What six skills and qualities does Miguel mention in his letter?

____________________ ____________________ ____________________

____________________ ____________________ ____________________

3. Is Miguel waiting for Ms. White to contact him? ______ What words in the letter tell you? ____________________________________

BONUS **Write a thank-you letter for a job that you have applied for in the past or that you would like to apply for. You can make up any information you don't know.**

Unit 3 Test

Before you take the test

ⒶⒷⒸⒹ Use the answer sheet for Unit 3 on page 209.

1. Print your name.
2. Print your teacher's name.
3. Write your student identification number, and bubble in the information below the boxes.
4. Write the test date and bubble in the information.
5. Write your class number and bubble in the information.

Listening I [Track 21]

Listen to the question or statement. What is the correct answer: A, B, or C?

1. A. I'm a manager.
B. It's fast-paced.
C. You need an appointment.

2. A. I'm looking for an entry-level position.
B. I want a position with more challenges.
C. I'm very good with people, and I work well on a team.

3. A. I can start working in two weeks.
B. I want to work full-time.
C. I speak Spanish, and I can use a computer.

4. A. Yes. What are the biggest challenges of the position?
B. Yes. Did I get the job?
C. Yes. Do you have any experience?

Listening II [Track 22]

Listen. Test items 5, 6, and 7 are on the audio CD.

Reading

Read. What is the correct answer: A, B, C, or D?

Carla was looking for a job as a hair stylist. She looked at the job ads in the newspaper each week. She applied to several jobs, but she never heard from any of the employers. Carla also told her friends she was looking for a job. One of her friend's cousins, Sarah, owned a salon. Carla's friend gave Carla the phone number of her cousin. Carla called Sarah, and they talked. A month later, Sarah called Carla. She said one of her workers had quit, and she needed a new stylist. Carla went to the salon for an interview. The next day Sarah offered her the job.

8. How did Carla get her job?

A. She answered an ad in the newspaper.

B. She networked.

C. She sent her resume to the company.

D. She started to work for a friend.

9. According to the story, what did Carla do before she was offered the job?

A. She completed an application.

B. She got some experience.

C. She sent in her resume.

D. She had an interview.

NATASHA TITOV
1142 15th St., Apt. 8A, Brooklyn, NY 11235
718-555-8462 ntitov@nycmail.com

JOB OBJECTIVE

To obtain a position as assistant manager of a hotel

WORK EXPERIENCE

Front Desk Clerk May 2008–present
Worthington Hotel

- Handle guest reservations by phone and in person
- Ensure a smooth process of registration, payment, and departure for all guests
- Organize and maintain reservations and other records
- Provide excellent customer service, including responding to customer questions, requests, and complaints

Manager/Crew Member May 2005–May 2008
Front Door Restaurant

- Achieved promotion from crew member to manager in just one year
- Managed crew of ten people in fast-paced environment
- Hired and trained new employees
- Organized and maintained records of orders and supplies

---

10. What information should Natasha add to this resume?

A. her date of birth

B. her employment history

C. her education

D. how much money she makes

11. What is Natasha's current job?

A. assistant manager of a hotel

B. front desk clerk

C. manager

D. crew member

12. What does Natasha's experience *not* include?

A. a job as an assistant manager of a hotel

B. providing customer service

C. a job as a crew member

D. hiring new employees

1300 Wall St., Apt. 32
Tampa, FL 33601
813-555-1486
mirasen@bop.mail.com

August 25, 2009

Jennifer Brady
ABC Medical Group
5083 Roosevelt Blvd.
Tampa, FL 33634

Dear Ms. Brady,

I am writing to express my interest in the position of medical assistant advertised in *The Tampa Tribune* on August 23, 2009. I have recently completed my education at Palm Technical School and received a certificate from their medical assistant program.

My training, skills, and experience make me an excellent candidate for the position. I am motivated, detail-oriented, and good with people. I have developed strong professional skills in my current job as a customer service assistant.

I have included my resume for your review. I will call your office next week to request a time to discuss how my qualifications may meet your company's needs. Thank you for your time and consideration.

Sincerely,

Mira Sen

Mira Sen

13. Why did Mira send the letter?

A. to thank the person for an interview

B. to say she is interested in a job

C. to thank the person for the job offer

D. to accept the company's job offer

14. Which sentence is correct?

A. Mira doesn't have any job experience.

B. Mira is good at paying attention to small things.

C. Mira will wait for Ms. Brady to call her.

D. Mira is now working as a medical assistant.

WANTED

Sales Assistant

PT 20 hrs./week
$11/hr., exc. bens.
min. 1 yr. exp.
biling. pref'd.
exc. refs. req.
Apply in prsn. at The Hot Spot.
Ask for mgr. No appt. nec.

15. What is required for this job?

A. overtime

B. benefits

C. experience

D. an appointment

16. How can a person apply for the job?

A. make an appointment

B. go to The Hot Spot

C. call the manager

D. get references

Unit 4 Safety and Emergency Planning

Lesson 1 **Fire Safety**
- Identify some ways to prevent fires
- Identify what to do in case of fire

Lesson 2 **Reporting an Emergency**
- Identify emergencies
- Answer questions and follow the instructions of a 911 operator

Lesson 3 **Emergency Evacuations**
- Plan for an emergency evacuation

Lesson 1 Fire Safety

Learn

Read these important fire safety tips. Check the ones you follow in your home.

☐ Keep space heaters at least three feet from anything that can burn. Never leave heaters on when you leave home or go to bed.

☐ Don't plug too many things into one outlet.

☐ Keep matches and lighters out of children's reach.

☐ Put smoke alarms on each level of your home and outside of each sleeping area. Check smoke alarms once a month and change their batteries twice a year.

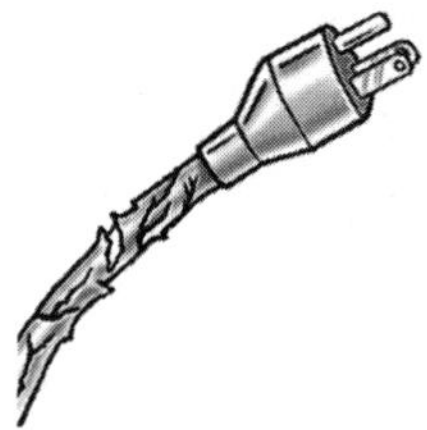

☐ Check all your electrical cords, and replace any that are cracked or frayed.

☐ Buy and learn how to use a fire extinguisher. Keep it near the entrance to your kitchen, away from the stove.

Practice

Look at the fire safety tips again. Then read the sentences. Circle *T* for *True* or *F* for *False*.

1. It's OK to keep a space heater on when you sleep if it's very cold. T (F)
2. It's OK to keep a space heater on when you leave the house for a short period of time. T F
3. It's important to keep matches in a place where children can't reach them. T F
4. If you have a cracked electrical cord, you should try to fix it. T F
5. You shouldn't plug in a lot of things in one outlet. T F
6. You need a smoke alarm in every room in your house. T F
7. You should check your smoke alarms twice a year to be sure they're working. T F
8. You should have a fire extinguisher in your home. T F

Learn

A **Do you know how to respond to a fire? What is the first thing you should do if there's a fire in your home? Put a check next to the correct answer. If you don't know, you can guess.**

☐ Get your wallet. ☐ Call 911. ☐ Get out of the building.

B **Now read the information below and check your answer.**

Responding to a Fire

- Plan two ways to get out of every room if there's a fire. Choose a place to meet after everyone is safely outside. Practice the plan with your family.
- If there's a fire that you can't quickly and easily put out, get out of the building immediately! Do not stop to call 911 or take anything with you.
- Never use an elevator if there's a fire.
- Do not open a door if it's hot; there may be a fire behind it. Leave another way.
- If you must exit through smoke, get on your hands and knees and crawl to the nearest safe exit. Heat and smoke rise, so the cleanest, coolest air is near the floor. If possible, cover your mouth and nose with a wet cloth.
- If your clothes catch on fire, don't run! Stop, lie down, and roll your body over and over on the ground to put out the fire. Cover your face with your hands.
- After you have left the building, call 911 from a cell phone or a neighbor's phone.*
- Never go back into a burning building for any reason. Tell firefighters about anyone still inside the building.

For more information on fire safety, go to http://www.fema.gov/areyouready/fire.shtm.

*See pages 64–65 for more information on 911.

Practice

Look at the information again. Complete the sentences. Use the words in the box.

crawl	go	leave	roll	take	touch	use

1. You should ____leave____ your home immediately if there's a fire.
2. Don't ________ anything with you.
3. When there's a fire, you should ________ any door before you open it.
4. If there's smoke, you should ________ on the floor to the closest safety exit.
5. If your clothes are on fire, you should ________ on the ground.
6. After you leave your home, ________ a cell phone or a neighbor's phone to call 911.
7. Never ________ into a building that's on fire.

Lesson 2 Reporting an Emergency

Learn

A *PAIRS.* **Look at the emergencies. Which ones do you know? Match the sentences with the pictures.**

a. He got burned.	e. There's a downed power line.	i. He's choking.
b. He's drowning.	f. He's having a heart attack.	j. There was a hit-and-run.
c. A house is on fire.	g. She needs an ambulance.	k. She swallowed poison.
d. She's unconscious.	h. Someone is breaking into a house.	l. There's a violent fight.

1. g

2. ____

3. ____

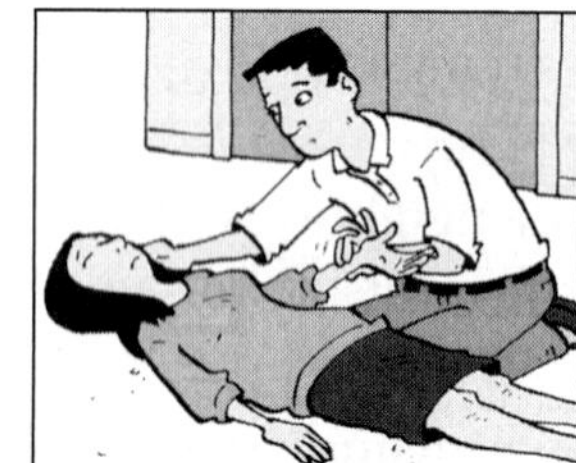

4. ____

5. ____

6. ____

7. ____

8. ____

9. ____

10. ____

11. ____

12. ____

B **Listen and check your answers.**

C *PAIRS.* **Which words do you know? Answer the questions.**

1. Do you **hang up** at the beginning of a phone conversation or at the end?

 ____

2. If someone is **on the way** to your house, is the person leaving your house, or is the person going to arrive there soon? ____________________

3. If you **stay on the line**, do you finish your phone call or continue to talk on the phone?

 ____

D **Read the information.**

Help Is Just a Phone Call Away

911 is an emergency response system in the United States. Dial 911 any time there is a medical emergency, a fire emergency, or a police emergency. You can call the number for free from any phone, including home phones, pay phones, and cell phones.

When you call 911, try to stay calm. The 911 operator will ask you some questions and then send the appropriate help (an ambulance, the fire department, or police officers). Be prepared to give the following information:

- **The type of emergency** (Say exactly what the emergency is, for example, *Someone is drowning, Someone is stealing a car, My apartment building is on fire.*)
- **The exact location of the emergency** (Give the address, including the apartment number. Give any other information you know, such as the building name or the color of the building. Give the cross streets or the closest intersection.)
- **Details about the emergency** (Give as much information as you can about what happened, what's being done, etc.)
- **Your name and the phone number you're calling from** (You can report a crime to 911 anonymously, that is, without giving your name, if you prefer.)

Do not hang up until help arrives. The 911 operator might have more questions or more instructions for you. The operator does not have to hang up with you in order to send help. While you are talking, help is already on the way.

Remember, an emergency is a situation that needs an immediate response. Do not call 911 unless there is an emergency.

Listen

CD1 TRACK 24

Read the questions below. Then listen to the 911 call. Check the questions the 911 operator asks.

- ☐ What's your emergency?
- ☐ What's the location of the emergency?
- ☐ What's the closest cross street?
- ☐ Where's the closest hospital?
- ☐ Is anyone inside your home?
- ☐ How old are you?
- ☐ How old is your son?
- ☐ What's your name?
- ☐ What's your son's name?
- ☐ What number are you calling from?

Practice

  **Oscar Montes is calling 911. Listen to the conversation and read.**

Operator: 9-1-1. What's your emergency?
Oscar: My daughter is choking.
Operator: OK. What's the location of the emergency?
Oscar: I'm at home. The address is 1820 Sabina Street. It's a big, red apartment building. The apartment number is 22.
Operator: OK. What's the closest intersection?
Oscar: Sabina Street and 18th Avenue.
Operator: All right. Is your daughter conscious?
Oscar: Yes, she is.
Operator: Is she breathing?
Oscar: No!
Operator: OK. How old is your daughter?
Oscar: She's seven.
Operator: And what's your name?
Oscar: Oscar Montes.
Operator: What number are you calling from?
Oscar: 619-555-2834.
Operator: All right, Oscar. Help is on the way. Stay on the line until an ambulance arrives.

 ***PAIRS.*** **Practice the conversation. Switch roles.**

Make It Yours

PAIRS. ROLE PLAY. **Create new conversations. Use the conversation above as a model and the information below.**

1. **Student A:** Your 75-year-old friend is having a heart attack. She isn't conscious, but she's breathing. Call 911. Use your own address and phone number.
   Student B: Answer the call. Ask questions about the situation.
2. **Student B:** Your friend's four-year-old son swallowed poison. He's not conscious or breathing. Call 911. Use your own address and phone number.
   Student A: Answer the call. Ask questions about the situation.

BONUS

1. **Imagine there's an emergency at your school. You need to call 911. Do you know the address and closest intersection of your school? If not, find out, and write them down.**
2. **Think of another place you go to often, such as your work or a friend or family member's home. Do you know the address and closest intersection of the place in case you needed to call 911? If not, find out, and write them down.**

Lesson 3 Emergency Evacuations

Learn

Note
>>>>>>

Emergencies such as hurricanes, tornadoes, earthquakes, and floods can cause a lot of damage to homes. During or after some weather emergencies, it might not be safe to stay in your home. It's a good idea to have some things ready to take with you in case you have to evacuate, or leave your home to go somewhere safe.

A *PAIRS.* **Look at some of the things you might need if you had to evacuate. Which words do you know? Write the correct words under the pictures. Use the words in the box.**

a can opener	a first-aid kit	a flashlight and batteries	utensils
a gallon of water	a hand-crank radio	hand wipes	
pillows and blankets	a pocket knife	non-perishable food	

1. 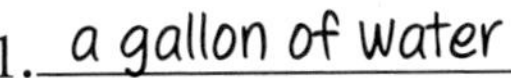

2. ____________
3. ____________
4. ____________

5. 
6. ____________
7. 

8. ____________
9. ____________
10. ____________

B **Read the article.**

If you have to leave your home because of a weather emergency, you probably won't have a lot of time to plan. You should always have some important things packed and ready to go in bags or containers in case you need to leave quickly.

✓ Pack enough water and food for at least three days. You need one gallon of water per person per day. You should have non-perishable food, that is, food that does not need to be refrigerated or cooked, such as canned or dried food. Also take a can opener, a pocket knife, paper or plastic cups and plates, and plastic utensils. Pack some plastic bags to use for trash.

✓ Make sure you have a battery-powered or hand-crank radio so you can get information and instructions from local government officials.

✓ Pack hand wipes and paper towels to stay clean so you don't get sick. Get a first-aid kit so you can take care of anyone who gets hurt or sick.

✓ Don't forget personal products such as prescription medication, extra contact lenses or eyeglasses, a toothbrush, toothpaste, diapers if you have a baby, etc.

✓ Pack a blanket and pillow for each person in your family. Have extra clothes for each family member. Take coats, hats, and gloves if the weather is cold.

✓ You'll want things such as books, puzzles, or games, especially if you have children, to keep the family entertained. Also take a flashlight and extra batteries.

✓ You should have identification, including birth certificates, passports, and/or social security cards for each person in your family. Also, make copies of insurance papers, bank account records, medical records, and children's school records. Make sure you have a map of the area. Take cash and credit cards.

It's important to plan where you would go if you had to evacuate. Some cities have shelters, or buildings where many people can stay in order to be safe. You can call the American Red Cross at 1-888-843-5748 to find the shelter nearest you. Shelters usually do not offer beds, food, or medical care. Also consider staying with a friend or family member who lives outside of the evacuation area.

Once you know where you would go, think about how you would get there. If you drove, what route, or way, would you take? Consider that many other people might also be evacuating, so there could be a lot of traffic. Some cities offer public transportation to evacuation shelters. You should know how and where to get this transportation if you need it.

Practice

A **Look at the article again. Complete the sentences. Circle the correct words or phrases.**

1. When you evacuate, you **stay in** / **leave** your home.
2. If you evacuate, you should take enough water for **two** / **three** days.
3. Each person needs one **quart** / **gallon** of water for each day.
4. You should take **fresh** / **canned** vegetables.
5. You should take copies of **important papers** / **a first aid kit**.
6. A shelter offers **safety** / **food**.

B **Look at the article again. Make sentences about things to take if you evacuate. Match the sentence beginnings and endings.**

1. Take a can opener so	you can stay clean.
2. Take hand wipes so	you have a place to put trash.
3. Take a radio so	you can open cans of food.
4. Take plastic bags so	you can get information.
5. Take a first aid kit so	you don't get too bored.
6. Take games and puzzles so	you can take care of someone who gets hurt.

BONUS

Find out about emergencies that are likely in your area. Make a plan with your family. Answer the questions below on a separate piece of paper. You can go to www.ready.gov or www.fema.gov/areyouready for more information. You can also contact the American Red Cross in your area (go to http://www.redcross.org/where/where.html to find one near you) for materials on community disaster education.

- What emergencies are likely in your area?
- Where would you go if you had to evacuate? (Consider shelters and the homes of family and friends outside the area.)
- How would you get there? (Do you have a car? What route would you take? Are there planned emergency evacuation routes in your area?)
- What would you take with you? (Make a list of supplies you'd need. Look at page 67 for ideas. Consider the needs of each person in your family.)

Unit 4 Test

Before you take the test

ⒶⒷⒸⒹ Use the answer sheet for Unit 4 on page 211.

1. Print your name.
2. Print your teacher's name.
3. Write your student identification number, and bubble in the information below the boxes.
4. Write the test date and bubble in the information.
5. Write your class number and bubble in the information.

CD1 Listening I [Track 26]

You will hear a conversation. Then you will hear three sentences. Which sentence is true: A, B, or C?

1. A. The man is going to evacuate.
B. Someone is going to call 911.
C. The man needs a fire extinguisher now.

2. A. This is an emergency.
B. The woman should evacuate.
C. A woman is drowning.

3. A. The person needs an ambulance.
B. The woman saw someone stealing a car.
C. Someone is trying to get into another person's home.

CD1 Listening II [Track 27]

Listen. Test items 4, 5, 6, and 7 are on the audio CD.

Reading

Read. What is the correct answer: A, B, C, or D?

Tao and his wife, Jing, live in California, in an area where there are sometimes weather emergencies, such as fires and earthquakes. Especially when there are fires, sometimes it isn't safe for Tao and Jing to stay in their home. They keep some important things packed and ready to go so they can evacuate quickly if it's necessary. They have enough water and non-perishable food for three days. They also have a radio, flashlights, and extra batteries. They made a first-aid kit with medical supplies and Jing's prescription medication. They also have copies of all their important papers, including their medical records, insurance papers, and bank account records.

If they ever have to evacuate, Tao and Jing plan to go to a shelter not too far from their house. The shelter will provide them with safety, but Tao and Jing know that they should take things that won't be provided at the shelter, like clothes, blankets, pillows, and food and water.

Tao and Jing hope they never need to evacuate. But if it's necessary, they'll be ready.

8. Why do Tao and Jing have an evacuation kit?

A. There was a fire, but they didn't evacuate.

B. They want to be ready in case they need to evacuate.

C. Jing takes prescription medication.

D. They know they always need to evacuate when there's an emergency.

9. What will Tao and Jing take with them if they evacuate?

A. fresh food for one week

B. their school records

C. pillows and blankets

D. shelter

Eva was outside watching her two sons play. One of them was climbing up a tree, and he fell. Eva went running to him. The boy was breathing but unconscious. Eva called 911 immediately. She told the 911 operator she needed an ambulance. The operator asked Eva some questions. Then he told her to stay on the line until the ambulance arrived.

10. What were the operator's instructions?

A. Don't hang up yet.

B. Call back.

C. Wait outside.

D. Hang up now.

One cold night last winter, Ganesh was watching TV in his living room. He was using a space heater to stay warm. Ganesh got very tired while he was watching TV. He turned off the television, but he forgot about the space heater, and he went to bed. Then Ganesh heard a very loud sound—the smoke alarm. His house was on fire! Suddenly Ganesh was very awake. There was a fire extinguisher in the kitchen, and he thought about getting it to put out the fire. He ran to the door of his bedroom, which was closed. He touched it, and it was hot. He knew that meant there was probably a fire on the other side of the door. He needed to get out of the house fast, so he escaped through a window. After he was outside, he went to a neighbor's house to call 911 and report the fire.

11. How did the fire probably start?

A. It probably started with matches.

B. It probably started with the space heater.

C. It probably started with the smoke alarm.

D. It probably started with the fire extinguisher.

12. How did Ganesh know there was a fire?

A. He heard the smoke alarm.

B. He saw the fire.

C. His neighbor called him.

D. His room was hot.

13. What did Ganesh do first?

A. He turned off the space heater.

B. He put out the fire.

C. He left the house.

D. He called 911.

14. Why did Ganesh leave through a window instead of the door?

A. The bedroom door was closed.

B. The 911 operator told him to use the window.

C. His neighbor told him the house was on fire.

D. There was probably a fire on the other side of the door.

Are you prepared?

Here are some things your family should have ready in case you need to make an emergency evacuation.

Staying healthy is a big concern after many emergencies, especially if a lot of people are evacuating to one area. Plan for the following if you have to evacuate:

- You may be somewhere without safe drinking water. Each person needs 1 gallon of water per day. Plan to take enough water for three days.
- You probably won't have a refrigerator to put food in. Many kinds of food go bad quickly when they're not cold. You can avoid this problem by having enough non-perishable canned or dried food for three days in your kit. Include a can opener if you have canned foods.
- You will need to find a way to stay clean. Make sure you have paper towels and hand wipes. Take bags for your trash.
- Pack a first-aid kit so you can take care of anyone who gets hurt or sick.

15. What is the purpose of this information?

A. to explain how to make a first-aid kit for an emergency

B. to explain what to do in an emergency

C. to explain how to use a first-aid kit in an emergency

D. to explain what you should pack for an emergency evacuation

16. How much water should you take for each person if you evacuate?

A. 1 gallon per person per day

B. water for each person

C. three days

D. 1 gallon each

17. What kind of food should you take if you evacuate?

A. cold food

B. non-perishable food

C. a can opener

D. food in the refrigerator

Unit 5 Smart Shopping

Lesson 1 **Researching Before You Buy**
- Research different products and prices before making a big purchase

Lesson 2 **Advertising Techniques**
- Recognize deceptive advertising techniques

Lesson 3 **Returns and Exchanges**
- Understand a store's return policy
- Give a reason for returning an item

Lesson 4 **Warranties**
- Understand warranties

Lesson 1 Researching Before You Buy

Learn

Note >>>>> *It's a good idea to do some research, or get information, before you make big purchases. (A big purchase is something you buy that's expensive). That can mean finding out about similar items and brands to compare their features, or important details. It can also mean looking at the prices of the same item at different stores or online. Sometimes you can use ads to help you research.*

A *PAIRS.* **Read the advertisements for washing machines. Then answer the questions. Use the context (pictures and other words) to help you.**

Clean CLX
$499.99
• Top-loading feature—easier to put clothes in and take them out.
• Four wash/rinse temperatures—gives you options.
• Short wash time—finishes in just 30 minutes.
• Compact size—ideal for small houses and apartments.
• Rated #1 washing machine under $500 by Happy Home magazine.

WASHING WIZ
$594.99
★ Front-loading model is gentler on clothing than traditional top-loading washers.
★ High-efficiency model uses less energy, detergent, and water than standard models.
★ Extra-large capacity lets you wash up to 12 pairs of jeans at once.
★ Delay feature lets you choose a later time to start the wash.

1. Where do you put the clothes in a top-loading machine? in the top of the machine
   In a front-loading machine? in the front of the machine
2. When you rinse something, do you clean it with soap or use water to remove the soap? __________
3. If something is compact, is it large or small? __________
4. Does a high-efficiency machine use a lot of energy or a little? __________
5. Does the capacity of a washing machine describe how much it can wash at one time or how well it cleans? __________
6. If you delay something, do you make it start earlier or later? __________

B **Look at the washing machine advertisements again. Answer the questions. Check *Clean CLX* or *Washing Wiz*.**

Which washing machine . . .	Clean CLX	Washing Wiz
1. is smaller?	☑	☐
2. cleans clothing quickly?	☐	☐
3. can wash a lot of clothing at one time?	☐	☐
4. is energy efficient?	☐	☐
5. is a favorite of magazine readers?	☐	☐
6. has more than three water temperatures?	☐	☐

Practice

Look at the advertisements again. Read the situations. Answer the questions.

1. Mrs. Martin has back problems, and it hurts her to bend down. Which washing machine would she probably prefer? the Clean CLX Why? It's a top-loading machine. It's easier to get clothes in and out because you don't have to bend over.
2. Cheng lives alone in a small apartment. Which washing machine would she probably prefer? ____________ Why? ____________
3. Dave and Kate have four children. Which washing machine would they probably prefer? ____________ Why? ____________
4. Marisol wants to do what's best for the environment. Which washing machine would she probably prefer? ____________ Why? ____________

Make It Yours

PAIRS. **Look at the advertisements again. Imagine you're going to buy a new washing machine. Which machine would you prefer? Why? Discuss.**

BONUS

GROUPS OF 3. **Do you do research before you make big purchases? If so, how do you get information?**

Lesson 2 Advertising Techniques

Learn

A **Read the article.**

BUYERS BEWARE!

Buyers beware—many companies can be deceptive in their advertisements, meaning that they try to make you believe things about their products that aren't true. Here are some common situations and advice on how to avoid them.

Situation: You're shopping for a cell phone. You see that Talk-A-Lot is offering a free cell phone if you sign a contract, or agreement, with the company. You go to the store, and you find out that you have to pay a $100.00 activation fee before your phone will work. Then you learn that there's a monthly maintenance fee of $70.00. And if you cancel your contract before the end of two years, you have to pay $350.00 Suddenly the "free" phone looks very expensive.

How to avoid this: Always read a contract carefully before you sign it. Ask exactly what fees there are.

Situation: You see that TVs are on sale at Electric City for 30% off, but you look at prices of TVs at a few other stores, too. You find out that the regular price of TVs at Electric City is about 30% more than the regular prices at most other stores. So even with a "sale" of 30% off, Electric City's prices aren't any better than other stores' prices.

How to avoid this: Before you buy, compare prices of the same or similar items at a few different places. You can go to stores, look at newspaper ads, or look online.

Situation: You see that Photo Fun is offering a good camera at a great price. You go into the store, and you find out that the price doesn't include the battery, something that is normally included in the price of a camera. The salesperson offers you a "special" (higher) price for the camera and the battery together. This "special" priceis more than you would pay for the camera and its battery at most other stores.

How to avoid this: Ask exactly what is included with any product you buy. Compare the price of products and other things they come with at different stores.

Situation: You want to buy fruit juice for your family, and you pick up a bottle of Fruity Juice Drink. The name has the word *juice* in it, but you check the ingredients on the label. The first ingredient is water, and the second is sugar. The label also says that the drink may contain up to 2% orange, apple, and grape juice. The "juice" drink actually contains only a very tiny amount of juice.

How to avoid this: Read labels carefully, especially the fine, or small, print for more information about the product.

B **Look at the article again. Complete the sentences. Circle the correct words or phrases.**

1. If someone tells you to beware, you should **listen carefully / be careful**.
2. A deceptive ad tells you something that **is / isn't** true.
3. When you sign a contract, you **agree to / don't** do something.
4. When you cancel a contract, you **start / end** the agreement.
5. A fee is money you **get / have to pay**.
6. Read the **fine print / product's name** on a label to get more information about the product.

Listen

CD1 TRACK 28 **Listen to each conversation. Then complete the sentence. Circle *a* or *b*.**

1. The man asks if _____.

   a. there are extra costs **b.** the item is on sale

2. The woman tells the man to _____.

   a. read the ingredients **b.** save his money

3. The woman wants to _____.

   a. buy the item now **b.** go to other stores

4. The man wants to know _____.

   a. what the price includes **b.** what kind of battery he needs

Practice

Look at the article again. Which suggestions does the writer of the article give? Check the sentences.

- ☐ 1. Don't buy anything on sale.
- ☐ 2. Don't sign a contract before you read it.
- ☐ 3. Ask questions. Find out all the details of a deal, including extra fees.
- ☐ 4. Research the cost of different things at different stores.
- ☐ 5. Make sure you know what is included with a product before you buy it.
- ☐ 6. Read the fine print.
- ☐ 7. Buy only things that are on sale.

Make It Yours

GROUPS OF 3. **Have you ever seen examples of deceptive advertising? Talk about your own experiences or things that have happened to other people.**

Lesson 3 Returns and Exchanges

Learn

A *PAIRS.* **Which words do you know? Complete the sentences. Use the words in the box.**

exchange	method of payment	policy	receipt	return
merchandise	original	purchase	refund	store credit

1. The things that a store sells are its ____merchandise____.
2. Your ____________ is how you pay for something, for example, cash, credit card, or a check.
3. When you ____________ something, you take it back to the store.
4. When you ____________ something, you take it back to the store and get something else instead.
5. If something is ____________, it's the first one, not a copy.
6. A ____________ is a piece of paper that shows you paid for something.
7. When you get ____________, you receive a card or piece of paper worth a specific amount that you can use instead of money in that store.
8. A ____________ is money given back to you when you return something to a store.
9. When you ____________ something, you buy it.
10. A company's ____________ is its rules about a certain thing.

B *PAIRS.* **Sometimes when you return things to a store, you have to give the reason for the return. Look at these reasons to return things. Match each reason with its meaning.**

____ 1. It doesn't work. a. I changed my opinion on the item.

____ 2. I changed my mind. b. It doesn't do what it's supposed to do.

____ 3. It doesn't fit. c. It's broken or not right in some way.

____ 4. It's damaged. d. It's not the right size.

Practice

Look at the store's return policy. Then read the questions. Write the correct answers.

Metro Mart

Return Policy

- Customers may return merchandise within 90 days of purchase in order to receive a refund.
- Refunds will be given for new merchandise with the original receipt. Refunds will be given in the original method of payment.
- After 90 days, no refunds will be given. Merchandise may be returned for store credit or exchanged.
- Customers returning an item without a receipt may exchange the item or receive store credit for the price of the item.

1. Can you return something to Metro Mart a month after you bought it? ___yes___
2. Do you need a receipt to get a refund for a returned item? ________________
3. If you paid for an item with a credit card, can you get a cash refund? ________________
4. What are your choices if you return something to Metro Mart more than 90 days after you bought it? ________________ or ________________
5. What can you do if you return something to Metro Mart but you don't have your receipt? ________________ or ________________

Listen to the conversation. Listen and read.

A: I'd like to return <u>this radio</u>.
B: OK. What's the reason for the return?
A: <u>It's damaged</u>.
B: Do you have your receipt?
A: <u>Yes, I do. Here it is.</u>
B: OK. Would you like to exchange this for another <u>radio</u>?
A: No, thanks. I just want <u>my money back</u>.

Make It Yours

PAIRS. ROLE PLAY. **Make new conversations. Use the conversation above as a model. Use the information in Metro Mart's return policy and the information below.**

1. **Student A:** You bought a jacket at Metro Mart. You want to return it because it doesn't fit, but you don't have your receipt. You want to get store credit.
   Student B: Help the customer.
2. **Student B:** You bought a toaster at Metro Mart yesterday. You want to return it because you changed your mind. You have your receipt. You want a refund.
   Student A: Help the customer.

Warranties

Learn

This month *Smart Consumer* magazine talks about warranties. Read the article and answer the questions. Circle *a, b,* or *c*.

WARRANTIES—*The Basics*

A warranty is a written promise that a company will fix or replace a product if it breaks within a certain period of time after you buy it. Depending on the product, warranties are generally for one to two years, although some may be longer.

A warranty generally covers, or takes care of, problems caused by mistakes the company has made. These mistakes may be problems with parts of the product (materials) or the way a product was made (workmanship). Many warranties do not cover parts of the product that typically wear out. For example, car warranties don't usually cover tires. Warranties usually do not cover any problems that are caused by using the product incorrectly.

Some companies also offer warranties on services they provide. For example, a mechanic's shop may guarantee the work on a car for 90 days.

1. If an item with a warranty breaks, the company will usually ____.
   - **a.** fix the item or give you a new one
   - **b.** give you a refund
   - **c.** both a and b
2. Warranties usually do not cover ____.
   - **a.** parts of a product that wear out
   - **b.** problems caused by not using a product correctly
   - **c.** both a and b

B ***PAIRS.*** **Which words do you know? Match the words with their meanings.**

__c__	1. defect	a. relating to a home
____	2. household	b. relating to a business
____	3. defective	c. a problem with a product
____	4. warranty claim	d. the use of something in a way it should not be used
____	5. commercial	e. not made correctly or not working correctly
____	6. abuse	f. a request by a customer for a company to fix or replace a defective product covered by a warranty

Practice

Read the warranty. Then read the sentences. Circle *T* for *True* or *F* for *False*.

Thank you for buying an LE Electronics product. Your satisfaction is important to us.

Warranty: LE Electronics products come with a one-year warranty against defects in materials and workmanship under regular, household use. LE Electronics will repair or replace the defective product covered by this warranty. Please keep your original sales receipt. You will need it to make a warranty claim.

This product is not for commercial use. The warranty does not cover damage caused by incorrect use, abuse, or accidents.

1. The company will give you your money back if there's a problem with the product. **T** (**F**)
2. The warranty covers damage that results from problems with the product's materials. **T F**
3. The warranty covers damage that results from problems in the way the product was made. **T F**
4. You need a copy of your receipt to make a warranty claim. **T F**
5. The product shouldn't be used in a business. **T F**
6. The warranty covers problems that result from using the product incorrectly. **T F**
7. The warranty covers problems that result from an accident with the product. **T F**

BONUS

GROUPS OF 3. **Read the questions below. Share your answers with your group.**

1. **When you're choosing a product to buy, do you consider whether or not the product has a warranty? Why or why not?**
2. **To make a warranty claim, you usually need the receipt that shows when you bought the product. After you buy a product with a warranty, do you usually keep the receipt? Why or why not?**

Unit 5 Test

Before you take the test

Ⓐ Ⓑ Ⓒ Ⓓ Use the answer sheet for Unit 5 on page 213.

1. Print your name.
2. Print your teacher's name.
3. Write your student identification number, and bubble in the information below the boxes.
4. Write the test date and bubble in the information.
5. Write your class number and bubble in the information.

Listening I [Track 30]

Listen to the sentence. Which of the following means the same as the sentence you heard: A, B, or C?

1. A. The pants aren't the correct size.
B. The woman changed her mind about the pants.
C. The pants are damaged.

2. A. There's a special sale each month.
B. You have to pay for the service each month.
C. You can cancel the service after one month.

3. A. You can't get a refund without your receipt.
B. You have to give a reason for the return.
C. You can't make an exchange.

Listening II [Track 31]

Listen. Test items 4, 5, and 6 are on the audio CD.

Reading

Read. What is the correct answer: A, B, C, or D?

Rachel wanted to buy a new dishwasher for her home. She knew it was going to be expensive, so she decided to do some research. She looked online to compare the features of different dishwashers. She found two that she liked. She made a chart of the features of each dishwasher to decide which one was best for her.

FEATURES	DISH WIZ	WASH PRO 2020
delay-start feature	✓	
quick-wash cycle		✓
quiet	✓	
energy-efficient	✓	
no-heat drying option	✓	
warranty	✓ (5-year)	✓ (2-year)
price	$594.99	$499.99

7. What is the purpose of this chart?

A. to compare the different features of two dishwashers

B. to find deceptive advertising

C. to decide whether she needs a dishwasher

D. to look at the same item at different stores

8. Which sentence is true?

A. The Dish Wiz is probably noisier than the Wash Pro 2020.

B. You can set both dishwashers to start to wash at a later time.

C. Both dishwashers offer the option to dry dishes without heat.

D. The Wash Pro 2020 probably uses more energy than the Dish Wiz.

Piper and Roxy Clothing Shop

Store Return Policy

Customers may return new, unused merchandise within 14 days of purchase. Refunds will be given only for merchandise returned with the original receipt. All refunds will be given in the original method of payment. Merchandise returned after 14 days may be returned only for store credit or exchange. Merchandise returned without a receipt may be returned for store credit or exchange.

9. Which of the following does a customer need to get a refund?

A. the original method of payment

B. an exchange

C. the receipt

D. store credit

10. What can a customer get when returning an item without a receipt?

A. exchange or store credit

B. cash

C. store credit only

D. a refund

11. Which sentence is true?

A. Customers may make returns one week after buying an item.

B. Refunds will only be given two weeks or more after an item is purchased.

C. Only one method of payment is accepted.

D. You must give a reason for return.

Local Stores Involved in Deceptive Advertising

Several phone companies with stores in this area have been using deceptive advertising to try to get customers to buy their products. One common situation is this: The store advertises free phones when you sign a contract with the phone company. But they may not tell you what the contract says about expensive fees you have to pay, such as an activation fee, a maintenance fee, or an early cancellation fee.

Here's another common situation: A store offers a great price on a cell phone. But this price doesn't include the battery, which is necessary for the phone to work, and is usually included in the price of a phone.

How can you avoid these situations? Ask questions. Make sure you know exactly what you're purchasing. Ask about additional fees. Always read every contract carefully before signing it.

---

12. What is the purpose of this article?

A. to tell shoppers where to get inexpensive cell phones

B. to explain typical fees

C. to tell shoppers to be careful

D. to explain why cell phones aren't necessary

13. What advice is given in the article?

A. Check prices at different stores before you buy an item.

B. Don't sign a contract until you read it carefully.

C. Don't buy a cell phone unless you really need one.

D. But a cell phone and battery at the same time.

HomeMakers Product Warranty

Thank you for buying a HomeMakers product. All of our products come with a two-year warranty that covers defects in materials and workmanship under normal, household use. HomeMakers will repair or replace the defective product covered by this warranty.

This product is for home use only. The warranty does not cover damage caused by accidents or by abuse of this product.

Please keep your original sales receipt from the purchase of this product. You will need it to make a warranty claim.

14. What does the warranty cover?

A. the original receipt

B. defects in materials

C. damage caused by abuse

D. damage caused by accidents

15. What will HomeMakers do if the product is defective?

A. make a warranty claim

B. cover the warranty

C. give you a two-year warranty

D. replace or repair it

Unit 6 Cars

Lesson 1 Buying a Car
- **Understand auto loans and financing**

Lesson 2 Car Problems and Maintenance
- **Describe some basic car problems**
- **Understand the importance of car maintenance**

Lesson 3 Reporting a Car Accident
- **Understand steps to take after a car accident, including reporting it to an insurance company or the police**

Lesson 1 Buying a Car

Learn

A **Read the article. Then complete the sentences. Use the words in the box.**

Car-Buying Basics

If you're like most people, you don't have enough money to just go out and buy a car—you'll probably need to get a loan, or borrow money. You can get a loan from the car dealership where you buy your car. You can also get a loan from a bank, a credit union (similar to a bank, but owned by its members), or an online lender.

Sometimes when you get a car loan, you're required to make a down payment. This is part of the price of the car that you pay immediately. Lenders generally require a down payment of 3% to 13% of the total price. You can also put more money down than the amount that the lender requires.

When you borrow money, of course, you have to pay it back. Most lenders require you to pay back some of the loan every month. This is called a monthly payment.

You also have to pay interest, or extra money, on the amount that you borrow. You might hear about the APR, or annual percentage rate, of a loan. This is the rate of interest that you have to pay back when you borrow money. For example, if you have a loan with an APR of 5% and you borrow $1,000, then each year you must pay $50 in interest until you pay back all the money. The average APR on a car loan is between 3% and 10%. Different lenders offer different interest rates, so it's good to talk to a few lenders and compare their interest rates before you choose one.

The term of your loan, or length of time it takes you to pay the money back, affects the total cost of the car. Car loans often have terms of 36 or 48 months.

dealership	down payment	interest	lender	loan	term

1. When you get a _____loan_____, you borrow money from a bank, credit union, etc.
2. When you borrow money, __________ is extra money that you must pay back.
3. A __________ is a business that sells a particular company's product, especially cars.
4. A __________ is a person or business that lets people borrow money.
5. A __________ is a payment that is only part of the full price of something, with the rest to be paid later.
6. The __________ of a loan is the length of time that the loan lasts.

Listen

Listen to the question. What is the correct answer? Circle *a*, *b*, or *c*.

1. **(a.)** $700 — **b.** 7% — **c.** 7 months
2. **a.** $550 — **b.** 5.5% — **c.** 55 months
3. **a.** $600 — **b.** 6% — **c.** 60 months
4. **a.** $1,000 — **b.** 10% — **c.** 10 months
5. **a.** $3,600 — **b.** 3.6% — **c.** 36 months

Practice

Look at the article again. Answer the questions.

1. Why do many people get loans for cars? ______________________________
2. What are four different types of lenders for car loans?

______________________ ______________________

______________________ ______________________

Make It Yours

PAIRS. **Read the story and the chart. Answer the questions on a separate sheet of paper.**

Imagine you're going to buy a car. You need to get a loan. The price of the car is $8,000, and you have an interest rate of 7%. You're still deciding whether to put down $500 or $1,000 for the down payment. You also need to choose a 36-month loan or a 48-month loan. You make a chart to look at the options and see how each one will affect your monthly payments and the total cost of the car.

Price of car	$8,000	$8,000	$8,000	$8,000
Down payment	$1,000	$500	$1,000	$500
Interest rate	7%	7%	7%	7%
Term	36 months	36 months	48 months	48 months
Monthly payment	$216.13	$231.51	$167.62	$179.59
TOTAL COST	$8,781.00	$8,834.00	$9,046.00	$9,120.00

1. What is one advantage to making a larger down payment? A smaller down payment?
2. What is one advantage to having a shorter-term loan? A longer-term loan?

Lesson 2 Car Problems and Maintenance

Learn

PAIRS. **Look at the car problems. Which ones do you know? Write the sentences from the box.**

The air conditioner doesn't work.	My brakes are squeaking.	My car is leaking oil.
The check-engine light is on.	The window is stuck.	My car won't start.
My car is making a strange noise.	My car is overheating.	

1. My car won't start.

2. ______________________

3. ______________________

4. ______________________

5. ______________________

6. ______________________

7. ______________________

8. ______________________

Practice

A CD1 TRACK 33 **Lydia Montalvo is talking to her mechanic. Listen to the conversation and read.**

Mechanic: Hello, Armando's Garage. Ricardo speaking.
Lydia: Hi. This is Lydia Montalvo. Can I bring my car in today?
Mechanic: What seems to be the problem?
Lydia: My car is overheating.
Mechanic: OK. Bring it in this afternoon.
Lydia: Great. Thanks.

B *PAIRS.* **Practice the conversation. Use your own name and the car problems in the box above. Switch roles.**

Learn

A *PAIRS.* **Which words do you know? Match the words with their meanings.**

____ 1. maintenance

____ 2. manual

____ 3. lubricate

____ 4. filter

a. put something such as oil on parts of a machine in order to make them move smoothly and easily

b. work that is necessary to keep something in good condition

c. something that you pass a liquid or air through in order to remove dirt or other things so it's clean or suitable to use

d. a book that gives instructions about how to do something, especially how to use a machine

B **Read the newspaper column. Then answer the questions.**

Q

My mechanic says I need to do regular maintenance on my car, including changing the oil. But I think he just wants to make money! Who's right?

A

The best way to avoid problems with your car is by doing maintenance on it regularly. Your car's owner's manual tells you what maintenance is needed on your car and when. Try to follow that maintenance schedule. It's cheaper and easier to maintain your car in good condition than to fix problems that result from not taking care of it.

One very basic, but very important, part of car maintenance is changing your car's oil and its oil filter. Oil lubricates and cools your car's engine. The oil filter collects dirt from the oil. When oil gets old and dirty, your car doesn't run as well and you need to change it. When you put new oil in your car, it's good to put a new filter in, too.

Different cars have different requirements for how often you need to change the oil. Most mechanics will say that a car's oil needs to be changed every 3,000–5,000 miles, depending on the car, how often you drive, and the kind of oil you use. The best advice is to follow the instructions in the owner's manual.

1. Why is it a good idea to maintain your car in good condition?

____

2. What happens to your car when the oil isn't clean?

____

3. How can you find out how often you should change the oil in your car?

____

Practice

Note
>>>>>

Some people like to take care of their cars themselves, but not everyone has the skills to do this. So, many people take their cars to a mechanic's shop or a service station to have maintenance done, or to get their cars "serviced." Service stations usually do a 14-point maintenance check for one price. Different stations may check different things, but a 14-point check usually includes checking fluid (liquid) levels, the air filter, and the tire pressure and changing the oil and oil filter.

A **Read the receipt a customer received from a 14-point service check.**

Oil change and auto maintenance
1200 Southern Blvd., Aurora, CO 80010
Open Mon.–Sat. 8–6, Sun. 10–4
No appointment needed!

Name: Diane Jackson Date: 4/18/10

Address: 5319 Telluride Court, Aurora, CO 80010

License: F1B1748 Make: Nissan Model: Pathfinder

Year: 2009 Engine: 3.0 Mileage: 39,782

14-POINT SERVICE

1 CHASSIS LUBE	**2** OIL CHANGE	**3** OIL FILTER
6	3.5 quarts	TFC523

SERVICE CHECK	OK	ADD/REPLACE	ADDED SERVICES
4 windshield washer fluid		✓	car wash
5 transmission fluid		✓	
6 air filter	✓		
7 wiper blades		✓	
8 differential fluid	✓		
9 tire pressure	✓		
10 brake fluid	✓		
11 battery	✓		
12 power steering fluid	✓		
13 coolant/antifreeze fluid	✓		
14 PCV valve (if needed)	✓		

NEXT SERVICE Date: 7/18/10 Mileage: 42,782

Mechanic: Dave Meeker

Notes: Engine oil was very low. Remember to check weekly.

B **Look at the car maintenance checklist again. Then answer the questions. Circle *a*, *b*, or *c*.**

1. When can you take your car to get it serviced?
   - **a.** Monday through Saturday, from 8:00 to 6:00
   - **b.** on Sunday after 4:00
   - **c.** only when you have an appointment
2. How many miles has the car been driven?
   - **a.** 2009
   - **b.** 3.0
   - **c.** 39,782
3. What did the mechanic add?
   - **a.** transmission fluid
   - **b.** differential fluid
   - **c.** He didn't add any fluids.
4. What instructions did the mechanic give to the car owner?
   - **a.** Add windshield washer fluid.
   - **b.** Buy a new air filter.
   - **c.** Check the oil every week.
5. When should the customer bring the car back for another 14-point check?
   - **a.** April 18, 2010
   - **b.** at 39,782 miles
   - **c.** at 42,782 miles

PAIRS. **Check your answers.**

Make It Yours

PAIRS. **If you have a car, what maintenance do you do on it? Do you do the work yourself or do you take your car to a service station to get it serviced? Have you ever taken your car to a service station for a 14-point check? What are some other things that mechanics might check?**

Lesson 3 Reporting a Car Accident

Learn

A **Read the article. Then answer the question. Check the correct answer.**

What Do I Do If I'm in a Car Accident?

- Stop. It's illegal to drive away from an accident, even a small one, without stopping. If you can, pull over to the side of the road. (*Note:* In some places it's illegal to move your car from an accident until the police arrive and investigate. It's good to know the laws where you live *before* you get into an accident.)
- Find out if anyone is hurt. If anyone has serious injuries, call 911. Do not move a person with injuries. Wait for an ambulance.
- Exchange names, addresses, phone numbers, driver's license numbers, license plate numbers, and insurance information with the other driver or drivers. Also get the names, addresses, and phone numbers of other people who saw the accident.

- Record details of the accident as soon as possible. Write down everything you remember, including the time, weather conditions, and exactly what happened. If you have a camera, take pictures. These details will help the insurance companies and the police decide who was responsible for the accident.
- Don't say the accident was your fault, even if you think it was. It's the job of the police and insurance companies to decide who was responsible. Don't sign anything unless it is given to you by your insurance company or the police.
- If you cannot drive your car away from the accident, call a tow truck to move it for you.
- Call your insurance company to report the accident. Don't wait too long to do this. Many companies require that you report accidents within 72 hours or less.
- Different states have different laws about who you need to report a car accident to. Usually you need to file a report with the police and your state's Department of Motor Vehicles (DMV), as well as with your insurance company. You can call your DMV or look online for information on the laws in your state.
- *Note:* If you have an accident with a parked car, leave a note with your name and telephone number on the windshield. It's illegal to drive away without leaving a note.

Who is this information for?

☐ all drivers

☐ insurance companies

☐ someone who has seen an accident

B **Look at the article again. Match the words and their meanings.**

d 1. pull over	a. physical damage to a person's body caused by an accident
____ 2. injury	b. tell someone about something
____ 3. exchange	c. a truck that takes disabled cars or other vehicles to another place
____ 4. record	d. move your car off the road
____ 5. tow truck	e. give something to someone who gives you something
____ 6. report	f. write down information about something

Practice

Read the article again. Answer the questions.

1. What is the first thing you should do after a car accident? Stop your car.
2. What should you do if anyone has been seriously injured?
   ____
3. What information do you need to get from other drivers after an accident?
   ____
4. What else should you write down after an accident?
   ____
5. Who decides who was responsible for a car accident? ______________________________
6. In most states, what are the three organizations you need to report a car accident to?
   ____
7. What do the letters DMV mean? ______________________________
8. What do you need to do if you hit a parked car?
   ____

Make It Yours

GROUPS OF 3. **Have you ever been in a car accident? What happened? Who did you call? What did you do? Talk about your experience.**

BONUS

Find out the laws where you live. (Look in the Blue Pages of your phone book for the phone number of your DMV or look online.) Are you allowed to move your car to the side of the road after an accident, or do you have to wait until the police arrive? Who do you have to report accidents to in your state? How much time do you have after an accident to make the report?

Unit 6 Test

Before you take the test

Ⓐ Ⓑ Ⓒ Ⓓ Use the answer sheet for Unit 6 on page 215.

1. Print your name.
2. Print your teacher's name.
3. Write your student identification number, and bubble in the information below the boxes.
4. Write the test date and bubble in the information.
5. Write your class number and bubble in the information.

Listening I [Track 34]

You will hear a conversation. Then you will hear a question about the conversation. What is the correct answer: A, B, or C?

1. A. They're stuck.
B. They're making noise.
C. They're getting too hot.

2. A. after a car accident
B. each month
C. when he bought the car

Listening II [Track 35]

Listen. Test items 3, 4, 5, and 6 are on the audio CD.

Reading

Read. What is the correct answer: A, B, C, or D?

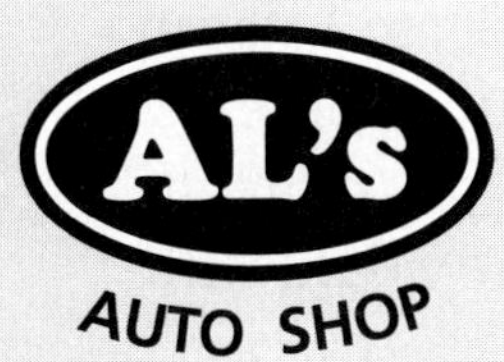

RECEIPT FOR STANDARD OIL CHANGE
(includes FREE 14-point inspection)

		CHECKED	ADDED/ REPLACED	NOTES
1	chassis lube	✓		
2	oil	✓	✓	replaced with 5 quarts of XTX brand oil
3	oil filter	✓	✓	replaced with Best Mark filter
4	windshield washer fluid	✓	✓	added
5	transmission fluid	✓		
6	air filter	✓		
7	wiper blades	✓		
8	differential fluid	✓		
9	tire pressure	✓	✓	filled tires
10	brake fluid	✓		
11	battery	✓		
12	power steering fluid	✓		
13	coolant	✓	✓	added
14	PCV valve (if needed)	✓		

7. What is the purpose of this information?

A. to show how often the car owner should do maintenance

B. to show the maintenance that was done on the car

C. to show the car owner how to do maintenance on the car

D. to show the parts of the car that the owner needs to check

8. Which of the following sentences is true?

A. The wiper blades weren't checked.

B. The air filter was replaced.

C. Best Mark brand oil was added.

D. Windshield washer fluid was added.

Esteban wanted to buy car. He found one that he liked for $4,000. He had $600 that he was going to use for a down payment, so he needed a loan for the other $3,400. Esteban talked to different lenders. He asked about interest rates at the dealership that was selling the car and at his bank. He also looked at online lenders. His bank offered him the best interest rate—8%, so Esteban decided to borrow the money from his bank. Then Esteban had to choose the term of his loan. He chose a 48-month loan. Over time, he'll pay more in total, but with a 48-month loan he'll pay less each month than he would with a 36-month loan.

9. How much money did Esteban need to borrow?

A. $4,000

B. $600

C. $3,400

D. $4,600

10. Which lender did Esteban choose?

A. the car dealership

B. his bank

C. a credit union

D. an online lender

Drive Sure Auto Insurance Company

We hope you never have a car accident. But if you do, it's important to know what to do. If you're in an auto accident, even a small one, follow these steps in order:

- Pull over to the side of the road and stop, even if it was a very small accident.
- Check for injuries. Call 911 if anyone is seriously hurt.
- Get the names, addresses, and phone numbers of everyone who saw or was involved in the accident. Get insurance information, driver's license number, and license plate number from the other driver(s).
- Make notes about the accident. Write everything that happened.
- Call Drive Sure Auto Insurance Company within 72 hours to report the accident. We'll need your insurance information, as well as information about the accident.

11. What is the purpose of this information?

A. to explain why drivers should report accidents to the police

B. to explain how to get information from other drivers

C. to explain why drivers should report accidents to their insurance companies

D. to explain what to do after a car accident

12. What should a person do first after an accident?

A. talk to other people in the accident

B. record details of the accident

C. move the car off the road

D. get out of the car

13. What *shouldn't* a person do after a car accident?

A. pull over

B. get information from other drivers

C. write down what happened in the accident

D. drive away without stopping

Trish was in a car accident. Someone hit her car from behind while she was stopped at a traffic light. She moved to the side of the road and expected the other driver to do that also. But instead of stopping, he drove away. Luckily Trish had a pen and a piece of paper with her, and she quickly wrote down the information she needed to give the police.

14. What did Trish write down?

A. the driver's insurance information

B. the driver's license plate number

C. the driver's phone number

D. the driver's name

Unit 7 Parenting

Lesson 1 Enrolling a Child in School
- Read and understand school registration information
- Identify documents required for registration
- Ask about enrolling a child in school

Lesson 2 Calling to Report an Absence
- Understand a school attendance policy
- Call school to report an absence

Lesson 3 Interpreting a Child's Report Card or Progress Report
- Interpret a social/learning skills progress report
- Evaluate a child's behavior

Lesson 4 Making Your Home Safe for Children
- Understand ways to make your home safe for children
- Give advice about making a home safe for children

Lesson 1 Enrolling a Child in School

Learn

A *PAIRS.* **Which words do you know? Match the words with their meanings.**

_f_ 1. school district
___ 2. proof of residency
___ 3. birth certificate
___ 4. immunization record
___ 5. physical examination form
___ 6. current address
___ 7. emergency contact
___ 8. legal guardian
___ 9. transcript

a. record of date, time and place of birth
b. place where someone is living now
c. record of grades and attendance
d. person who has legal responsibility for a child
e. evidence that someone lives in a particular place
f. an area—usually a town or city—that controls local public education
g. document showing results of medical tests
h. document listing vaccinations received
i. a parent or other adult who can be called if there is a problem during school hours

B **Most school districts in the United States have websites to provide information to parents, students, and the general public. Read the website below.**

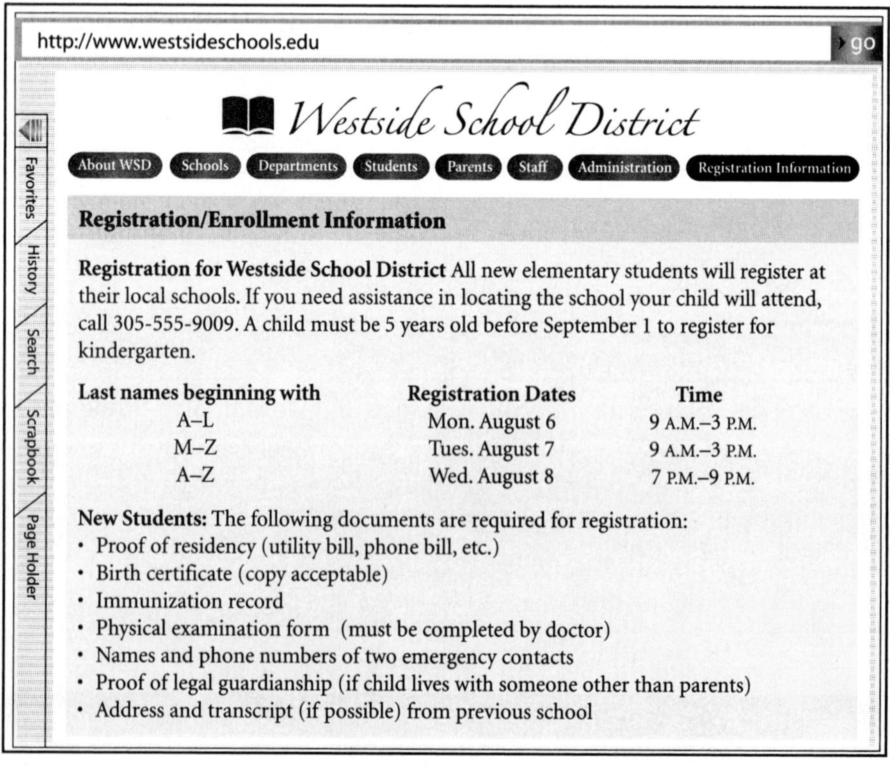

http://www.westsideschools.edu go

Westside School District

About WSD | Schools | Departments | Students | Parents | Staff | Administration | Registration Information

Favorites | History | Search | Scrapbook | Page Holder

Registration/Enrollment Information

Registration for Westside School District All new elementary students will register at their local schools. If you need assistance in locating the school your child will attend, call 305-555-9009. A child must be 5 years old before September 1 to register for kindergarten.

Last names beginning with	Registration Dates	Time
A–L	Mon. August 6	9 A.M.–3 P.M.
M–Z	Tues. August 7	9 A.M.–3 P.M.
A–Z	Wed. August 8	7 P.M.–9 P.M.

New Students: The following documents are required for registration:
- Proof of residency (utility bill, phone bill, etc.)
- Birth certificate (copy acceptable)
- Immunization record
- Physical examination form (must be completed by doctor)
- Names and phone numbers of two emergency contacts
- Proof of legal guardianship (if child lives with someone other than parents)
- Address and transcript (if possible) from previous school

Practice

A **Skim the website for answers to the following questions. Circle *Y* for *Yes* if the answer is on the website. Circle *N* for *No* if the answer is not on the website.**

1. When can I register my child for school? (Y) N
2. When is the first day of class? Y N
3. What do I need to bring to registration? Y N
4. What is the name of our neighborhood school? Y N
5. Where can I register my child for school? Y N
6. What time do classes start? Y N
7. When will my child catch the bus in the morning? Y N

B  CD2 TRACK 2 **Mrs. Chen is talking on the phone to a receptionist at Arden Elementary School. Listen to the conversation and read.**

A: Thank you for calling Arden Elementary School. How may I help you?
B: We just moved here, and I need to enroll my daughter in school. She's ten years old, and she'll be in fifth grade.
A: What's her name?
B: Tina Chen.
A: Chen. OK. Students are registered alphabetically by last name. You need to register your daughter on Tuesday, August 6 between 9:00 A.M. and 3:00 P.M. in the cafeteria.
B: All right. What do I need to bring?
A: You'll need her birth certificate, her immunization record, and proof of residency. Has she had a physical exam?
B: Yes.
A: Good. Bring that form from your doctor.
B: OK, thanks. We'll be there on August 6.

Listen

 CD2 TRACK 3 **Different school districts require different documentation when students register. Listen to the conversations. Check the documentation that each student will need.**

	Birth Certificate	Proof of Residency	Immunization Record	Proof of Legal Guardianship	Physical Examination Form	Transcript
Student 1						
Student 2						

Lesson 2 Calling to Report an Absence

Note 

School attendance is mandatory, or required, for all children in the United States. But each state defines age requirements and how many days students must attend. Local school districts provide specific attendance policies.

Learn

A **Read the attendance policy of one school district.**

Summerville School District Attendance Policy

Parents or legal guardians are responsible for their children's attendance. To insure that any absences are officially approved, parents should follow these procedures:

1. If you know that your child will be absent or late, please notify the attendance office in advance by phone (305-555-1122) or in writing.
2. When advance notice is not possible, you must contact the attendance office *within one day* if your child has been absent or arrived late. An absence is considered unexcused if a call or note is not received from a parent or legal guardian within two days.
3. After an absence or in the case of late arrival, have your child report immediately to the attendance office to obtain an admission slip signed by the attendance staff. Students will not be allowed to return to class without an admission slip.
4. A doctor's note is required for absence due to illness lasting five days or more.
5. If a student has missed more than three consecutive days, arrangements should be made with each teacher to pick up homework.

Absences or late arrivals for the following reasons will be excused. Any absence or late arrival that is not listed below will be considered unexcused.

- Illness or medical emergency
- Family emergency
- Established special days on a religious calendar
- Prearranged medical or dental appointment
- Prearranged school activity
- District emergency (for example, school closing due to bad weather)

B **Galina is a student in the Summerville School district. Her grandmother died. Read the sentences about Galina's one-day absence for the funeral. Circle *T* for *True* or *F* for *False*.**

1. Galina can be excused to attend her grandmother's funeral. (T) F
2. Galina's parents must notify the school with a call and a written note. T F
3. An admission slip is a note that will allow Galina to return to class. T F
4. Galina will need to bring a doctor's note to return to class. T F
5. Galina's parents will not make arrangements to pick up homework. T F

Practice

A mother is calling to report her daughter's absence from school. Listen and read.

A: Hello. Washington Elementary School. May I help you?
B: Yes. My daughter can't come to school today. She's coughing and has a slight fever.
A: Oh, I'm sorry. What's her name?
B: Maria Cardona.
A: Are you her mother?
B: Yes, I'm Mrs. Cardona.
A: When do you think she'll return?
B: Probably tomorrow, but I'm not sure. I'm taking her to the doctor today.

Listen

A **Listen to the conversations. Complete the sentences. Circle the correct information.**

1. Ben Fu will be **late / absent** because he **is sick / has a dental appointment**. He'll miss **half a day / a day** of school.
2. Zari Kashani is going to be **late / absent** today for a **religious holiday / doctor's appointment**. She'll be back to school **tomorrow / later today**.
3. Elena Baranova will be **absent / late** to school because she **has a medical appointment / overslept**. She'll be about **half an hour / an hour** late.

B ***PAIRS.*** **Discuss the reasons for absence or late arrival in the conversations above. Which ones are excused? Which is not excused?**

Make It Yours

PAIRS. **Write a short phone conversation using the one in Practice as an example. Practice the conversation. Present your conversation to the class.**

Lesson 3 Interpeting a Child's Report Card or Progress Report

Learn

Note >>>>> *Report cards and progress reports explain how well your child is doing in different subject areas and often include a section about your child's behavior. The* Social and Learning Skills *report below is an example. Report cards and progress reports are given at the end of each term—usually three or four times a year, depending on the school district.*

Westside School District
Fuller Elementary School | Elementary Progress Report

Student: Alberto Morales		**Grade:** 5	
Teacher: Leslie Sato		**School Year:** 2009–2010	
	Fall	**Winter**	**Spring**
Social and Learning Skills	**1st**	**2nd**	**Year-End**
a. Respects others	E		
b. Takes responsibility for learning	D		
c. Follows directions	E		
d. Cooperates with others	E		
e. Uses time effectively	S		
f. Shows positive attitude	E		
g. Completes homework	U		
h. Demonstrates problem-solving abilities	U		

Social and Learning Skills Key
E = Exceptional: Behavior always observed
S = Satisfactory: Behavior usually observed
D = Developing: Behavior sometimes observed
U = Unsatisfactory: Behavior rarely observed

A **Match these explanations with the teacher's comments in the progress report.**

<u>a</u> 1. Alberto is always polite to his classmates.
_____ 2. Alberto always works well with other classmates.
_____ 3. Alberto always has a positive way of behaving and thinking.
_____ 4. Alberto sometimes takes responsibility for his own learning.
_____ 5. Alberto rarely does all of his homework before class begins.
_____ 6. Alberto rarely takes the necessary action to solve problems effectively.
_____ 7. Alberto usually makes good decisions about the way he spends his time in class.

B **Look at Alberto's progress report again. Then on a separate sheet of paper answer these questions about Alberto's progress in the first term.**

1. Which of Alberto's social and learning skills are excellent?
2. Which of Alberto's social and learning skills need improvement?

Practice

PAIRS. **Read the situation for each child. Look at the Social and Learning Skills Key on page 108. Then grade each child's social and learning skills.**

1. Henry likes to talk a lot. He doesn't hear the teacher giving directions because he is usually talking to another student. His talking bothers the students around him.
   _____ Respects others
   _____ Follows directions

2. Jasmine always wants to be the leader in class. Instead of working together with other students, Jasmine usually tells them what to do and how to do it. Some of Jasmine's classmates don't like to work with her. Jasmine isn't able to solve her problems with other students. She always wants the teacher to get involved.
   _____ Respects others
   _____ Cooperates with others
   _____ Demonstrates problem-solving abilities

3. Although Jane does all of her homework before class, she often answers many questions incorrectly. She doesn't like to work with her classmates because they work too slowly. She usually wants to work alone. She does her class assignments quickly and then sits at her desk daydreaming. The teacher tells her to check her work, but she does this only some of the time, so she often has many careless mistakes.
   _____ Cooperates with others
   _____ Follows directions
   _____ Uses time effectively
   _____ Completes homework

Make It Yours

A *PAIRS.* **Write suggestions to help each child improve his or her behavior.**

B *GROUPS OF 4.* **Share your suggestions with another pair of students in class.**

Note >>>>>

Public schools generally provide special services for children with ongoing learning and behavior problems. School counselors work with students, teachers, and parents to identify and understand problems. Sometimes this includes learning about family situations that might affect students' behavior or progress in and out of school. Counselors can help with many different kinds of problems, including social skills, anger management, and drug and alcohol prevention. Their goal is to help students develop self-understanding and positive habits and to provide the necessary resources to do that.

BONUS

Look online or talk to a school counselor to identify other resources in your area that can help a child with behavior problems. Share your information with the class.

Lesson 4 Making Your Home Safe for Children

Learn

Note >>>>> *The U.S. government reports that approximately 2 million children are injured or killed at home each year. Here are some safety precautions you can take to make your home safer for children.*

A **Which safety precautions do you know? Match the rules to the pictures.**

a. Put nonskid strips in the bathtub.
b. Remove poisonous plants.
c. Use safety gates to keep children away from dangerous areas.
d. Keep cords from window blinds and shades out of children's reach.
e. Cover electrical outlets with safety plugs.
f. Store medicines out of children's reach.
g. Install childproof latches on cabinets and drawers.
h. Stick decorative decals on glass doors.

1. g

2. ____

3. ____

4. ____

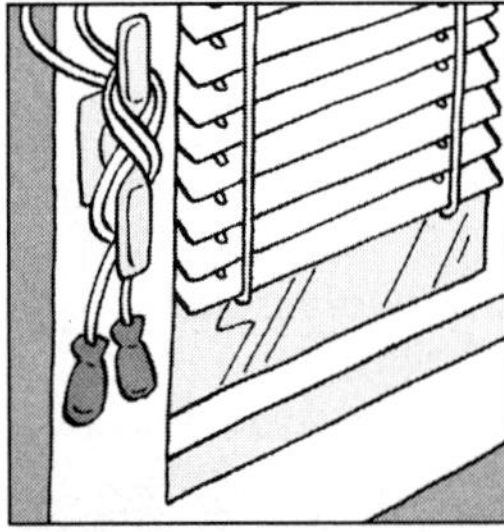

5. ____

6. ____

7. ____

8. ____

B *PAIRS.* **Tell your partner the safety precaution each picture shows. Take turns.**

C *CLASS.* **Discuss these questions: Are these safety precautions important? What experiences have you had with them?**

Practice

PAIRS. **Look at the pictures. Student A, choose a picture and say what could happen. Student B, say what the parents should do to prevent an accident.**

Example:

A: The baby might get an electrical shock.
B: Her parents should cover the electrical outlets with safety plugs!

1.

2.

3.

4.

5.

Make It Yours

GROUPS OF 3. **What are some other ways to make your home safer for children? On a separate piece of paper write three new recommendations. Share your group's ideas with the class. Then decide which precautions you might take in your own home.**

BONUS

Look online for a checklist of home safety precautions. Did you find any new ones that you think are worth following? Report back to the class.

Unit 7 Test

Before you take the test

ⒶⒷⒸⒹ Use the answer sheet for Unit 7 on page 217.

1. Print your name.
2. Print your teacher's name.
3. Write your student identification number, and bubble in the information below the boxes.
4. Write the test date and bubble in the information.
5. Write your class number and bubble in the information.

Listening I [Track 6]

You will hear a conversation. Then you will hear a question about the conversation. What is the correct answer: A, B, or C?

1. A. on August 9, from 9:00 to 3:00
B. on August 9, from 8:00 to 3:00
C. on August 8, from 9:00 to 3:00

2. A. a physical exam form
B. a note from the doctor
C. the child's birth certificate

3. A. He has a dentist appointment.
B. He's sick.
C. It's a holiday.

Listening II [Track 7]

Listen. Test items 4, 5, and 6 are on the audio CD.

Reading

Read. What is the correct answer: A, B, C, or D?

Taylor Elementary School

2009–2010
Progress Report

Student's name: Bloom, Kristen				**Grade:** 2
Teacher's name: R. Duval				
Social and Learning Skills	**1st quarter**	**2nd quarter**	**3rd quarter**	**4th quarter**
Shows positive attitude	S			
Respects others	S			
Cooperates with others	S			
Follows directions	D			
Uses time effectively	D			
Completes homework	D			
Demonstrates problem-solving abilities	E			
Takes responsibility for learning	U			

Social and Learning Skills Key
E = Exceptional: Behavior always observed
S = Satisfactory: Behavior usually observed
D = Developing: Behavior sometimes observed
U = Unsatisfactory: Behavior rarely observed

---

7. Which behavior does Kristen always show?

A. the ability to solve problems well

B. a positive way of acting and thinking

C. working well with her classmates

D. politeness to her classmates

8. In which area does Kristen most need to improve?

A. showing a positive attitude

B. using time effectively

C. solving problems

D. taking responsibility for learning

9. Which sentence is true?

A. Kristen never completes her homework.

B. Kristen usually respects other students.

C. Kristen always follows directions well.

D. Kristen usually takes responsibility for her own learning.

Children are naturally very curious. One way that young children learn about the world is by putting things in their mouths. If you've spent much time with babies or young children, you know that they put *everything* in their mouths—even things that taste bad. Many common household and personal products, including cleaning products, cosmetics, and medications, can be poisonous or even deadly to children if eaten. Keep all of these things out of children's reach. That could mean putting them up high or in cabinets and drawers with childproof latches.

---

10. Why should you put childproof latches on cabinets and drawers?

A. Products inside the cabinets and drawers can be dangerous for children.

B. Children might put cabinets and drawers in their mouths.

C. You should put latches up high.

D. Many household and personal products are common.

11. Which of the following should you keep out of reach of children?

A. everything

B. childproof latches

C. cleaning products

D. cabinets

Hillsdale Unified School District

Kindergarten

Student Registration Information

Students must be 5 years old on or before September 1 to register for kindergarten.

Please report to your local elementary school for kindergarten registration. Call 909-555-2548 for information on locating the school your child will attend.

Last names beginning with	Registration Date	Time
A–I	Monday, April 5	8:00 A.M.–2:30 P.M.
J–R	Tuesday, April 6	8:00 A.M.–2:30 P.M.
S–Z	Wednesday, April 7	8:00 A.M.–2:30 P.M.
A–Z	Thursday, April 8	6:00 P.M.–9:30 P.M.

The following documents are required for registration of kindergarten students:

- birth certificate (copy acceptable)
- proof of residency (utility bill, phone bill, etc.)
- proof of legal guardianship (if child lives with someone other than parents)
- physical examination form (must be completed by doctor)
- immunization record
- names and phone numbers of two emergency contacts

12. On which days may Julia Ochoa register her daughter, Carmen Ochoa, for school?

A. Monday and Tuesday

B. Monday and Wednesday

C. Tuesday and Thursday

D. Wednesday and Thursday

13. Which of the following is *not* needed in order to register a child for kindergarten?

A. the child's birth certificate (copy or original)

B. a form completed by a doctor

C. a utility bill that shows the parent/legal guardian's address

D. a driver's license

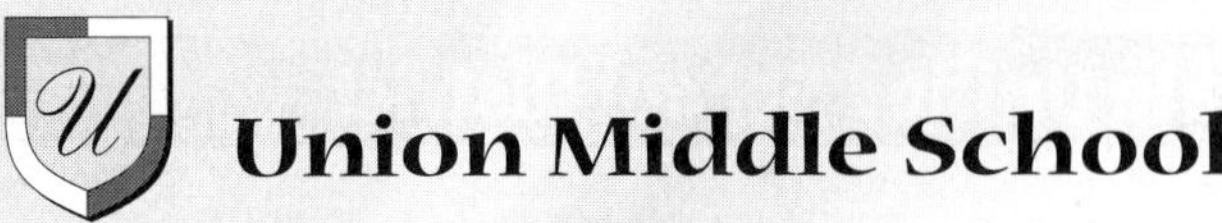

Union Middle School

Attendance Policy

Absences and late arrivals for the following reasons will be excused. Any absence or late arrival for any other reason will be considered unexcused.

- Illness or medical emergency
- Prearranged medical or dental appointment
- Special days established on a religious calendar
- Prearranged school activity
- Family emergency

Parents are responsible for their children's attendance. Follow the guidelines below to avoid unexcused absences and late arrivals.

- If you know that your child will be absent or late, please call or send a note to the attendance office in advance. If you write a note, include the student's first and last name, the date of the absence or late arrival, and the reason.
- When it's not possible to notify the attendance office in advance, you must contact the attendance office within one day of your child's absence or late arrival. Absences and late arrivals are considered unexcused if a call or note is not received from a parent or legal guardian within two days.

14. Who is this information for?

A. parents of students

B. workers at the attendance office

C. students with unexcused absences

D. students with medical appointments

15. Which of the following is considered an unexcused absence?

A. A student is absent because he's sick.

B. A student has an appointment at the doctor's office.

C. A student was absent three days ago and his parents haven't called or written a note.

D. A student has been absent for more than five days.

16. Which sentence is true?

A. A student's parents must go to the attendance office after the student's absence.

B. If a student misses school for a doctor's appointment, he or she must bring a note from the doctor.

C. A student's parents should call or write a note if the student is going to be late.

D. Arriving to school late because of a family emergency is considered an unexcused absence.

Unit 8 On the Job

Lesson 1 **Giving and Following Instructions**
- Give and follow multistep instructions

Lesson 2 **Correction at Work**
- Respond to criticism

Lesson 3 **Workplace Safety**
- Understand workplace safety rules, signs, and procedures
- Report unsafe working conditions
- Report on-the-job accidents

Lesson 4 **Getting Paid**
- Understand a pay stub

Lesson 1 Giving and Following Instructions

Learn

  **Look at the picture and listen. Listen and read.**

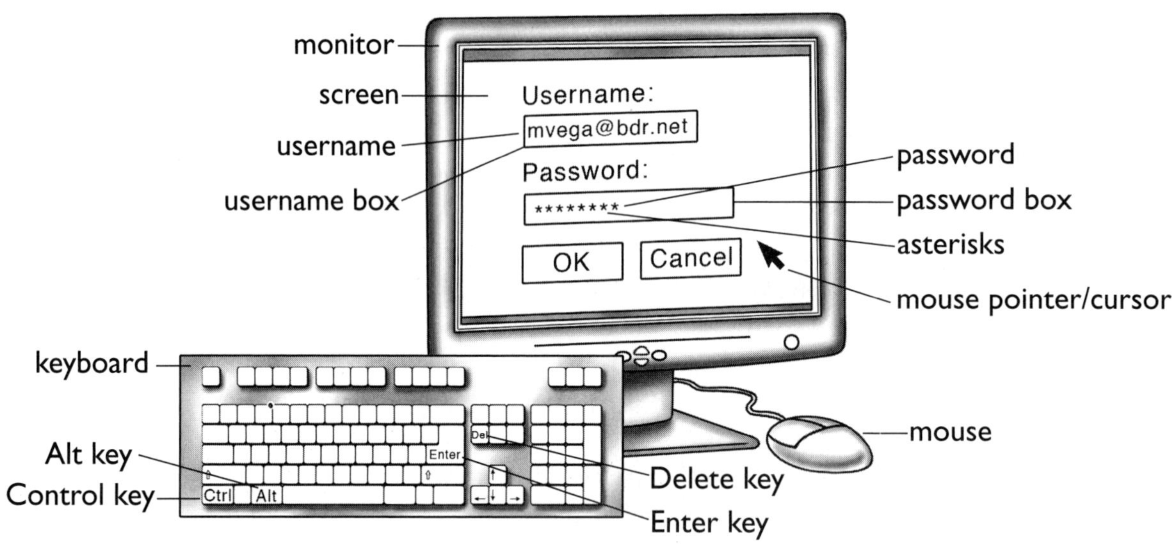

B **Today is Maria Vega's first day at work. She's following instructions to log on to her computer. Listen to the conversation and read.**

Maria: Excuse me, Mr. Lee, can you help me log on to my computer?
Mr. Lee: Sure. Do you have a username and password?
Maria: Yes.
Mr. Lee: OK. First of all, you need to turn on the computer and then wait until it boots up.
Maria: Boots up?
Mr. Lee: Yes. That means when it *starts up*.
Maria: OK.
Mr. Lee: Be patient. It may take a minute for the logon screen to load. *Load* means *to appear*. Now put your hand on the mouse. Move the mouse pointer on the computer screen to the username box and click on the username box.
Maria: OK. What do I do next?
Mr. Lee: Type your username. Be careful to type accurately. The computer doesn't recognize words if there are spelling mistakes.
Maria: I'm done.
Mr. Lee: OK. Now move the mouse pointer to the password box and click on the box. Type your password. You won't see your password on the screen. You'll see only asterisks. Then click or press *Enter* to submit your username and password.
Maria: It worked. Thanks, Mr. Lee.
Mr. Lee: You're welcome.

 *PAIRS.* **Practice the conversation. Switch roles.**

Practice

CD2 TRACK 10 **Listen to the conversation again. Number the logon instructions in the order you hear them.**

_____ Move the mouse pointer to the password box and click.

_____ Put your hand on the mouse.

_____ Turn on the computer and wait until it boots up.

_____ Press *Enter* to submit your logon information.

_____ Type your password accurately.

_____ Move the mouse pointer to the username box and click.

_____ Type your username accurately and click.

Learn

Read this tip on improving your communication skills.

When you're listening to instructions, it's your responsibility to let the speaker know what kind of help you need to understand better. Tell the speaker when you understand something, and be sure to ask questions if you don't understand. Ask the speaker to repeat, slow down, spell, or give more explanation when necessary. Repeat the information to confirm your understanding.

Listen

A CD2 TRACK 11 **Look at the picture on page 118. Locate the CTRL, ALT, and DEL keys on the keyboard. Maria's computer is not working. Listen to her conversation as she calls the computer help desk. Then answer the question.**

1. Did Maria get the information she needed? _______________
2. Maria practiced active listening skills in her conversation. Check the things she did.

- ☐ She asked the person to slow down.
- ☐ She told the person when she understood.
- ☐ She repeated information she heard.
- ☐ She asked the person to spell something.

B CD2 TRACK 11 **Listen to the conversation again. Pay attention to Maria's use of active listening. Fill in the missing words.**

1. You're going _______________.
2. _______________ which keys you mean.
3. _______________. OK, I found it.
4. Can you _______________?

Lesson 2 Correction at Work

Learn

A Read the article.

Workplace Tip: Responding to Criticism

Negative feedback, or criticism, can be painful to receive. At work, employees need to accept supervisors' corrections and respond appropriately. In most cases, criticism from a supervisor is meant to be constructive, or helpful. With an open and positive attitude, employees can learn and improve job performance. Here are some tips for doing that:

Remain calm. Try not to get upset when you receive criticism. If your supervisor is angry, do not respond with anger. An angry response makes the situation more difficult.

Listen carefully to the criticism and try not to get defensive. That means that you shouldn't offer a lot of excuses. Accept responsibility for your mistakes. Don't blame others. It's fine to give an explanation if you need to, but your main goal should be to show that you are interested in hearing what your boss has to say and that you will take responsibility for making things better. Ask questions if necessary to make sure that you understand.

Take time to respond carefully and politely. Apologize if appropriate. Thank your supervisor for being honest. Tell your supervisor about the positive steps you plan to take in response to the criticism. Constructive criticism requires a constructive response!

Think about the criticism and ask your supervisor for suggestions. You can also ask co-workers for advice.

What if your supervisor is wrong? Sometimes people make mistakes. If the information your supervisor has is wrong or if you are being criticized for something you didn't do, of course, you need to say something. However, it's still important to try to understand your boss's concerns and to show that you're interested in helping to improve the situation.

B Match the words from the article with their meanings.

__c__ 1. constructive criticism
____ 2. open attitude
____ 3. positive attitude
____ 4. blame
____ 5. concerns

a. believing people can make good things happen even in difficult situations
b. feelings of worry about something
c. negative feedback that is meant to be helpful
d. accepting of new ideas, willing to try new things
e. say someone else is responsible for something bad

Practice

Use what you learned in the article to choose the best response to the supervisor's criticism in each conversation.

1. **Supervisor:** Ali, I'd like to talk to you about something.
   Employee: Of course, Mr. Nuñez, what is it?
   Supervisor: I've noticed that you've been late to work several times this week. Is there some kind of problem that I can help you with?

   a. I'm sorry, but I'm not the only one who is late.
   b. I'm sorry, Mr. Nuñez. I know it's important to come to work on time. I had a problem with my car, but it's fixed now.
   c. I know that I've been late several times, but it's not my fault. I had car problems.

2. **Supervisor:** Mia, there's something we need to discuss.
   Employee: Oh, what is it, Mr. Smith?
   Supervisor: Some of your co-workers feel uncomfortable because you don't talk at meetings. I'm concerned because good communication is important in the workplace.

   a. I didn't know it was important to speak up. Other people have better ideas than I do.
   b. I'm sorry.
   c. Thank you for telling me. I didn't know I was making them uncomfortable. I have trouble understanding what my co-workers are saying sometimes. Do you have any suggestions?

3. **Supervisor:** Young, do you have a moment to speak with me?
   Employee: Of course, Ms. Tan.
   Supervisor: I think that you're a good worker, but it's taking you too long to complete some of your tasks.

   a. I didn't realize that, Ms. Tan. Can you give me some examples? Maybe we can discuss how I can improve.
   b. I'm just trying to do a good job, and that takes time. Is it causing trouble?
   c. I'm not the only one who works slowly. Are you discussing this with other people, too?

PAIRS. **Discuss the responses in each conversation. What made the "good" responses constructive? What was wrong with the other responses?**

Make It Yours

PAIRS. **Tell your partner about a time you received criticism and how you responded. Would you do anything differently if the situation happened again?**

Lesson 3 Workplace Safety

Learn

PAIRS. **Which workplace safety rules do you know? Match the rules to the pictures.**

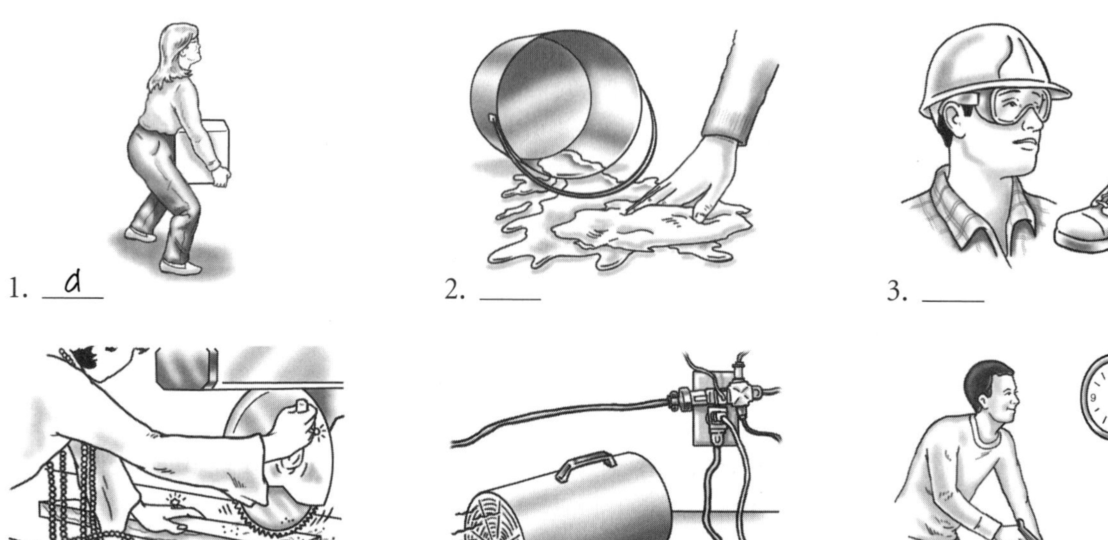

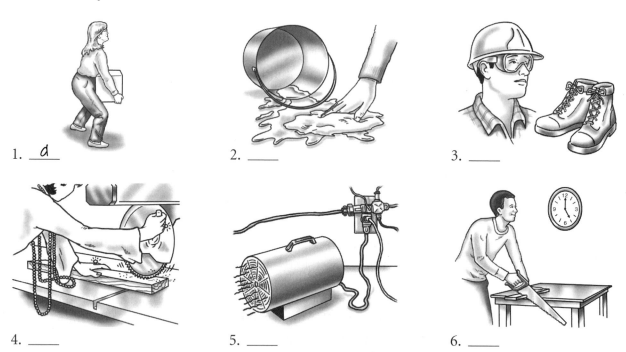

1. d
2. ____
3. ____
4. ____
5. ____

6. ____

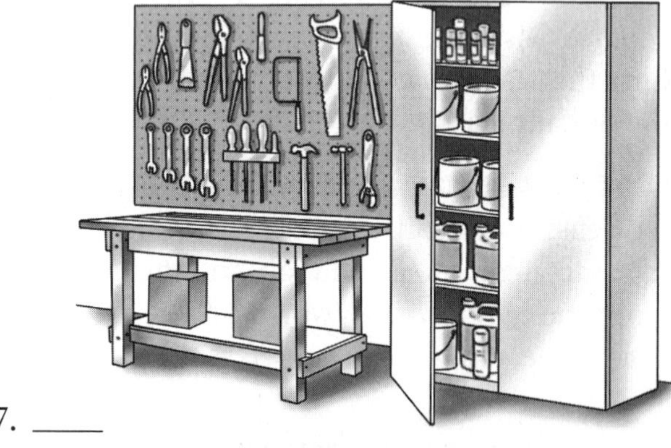

7. ____

a. Store supplies and equipment properly. Put items back in their place after use.
b. Don't overload electrical circuits. This means not using an adapter in an outlet to plug in extra equipment.
c. Wipe up spills immediately.
d. Lift heavy items properly. Use your legs and not your back. Ask for help if something is too heavy for you.
e. Don't wear loose clothing, and remove jewelry before working with machinery.
f. Focus on your task. Do not get distracted by talking to a co-worker or looking away when operating machinery.
g. Wear protective gear (hard hats, goggles, and steel-toed shoes).

B *PAIRS.* **Which of these workplace signs do you know? Match the signs with their meanings.**

1. ____

2. ____

3. ____

4. ____

a. Smoking is prohibited in this area because there are materials that can catch on fire and burn easily.
b. Pay attention. You must have special permission to enter this area.
c. Don't touch this. You might get a strong electrical shock.
d. Watch out! The floor is wet, and you could fall down.

Practice

A *PAIRS.* **Take turns describing the numbered safety violations in the picture.**

B **Look at the safety rules on page 122 again. Write the letter of the rule that is being violated next to each number.**

Make It Yours

C *GROUPS OF 3.* **Look at the picture again. Can you identify other safety hazards? Discuss.**

Listen

CD2 TRACK 12 **Review the words below. Then listen to the introduction to a training session on handling hazardous materials. Write the words you hear in the blanks.**

authorized	flammable	hazardous	spills
directions	gear	smoking	store

All employees of this company need specialized training with (1) ____________________ materials. You will see many signs in this workplace that say "(2) ____________________ personnel only." That means you must complete this training successfully to enter these areas. In our business we work with many (3) ____________________ materials. If you do not follow (4) ____________________ when you use flammable materials or (5) ____________________ them properly, you can cause a fire. We will discuss what kind of protective (6) ____________________ you need to wear and when you will need to wear it. We will cover how to properly wipe up (7) ____________________ of liquid flammables such as gasoline to prevent fire. And remember, you will see signs all over this work site that prohibit you from (8) ____________________. Be sure to obey them, or you could be responsible for starting a fire.

Practice

Read the following notice about how to lift things safely. Then do the activity below.

Safe Lifting Procedures

Save your back. Use safe lifting procedures.

Plan before you lift any heavy object.
Do you need help to push, pull, or roll it?
Both feet need to be flat on the ground.
Find the best way to lift the object. Look for handles.
When you bend down, keep your back straight.
Tighten your stomach muscles and lift with your legs.
Lift slowly, holding the object close to your body.
Set the object down carefully. Use your legs and keep your back straight.
Ask for help if you need it. Use a lifting tool if necessary.

B *PAIRS.* **Imagine you're lifting something heavy. Demonstrate safe lifting procedures.**

Note

The American workplace is becoming safer. Avoiding accidents and injuries, obeying safety signs and procedures, and reporting unsafe working conditions is the responsibility of each employee. The Occupational Safety and Health Administration (OSHA) is the federal agency that assures the health and safety of nearly every American worker. In 2007, it reported that injuries and job-related accidents decreased by 17%. At the same time, fatalities (injuries causing death) in the workplace also decreased.

C **Most workplaces have procedures that allow employees to report unsafe conditions. Look at Javier's unsafe condition report.**

Name: Javier Ortega	Date: 4/19/2010
Description of unsafe condition: There are too many electrical cords plugged into an adapter in one outlet.	
Suggestion for improvement: Install more outlets in the room. Place a caution sign over the electrical outlet.	
Signature: Javier Ortega	

D **Look at the picture on page 123. Report an unsafe condition on the form below. Use your own name and the actual date.**

Name:	Date:
Description of unsafe condition:	
Suggestion for improvement:	
Signature:	

Make It Yours

PAIRS. **Look around your workplace, your school, or another location. Identify an unsafe condition. Report it on this form. Share your unsafe condition report with a partner.**

Name:	Date:
Description of unsafe condition:	
Suggestion for improvement:	
Signature:	

Learn

A **When an accident happens at work, employees are usually required to complete a form and report the accident to a supervisor. Read Li's accident report form.**

ACCIDENT REPORT FORM FOR FINANCIAL SERVICES INCORPORATED

SECTION 1: Employee Information		
Last Name: Zhang	**First Name:** Li	**Social Security Number:** 555-55-5555
Sex: (F) M	**Age:** 26	**Date of Birth:** 5/12/82
Job: Bookkeeper	☑ **Full-time** ☐ **Part-time**	**Work Phone:** 206-555-4621

SECTION 2: Accident Information	
Accident Date: January 22, 2010	**Time:** 8:00 A.M.
Location of Accident: Outside of Office R1305 in the Financial Services Building at 1220 N. Spring St., Seattle, WA 98016	
Bodily part injured? I have a lump on my forehead over my right eye. I also have a black eye.	
What happened? (Be specific. Give as many details as possible.) As I was coming to work on January 22 at 8:00 A.M., I was carrying a box of files, and I was in a hurry to get to my office. I had my office keys in my right hand, ready to open the door. As I came toward the door, I noticed a bucket and a mop nearby that had been left in the hallway. I saw the floor was wet. Someone didn't wipe up water that had spilled on the floor. I slipped and fell and hit the right side of my forehead on the frame of my office door. I was faint. My co-worker Mai Nguyen was carrying another box of files and saw me fall.	
Medical provider? Healthwise Care of America	**Witnesses (Name and Phone No.):** Mai Nguyen 425-555-6636
Report completed by: Li Zhang	**Date:** Jan. 22, 2010
Suggestions for improvement: The cleaning staff needs to be more careful and wipe up spills immediately.	

SECTION 3: Supervisor	
This accident was reported to me on January 22, 2010 (Date) at 8:30 A.M. (Time)	
Follow-up: Investigated the accident and who was responsible. Reviewed safety procedures with cleaning staff and implemented a new training plan.	
Supervisor's signature: John Morris	**Date:** Jan. 22, 2010

B **Look at Li's accident report form again. Match the words with their meanings.**

____ 1. specific	a. a way to do something that people agree on
____ 2. to be faint	b. someone who sees something happen
____ 3. witness	c. detailed, exact
____ 4. investigate	d. begin to make something happen
____ 5. implement	e. carefully examine something that has happened
____ 6. procedure	f. feel weak and dizzy

Practice

A **It's important to be specific when you fill out an accident form. Look at Li's accident form again. Answer the questions using the detailed information she gave.**

1. When did the accident occur?

   on January 22, 2010 at 8:00 A.M.
2. Where did the accident happen?

   ____
3. What was Li doing when the accident occurred?

   ____
4. What was the cause of the accident?

   ____
5. What happened?

   ____
6. What parts of her body did Li injure?

   ____

B *PAIRS. ROLE PLAY.* **Role-play the conversation Li had with her supervisor when she reported the accident. Student A, you're Li's supervisor. Ask the questions in Exercise A. Student B, you're Li. Give answers using the information above. Switch roles.**

Note >>>>>

Employers must follow OSHA (Occupational Safety and Health Administration) rules and regulations. They must make sure that the workplace is safe and that employees are trained in safety procedures. OSHA inspectors come to work sites to identify hazards and unsafe practices. Any employee who feels that the work environment is not safe can file a complaint (report) with OSHA.

Make It Yours

PAIRS. ROLE PLAY. **Think of an accident that could happen at your workplace or school. Role-play reporting the accident to your supervisor or a school official. Student A, ask the questions in Exercise A. Student B, give your own specific answers. Switch roles.**

Lesson 4 Getting Paid

Learn

A **Look at the pay stub. Match the words with their meanings.**

City Center Hospital

Name Pulman, Nava				**Pay date** 4/5/10		
Social Security # 123-45-6789				**Pay Period** March 26–April 4, 2010		
				Net $922.43		
Earnings				***Deductions***		
Pay type	**Hours**	**Current Amount**	**Year-to-Date Amount**	**Type**	**Current Amount**	**Year-to-date Amount**
Reg. Pay—Salary	80	$1250.00	$8750.00	FICA	$68.61	$480.27
				Fed. Tax	$90.39	$632.73
				State Tax	$32.50	$227.50
				SDI	$22.07	$154.49
				Union Dues	$37.50	$262.50
				Medical Ins.	$14.00	$98.00
				401K	$62.50	$437.50
Total Gross		$1250.00	$8750.00	**Total Ded.**	$327.57	$2292.99

_e_ 1. net (pay)
____ 2. current earnings
____ 3. year-to-date
____ 4. FICA
____ 5. fed. tax
____ 6. SDI
____ 7. union dues
____ 8. medical ins.
____ 9. 401K
____ 10. total gross (pay)
____ 11. ded.

a. Federal Insurance Contributions Act: Social Security retirement benefits

b. from the beginning of the year until now

c. State Disability Insurance: money taken for medical care if you can't work because of an injury or illness not related to your job

d. federal income tax, taken by the U.S. government

e. amount of pay after deductions are taken out, also called *take-home pay*

f. deductions: amounts that are subtracted from your gross pay for taxes and other things

g. amount you earned before deductions

h. an account that allows employees to put aside money until they retire, or leave the company. Employees do not pay taxes on this money until they withdraw it.

i. amount taken out of your paycheck to support the union you belong to (if you belong to a union)

j. your pay this period

k. amount you pay for health insurance

B *PAIRS.* **Check your answers.**

Practice

A **Look at the pay stub again. Answer the questions for this pay period.**

1. What was Ms. Pulman's take-home pay this pay period? ____$922.43____.
2. What were her current earnings before deductions? ______________
3. What are her year-to-date earnings? ______________
4. How many deductions were there on her paycheck? ______________
5. How much has she paid for Social Security this year? ______________
6. What did she pay for State Disability Insurance this pay period?

   ____
7. What did she pay for health insurance this pay period? ______________

B *PAIRS.* **Check your answers.**

Note >>>>>

A union is an organization formed by workers to protect their rights. At some places of employment, all workers are required to join the union. This is called a closed shop. *At other places of employment, employees can choose whether or not to join the union. This is called an* open shop.

Make It Yours

PAIRS. **Discuss. Do you or does anyone you know belong to a union? What are the advantages and disadvantages of being a union member?**

Unit 8 Test

Before you take the test

ⒶⒷⒸⒹ Use the answer sheet for Unit 8 on page 219.

1. Print your name.
2. Print your teacher's name.
3. Write your student identification number, and bubble in the information below the boxes.
4. Write the test date and bubble in the information.
5. Write your class number and bubble in the information.

Listening I [Track 13]

Listen to the sentence. Which of the following means the same as the sentence you heard: A, B, or C?

1. A. Let the speaker know when you understand, and ask questions when you don't.
B. Speak slowly and clearly.
C. Write down everything the person says.

2. A. Workers have to use special clothing and equipment.
B. Workers must store equipment properly.
C. Workers must remove jewelry before using the equipment.

3. A. I have to pay $500.
B. I'm going to be paid $500.
C. My taxes are $500.

Listening II [Track 14]

Listen. Test items 4, 5, and 6 are on the audio CD.

Reading

Read. What is the correct answer: A, B, C, or D?

Nida is a worker in a factory. Last week, her boss, Mrs. Key, noticed that Nida hadn't met her production goals on two different days. She saw that Nida was talking a lot to a new worker named Helen. Mrs. Key called Nida into her office to talk to her about the situation.

Nida apologized for missing her production goals. She explained that another worker, Helen, hadn't understood some of her job duties and that she had asked Nida for help. Nida had been helping Helen all week, which is why she sometimes didn't finish her own work.

Mrs. Key thanked Nida for explaining the problem. She suggested that they make a schedule for Nida to give Helen some training each day. She reduced Nida's production goals during the training period.

7. Why did Mrs. Key want to speak to Nida?

A. Nida had a very open attitude.

B. Nida was very defensive.

C. Nida wasn't getting enough work done.

D. Nida didn't take responsibility for the situation.

8. What happened during Mrs. Key's conversation with Nida?

A. Nida offered constructive criticism.

B. Nida blamed Mrs. Key for the situation.

C. Nida criticized Helen's work.

D. Nida explained the situation to Mrs. Key.

Green's Landscaping Company

Name Goodman, David				Social Security number 888-55-0123		
				Pay Period 3/26/10 – 4/4/10		
Net pay $922.43				Pay date 4/5/10		
Earnings				*Deductions*		
Pay type	**Hours**	**Current Amount**	**Year-to-Date Amount**	**Type**	**Current Amount**	**Year-to-Date Amount**
Regular	80	$1,250.00	$8,750.00	Federal Tax	$90.39	$632.73
				FICA	$68.61	$480.27
				State Tax	$32.50	$227.50
				State Disability Ins.	$22.07	$154.49
				Medical Insurance	$14.00	$98.00
				401K	$62.50	$437.50
				Union Dues	$37.50	$262.50
Total Gross Pay		$1,250.00	$8,750.00	**Total Deductions**	$327.57	$2,292.99

9. Which of the following was taken out of David's paycheck?

A. earnings

B. regular pay

C. gross pay

D. state tax

10. How much money has David earned before deductions this year?

A. $1,250.00

B. $8,750.00

C. $327.57

D. $2,292.99

11. What is the amount of David's paycheck for this pay period?

A. $922.43

B. $1,250.00

C. $8,750.00

D. $327.57

12. What does the sign mean?

A. No one may enter this area.

B. You need special permission to enter this area.

C. You must read the rules before you enter this area.

D. Do not enter this area without protective gear.

What happened? (Be specific. Give as many details as possible.)
I was carrying a box through the workroom. It was big, and I couldn't see over it or around it. As I was walking, I tripped over a can of paint, and I fell onto my hands and knees. Someone hadn't stored the paint properly; the person had left the paint in the middle of the floor. My co-worker Bruce Tilman saw me fall and came over to help me up.

Bodily part injured? My left knee hurts a lot. I have trouble walking.

Witnesses (Name and Phone #) Bruce Tilman 602-555-1825

Report completed by:
(employee's signature) John Selec **Date:** May 20, 2010

This accident was reported to me on
May 20, 2010 (date) at 3:00 P.M. (time).

Supervisor's signature: Steven Parson **Date:** May 20, 2010

13. What is the purpose of this form?

A. to explain a procedure
B. to report an accident
C. to suggest a way to improve an unsafe condition at work
D. to criticize a worker

14. Who was in the workroom when the accident happened?

A. only John Selec
B. John Selec and Steven Parson
C. John Selec and Bruce Tilman
D. Bruce Tilman and Steven Parson

Managing Your Money

Lesson 1 **Personal Expenses**
- Identify and track fixed and variable personal expenses

Lesson 2 **Preparing a Monthly Budget**
- Make a budget for personal expenses
- Compare budgeted and actual expenses

Lesson 3 **Banking**
- Choose an account with the right services for your needs

Lesson 4 **Applying for an Educational Loan**
- Understand the requirements for applying for an educational loan
- Identify different kinds of educational loans
- Fill out a financial aid form

Lesson 1 Personal Expenses

Learn

A *PAIRS.* **Which words do you know? Match the words with their meanings.**

_f_ 1. expenditure
____ 2. fixed expense
____ 3. variable expense
____ 4. co-pay
____ 5. household items
____ 6. discretionary income

a. a fixed amount that someone with medical insurance has to pay for using certain medical services
b. a cost that changes from month to month
c. things that you use every day at home
d. a cost that stays the same from month to month
e. money that you can spend in any way you want
f. the total amount of money spent on something

B **Read the story about Olga.**

Olga moved to the United States two years ago. Her family still lives in Russia, and she has been living by herself in a small one-bedroom apartment in the city. She is working as an administrative assistant, but she hopes to become a project manager, so she wants to save money to get a business degree at a local community college. She has decided to make a budget for herself so that she can start saving. As a first step, she is figuring out what her actual expenses are. For the last month, she has saved all her receipts and kept a record of her expenditures. She has divided them into two categories: *fixed* for expenses that stay the same every month, and *variable* for expenses that change.

Olga pays $900 for rent every month. Last month, Olga paid $50 for gas, $35 for electricity, and $48 for telephone. She pays $20 monthly for Internet service.

Olga earns a net income of $2,100 per month. One of the benefits she receives as an employee is health insurance. She pays $75 per month for medical, dental, and vision care. She had to see the doctor last month and paid a co-pay of $10 for the office visit. Every month, she sends $200 home to her parents for their living expenses. Since Olga lives in the city, she doesn't have a car. She relies on the bus to go to work. Her monthly bus pass costs $60. Olga needs to look professional at her job. Last month she spent $20 on dry cleaning and $80 on clothes, cosmetics, and a haircut. And she spent $280 on groceries and household items.

Olga's salary allows her to have some discretionary income. One way Olga likes to spend her money is eating out with her friends and going to the movies. She likes to rent videos and download music onto her MP3 player. Last month she spent about $200 on eating out and $30 on other kinds of entertainment.

C **Read Olga's story again. Answer the question below. Complete Olga's monthly expense record. Then calculate her total expenses.**

What is Olga's net income? ____________________

Monthly Expenses	
Fixed Expenses	Amount
Rent	$900
Internet	
Health insurance	
Transportation (bus pass)	
Contribution to parents	
TOTAL Fixed Expenses	
Variable Expenses	
Utilities (gas, electricity)	
Telephone	
Groceries and household items	
Medical (co-pays, prescriptions)	
Personal (dry cleaning, clothes, cosmetics, hair, etc.)	
Entertainment (eating out, DVD rentals, movies, music, etc.)	
TOTAL Variable Expenses	
TOTAL EXPENSES (Variable + Fixed)	

Practice

A **Look at Olga's expense record again. Answer the questions.**

1. What is Olga's biggest fixed expense? rent
2. What is the total amount of her fixed expenses? ______
3. What is Olga's biggest variable expense? ______
4. What is the total amount of her variable expenses? ______
5. What is the combined total of her fixed and variable expenses? ______
6. After paying all her monthly expenses, how much does Olga have left? ______

B *CLASS.* **Discuss what Olga could do to decrease her variable expenses.**

BONUS

At home, keep a list of all your expenses for one month. At the end of the month see how you're spending your money. What do you spend the most money on? Are there any ways to reduce your spending in some areas? What could you do with the money you would save?

Lesson 2 Preparing a Monthly Budget

Learn

A budget is a plan for how you're going to spend money. To make a personal budget, first look at your fixed and variable expenses. Second, create a realistic plan for spending and paying all your bills, being sure to save some money for future goals and emergencies that may come up. Third, try to spend only your budgeted amount or less. Last, at the end of each month compare the amount you actually spent to your budgeted amount.

Learn

Read more about Olga, and look at her budget.

After Olga figured out her fixed and variable expenses, she created a budget using her last month's expense record as a guide. She decided to budget $125 for savings. This means that in some areas she budgeted less than the amount she spent last month.

Net Income			$2,100
Fixed Expenses	Budgeted	Actual	Difference
Rent	$ 900	$900	
Internet	20		
Health insurance	75		
Transportation (bus pass)	60		
Contribution to parents	200		
Savings	125		
TOTAL	$1380		
Variable Expenses	Budgeted	Actual	Difference
Utilities (gas, electricity)	$ 85		
Telephone	50		
Groceries and household items	275		
Medical (co-pays, prescriptions)	10		
Personal (dry cleaning, clothes, cosmetics, hair, etc.)	100		
Entertainment (eating out, DVD rentals, movies, music, etc.)	200		
TOTAL	$720		

B **Read how Olga actually spent her income. Fill in the amounts that she spent in the "Actual" column of her budget.**

This month Olga paid her fixed bills, but her mother in Russia had an emergency and asked for an extra $50 in addition to the $200 Olga had budgeted as a contribution to her parents. Her utilities were $85, and her bus pass was $60, as budgeted. She didn't make any long distance calls, so her telephone bill came to $35. And she didn't go to the doctor this month, so she had no medical expenses. Olga spent a little more on groceries than she had planned—$280 instead of $275. She spent $130 for personal items because she is looking for a new job and needed to buy a suit. A friend came to visit her from Russia, so her entertainment expenses came to $265. This left Olga without any money to put into savings this month. But she has promised herself she will start saving next month.

Practice

A **Look at Olga's budget again. Answer the questions. Then write the amounts in the correct places on Olga's budget.**

1. What was Olga's total expenditure for fixed expenses? ____________________
2. What was Olga's total expenditure for variable expenses? ____________________

B **Look at Olga's budget again. Compare the amount that she budgeted for each expense with how much she actually spent. Write the difference between the budgeted amount and the actual amount in the "Difference" column of her budget.**

C *PAIRS.* **Check your answers. Look at Olga's budget line by line and compare her actual expenses to what she budgeted.**

Example:
A: Olga spent $50 more on her contribution to her parents than budgeted.
B: Yes, and she saved $125 less than planned!

D *GROUPS OF 3.* **Work together to answer these questions:**

1. Olga's goal is to get a degree in business. Yearly tuition at the community college is $3,000. If Olga is able to save $125 a month, how long will it take her to save enough to pay for the first year of college?
2. Do you think Olga could save more than $125 a month? How much more could she save? What changes should Olga make to her budget in order to save more?

Make It Yours

PAIRS. **Discuss these questions: Are you spending your money the way you want to? Is there a future goal you want to save for? Are there some things you think you should spend less on?**

Lesson 3 Banking

Learn

A *PAIRS.* **Which words do you know? Match the words with their meanings.**

__f__	1. deposit	a. money taken out of a bank account
____	2. debit card	b. keep
____	3. transaction	c. a business deal or action
____	4. fee	d. the amount that a bank charges for a service
____	5. maintain	e. smallest amount you can keep in a bank account without having to pay a fee
____	6. minimum balance	f. put money into a bank account
____	7. withdrawal	g. a plastic card with your signature that you use to pay for things or to take money from an ATM (the money is taken directly from your bank account)

B **Read the article about choosing a bank account.**

How to Choose the Right Bank Account FOR YOU

Banks offer two main types of accounts: savings and checking. Savings accounts usually give you a higher interest rate than checking accounts. Savings accounts are best for depositing money that you can leave in the bank for a while. If you have some money that you're not going to need immediately, a savings account might be good for you.

Checking accounts are convenient since they allow you to pay for things by check and debit cards. Banks offer many types of checking accounts. Most of them allow your employer to directly deposit your paycheck into your account. Most banks also offer a free debit card with any checking account.

To find the right kind of checking account for you, think about these questions: What kinds of transactions do you make at the bank? Do you write a lot of checks? How much are you willing to pay in monthly fees? Can you maintain a minimum balance in the account? Do you sometimes "bounce" checks by writing a check for an amount greater than is in your account? Will you need teller service? How often do you make withdrawals? Is there a fee to use ATMs?

Practice

First Union Bank offers three different kinds of checking accounts. Read this brochure. Then answer the questions.

First Union Bank has answers to your questions!

	Regular Checking	Basic Checking	Online Checking
What is the minimum opening balance?	$200	$25	$100
What is the minimum monthly balance I have to keep in the account?	$200	$.01	None
What is the monthly service fee?	$8 ($0 if minimum balance kept)	$3.00	$3.00
What is the fee for bounced checks?	$25 per check*	$25 per check*	$25 per check*
What is the fee to see a teller?	None	10 free transactions/mo. ($3 per transaction after that)	$3 per transaction
How many withdrawals can I make every month?	Unlimited	8 free and then $.25 per withdrawal	Unlimited
What is the fee for ATM service?	None	10 free transactions/mo. ($1.50 per transaction after that)	None

*No fee if account is connected to a credit card or savings account.

UNION BANK

1. With a regular checking account, what is the monthly service charge if the minimum balance of $200 is kept? ____________________
2. Which account always charges for teller service? ____________________
3. How can you avoid paying a fee if you bounce a check? ____________________

Listen

Listen to each conversation and decide which type of account the customer is probably going to open.

	Regular	Basic	Online
1. Conversation 1	☐	☐	☐
2. Conversation 2	☐	☐	☐

Make It Yours

PAIRS. **Look at the three different types of checking accounts again. Which type of checking account would be good for you? Explain your answer.**

Go to two different banks and find out about the kinds of checking accounts they offer. Ask the questions in the brochure or your own questions. Share the information with the class.

Lesson 4 Applying for an Educational Loan

Note

If you want to continue your education but don't have the money, you might think about applying for an educational loan. As with other types of loans, not only will you have to pay back the amount you borrow, or the principal, but you'll also have to pay interest. However, educational loans usually have low interest rates and long-term repayment plans, meaning you can pay back the money over a long period of time.

A *PAIRS.* **Which words do you know? Match the words with their meanings.**

_f_ 1. principal
____ 2. interest rate
____ 3. qualify
____ 4. eligible
____ 5. Selective Service
____ 6. federal income tax return

a. report filed with the Internal Revenue Service that shows your earnings and the taxes you owe for the year
b. able or allowed to do or have something
c. have the right to have or do something
d. the U.S. government's system for calling people up for military service
e. the percentage amount charged when you borrow money
f. the original amount of money that is lent to someone, not including any of the interest that is charged

B **Read the newspaper column questions and answers. Then, on a separate piece of paper, write any questions you'd like to ask.**

Michael Thomas, *financial expert, answers your money questions every week. This week's topic is student loans.*

Q: How do I apply for an educational loan?
A: You need to complete a financial aid form called the Free Application for Federal Student Aid, or FAFSA, form. You can apply online at www.fafsa.ed.gov or call 1-800-433-3243, and they will send you a form.

Q: Can anyone qualify for an educational loan?
A: No. First, you need to show that you have financial need. Second, you need to be enrolled in school and working toward a degree or certificate. Third, you need to be a U.S. citizen or eligible noncitizen. Also, if you are a male between the ages of 18 and 25, you need to be registered with Selective Service. And, of course, the money must be used for education.

Q: What kind of information do I have to give on the FAFSA form?
A: You have to provide information about your finances. You'll need a copy of your most recent federal tax return to do this.

Practice

Read the newspaper column again. Then read the sentences. Circle *T* for *True* or *F* for *False*.

1. You need to fill out a FAFSA form to ask about educational loans. **T (F)**
2. Only U.S. citizens may apply for education loans. **T F**
3. You must be registered for classes in order to receive an education loan. **T F**
4. You can only get an education loan if you're studying to get a college degree. **T F**
5. Anyone applying for an education loan must register with Selective Service. **T F**
6. You can use the money from an education loan to pay for other things such as a car or a house. **T F**
7. You need a federal tax return in order to apply for an education loan. **T F**

Learn

Read more about student loans. Then answer the question. Check the correct answer.

There are two kinds of educational loans: subsidized and unsubsidized. Both have low interest rates set by the federal government. Both also have long-term repayment plans and allow you to delay repayment of the principal for 6 months after completing your studies. With subsidized loans, you aren't charged interest on the loan while you are enrolled at least half-time in an eligible school. Interest charges begin only after you leave school. Unsubsidized loans are different. With these loans, you're charged interest immediately—while you're enrolled in school. There are limits on the amount of money you can get from a subsidized loan each year. It usually isn't enough to cover the cost of going to school, so most students receive both subsidized and unsubsidized loans.

What is one advantage of a subsidized loan over an unsubsidized loan?

- ☐ You don't have to start paying back a subidized loan until you leave school.
- ☐ You aren't charged interest in a subidized loan until after you leave school.
- ☐ You can usually get enough money from a subsidized loan to pay all of your school costs.

BONUS

Visit your school's financial aid office or career center and ask them for information about FAFSA, scholarships, and other forms of financial aid such as grants.

Learn

A *PAIRS.* **Financial aid forms use a lot of specialized vocabulary. Which words do you know? Match the words with their meanings.**

__a__ 1. widowed
_____ 2. IRS
_____ 3. adjusted gross income
_____ 4. current balance
_____ 5. net worth
_____ 6. investments

a. Internal Revenue Service; the department of the U.S. government that collects national taxes
b. money that you give to a company, bank, etc., in order to get a profit later
c. the amount of money remaining now
d. having lost a husband or wife because of death
e. income from wages, interest, investments, certain retirement accounts, etc.
f. the value of all the things a person owns, minus the amount of debt the person owes

B **Financial aid forms have many sections. Maria is just finishing a section about her finances. To complete this section, she needed to use her federal income tax return. Read Maria's application. Then answer the questions on the next page.**

PART TWO
Answer the questions about yourself (the student) if you are single, separated, divorced, or widowed. Include information about your spouse if you are married.

Have you completed your IRS income tax return?
I have already completed my return. ☑
I will file, but I have not yet completed my return. ☐
I'm not going to file. ☐

What income tax return did you file or will you file?
IRS 1040 ☐ A foreign tax return ☐ IRS 1040A or 1040EZ ☑
A tax return with Puerto Rico or another U.S. territory ☐

	DOLLARS
What was your (and spouse's) adjusted gross income for the year?	36,000
Enter your (and spouse's) income tax for the year.	4,621
How much did you earn from work for the year?	12,000
How much did your spouse earn from work for the year?	24,000
As of today, what is your (and spouse's) total current balance of cash, savings and checking accounts?	500
As of today, what is the net worth of your (and spouse's) investments, including real estate? This does not include the home you are currently living in.	0

Practice

A **Look at the financial aid form again. Then read the sentences. Circle *T* for *True* and *F* for *False*.**

1. Maria hasn't filed her taxes yet. T (F)
2. Maria plans to file a foreign tax return. T F
3. Maria and her husband's income from wages and interest is $36,000. T F
4. Maria and her husband have $4,621 in their savings account. T F
5. Maria and her husband do not have any investments to report. T F
6. Maria and her husband have a total of $500 when they add up the amount in their savings and checking accounts. T F

B **Look again at the section of the financial aid form entitled "Have you completed your IRS income tax return?" Match each sentence to its meaning.**

____ 1. I have already completed my return.

____ 2. I will file, but I have not yet completed my return.

____ 3. I'm not going to file.

a. I'm planning to fill out a federal tax return.

b. I'm not planning to fill out a federal tax return.

c. I already filled out my federal tax return.

Make It Yours

CLASS. **Do you know anyone who has applied for an educational loan? What information did the person need to complete the application? Did the person get the loan? Discuss any experiences you've heard about.**

BONUS **Go to www.fafsa.ed.gov and download the *FAFSA on the Web Worksheet*. Complete the worksheet. Discuss questions you don't understand with your class.**

Unit 9 Test

Before you take the test

Ⓐ Ⓑ Ⓒ Ⓓ Use the answer sheet for Unit 9 on page 221.

1. Print your name.
2. Print your teacher's name.
3. Write your student identification number, and bubble in the information below the boxes.
4. Write the test date and bubble in the information.
5. Write your class number and bubble in the information.

Listening I [Track 16]

You will hear a conversation. Then you will hear three sentences. Which sentence is true: A, B, or C?

1. A. The woman saved $200 last month.
B. The woman spent an extra $100 last month.
C. The woman plans to save $200 each month.

2. A. Only citizens can apply.
B. Some non-citizens can apply.
C. Students can't apply.

3. A. The minimum opening balance is $25.
B. The fee is $0 if the minimum balance is kept.
C. You get five free transactions.

Listening II [Track 17]

Listen. Test items 4, 5, and 6 are on the audio CD.

Reading

Read. What is the correct answer: A, B, C, or D?

Attention Students!

Need money for school?

You might be eligible to receive financial aid from the U.S. federal government.

In order to apply, you must

- ☑ be a U.S. citizen or eligible non-citizen.*
- ☑ be registered with Selective Service if you are a male between the ages of 18 and 25.
- ☑ be enrolled in school and working toward a degree or certificate.
- ☑ be able to show financial need.
- ☑ have a federal income tax return.

If you qualify, stop by the Career Center today to learn more about FAFSA (Free Application for Federal Student Aid) forms.

*Get more information on which non-citizens are eligible to apply at the Career Center.

7. What is the purpose of this notice?

A. to provide information about registering for the Selective Service

B. to provide information about completing a federal income tax return

C. to provide information about the Career Center

D. to provide information about applying for educational loans

8. Which of the following is true?

A. You must fill out a FAFSA form before you complete your federal income tax return.

B. Only U.S. citizens can get educational loans.

C. More information about FAFSA forms is available at the Career Center.

D. Only males are eligible to complete FAFSA forms.

First Bank of Washington has the right account for you. We offer a variety of accounts so you can choose the one that best meets your needs.

	Minimum Opening Balance	Minimum Monthly Balance	Monthly Service Fee	ATM Fee	Bounced Check Fee	Teller Fee
Online Checking	$100	$0	$5	$0	$25 per check	$3 per transaction
Standard Checking	$25	$5	$5	10 free transactions per month, $2 each after that	$25 per check	10 free per month, $3 each after that
Upgrade Checking	$200	$200	$10 (free if minimum balance is kept)	$0	$25 per check	$0

9. How much money do you need to open a Standard Checking account?

A. $5

B. $25

C. $100

D. $200

10. How much will you be charged for seeing a teller twice with an Online Checking account?

A. $0

B. $3

C. $6

D. $25

11. With an Upgrade Checking account, how much will you be charged if you write a "bad" check (a check you don't have enough money in your account to cover)?

A. $0

B. $10

C. $25

D. $200

Monthly Expenses

	Budgeted	June Actual	July Actual
rent	$1,100	$1,100	$1,100
car payment	185	185	185
utilities (gas, electricity, water)	100	87	95
Internet and phone	60	65	57
cell phone	45	45	45
entertainment	75	112	60
groceries	75	75	72
personal	100	89	102
savings	250	200	255

12. Which of the following is probably a fixed expense?

A. rent

B. entertainment

C. groceries

D. personal

13. How much money does the person plan to save each month?

A. $100

B. $200

C. $250

D. $255

14. Which of the following is true?

A. The person spent less than he had budgeted for entertainment in June.

B. The person spent the amount he had budgeted for Internet and phone in July.

C. The person spent the amount he had budgeted for groceries in June.

D. The person spent more than he had budgeted for the utilities in June.

Josef and Kamila are expecting a baby. They know that there will be a lot of extra costs when the baby comes, so they want to start saving some money now. They decided to make a budget to help them plan how'll they spend their money and how much they'll be able to save.

They started out by recording all the money they spent for a month. They saw that they were spending a lot of money on personal items and entertainment. They decided to budget less for those things and make sure they spent less. That way they'd have more for their savings.

For the next month, Josef and Kamila tracked their expenses again. Then they compared the amount they spent to the amount they had budgeted for each thing. They met their budget for fixed expenses, and they were under budget for variable expenses. So for that month, they had even more money to put into savings.

15. Why did Josef and Kamila make a budget?

A. They wanted to see how they were spending their money.

B. One month they had a lot of extra costs.

C. Their fixed expenses were too high.

D. They wanted to make a savings plan.

16. What did Josef and Kamila do first?

A. make a budget

B. track their expenses

C. reduce their variable expenses

D. open a savings account

Unit 10 Health and Wellness

Lesson 1 Good-Health Basics
- Identify basic factors of preventative health care

Lesson 2 Food and Nutrition
- Identify basic factors of good nutrition
- Make healthy food choices
- Identify healthful methods of food preparation

Lesson 3 Food Safety
- Understand precautions that can help prevent food-related illnesses

Lesson 4 Finding Health Care Providers
- Identify low-cost health care providers
- Identify health care services in the community

Lesson 5 Communicating with Your Doctor
- Describe symptoms to a doctor

Lesson 6 Medical History Forms
- Complete a medical history form

Lesson 7 Drug Labels
- Interpret directions and warnings on drug labels

Learn

Read the article. Then answer the question on page 153. Check (✓) the correct answers. (Note: There is more than one correct answer.)

Good Health and Living Well

What is "good health"? It's more than not being sick. And it's more than just eating healthy foods.* It's being well in mind, spirit, and body. Living well means that you balance, or give the right importance to, different parts of your life. Work is a large part of life, but you also need to spend time with your family and friends. And you need to make time for healthy activities daily.

Regular exercise is important to overall, or complete, wellness. It keeps your body strong and healthy, helps you manage, or control, your weight, and makes you feel happier. It can even help with depression. Find activities you like to do. You could try doing yoga, walking, running, riding a bike, dancing, or lifting weights. Even gardening and cleaning the house can be forms of exercise. Try different activities so you don't get bored. You can make exercise more fun by doing it with a partner. Sunshine is also important for your health, so be sure to include some outdoor activities.

Sleeping well provides the mind and body with needed rest. Adults who get seven to eight hours of sleep think more clearly and have more positive attitudes and better health than those who sleep less. To get a good night's sleep, don't drink caffeinated drinks (such as coffee, tea, or soda) or alcohol before going to bed. Do something relaxing, such as taking a warm bath or reading a book for pleasure before bedtime. To get the most benefits from your sleep, try to go to bed and wake up at the same time every day.

Stress, or feelings of worry, has a role in every illness. When we feel stressed, we don't breathe well, we tighten our muscles, our heart works harder, and so on. When this happens often, changes occur in our body that can make us sick. Learning how to manage and reduce stress is key to maintaining health. One of the best ways to reduce stress is to exercise. It's also important to pay attention to your body. Notice your breath as it goes in and out. Practice relaxing your muscles. Notice if there is tightness in different parts of your body—your jaw, your neck, your shoulders—and let it go. Relaxation helps reduce stress.

Wellness also includes doing something meaningful with your life. This means thinking about what is important to you and setting goals for your work life and your personal life. Finding work that is satisfying is a major part of happiness and health.

Finally, family and friends help us build loving relationships for support, or help. Loving well brings meaning to your life.

*See pages 155, 157, and 159 for more information on healthy food and nutrition.

According to the article, which of the following are important for wellness? Check the correct answers.

☐ exercise

☐ sleep

☐ a meaningful life

☐ friends and family

Practice

Read the article again. Answer the questions by putting a checkmark by the correct answers. (Note: Some questions have more than one correct answer. Check all the correct answers for each question.)

1. Which of the following things does the article say about good health?
   - ☐ Good health just means that you're not sick.
   - ☐ The only thing you need to do to be healthy is to eat food that's good for you.
   - ☑ Good health means you have a healthy spirit and mind, as well as a healthy body.
2. Which of the following things does the article say about exercise?
   - ☐ It's best to do only one kind of exercise.
   - ☐ Exercise makes you feel hungrier.
   - ☐ Exercise helps reduce stress.
3. Which of the following things does the article say about sleep?
   - ☐ If you get eight hours of sleep, you'll be able to think more clearly than if you get five hours of sleep.
   - ☐ Drinking alcohol can help you sleep well.
   - ☐ It's good to get up later on weekends than during the week.
4. Which of the following things does the article say about stress?
   - ☐ Stress causes changes in the body.
   - ☐ Stress can make you sick.
   - ☐ You can reduce stress by relaxing.
5. Which of the following things does the article say about wellness?
   - ☐ Balance in your life is an important part of wellness.
   - ☐ Wellness includes setting personal goals.
   - ☐ Your job is a big part of your wellness.

Make It Yours

GROUPS OF 3. **What healthy habits do you have? What can you do to become healthier? Talk about your habits and your health.**

Lesson 2 Food and Nutrition

Learn

A *PAIRS.* **Which words do you know? Match the words with their meanings.**

__e__ 1. preservatives
_____ 2. whole grains
_____ 3. fiber
_____ 4. protein
_____ 5. poultry
_____ 6. lean
_____ 7. processed foods
_____ 8. nutrients

a. foods that have been prepared in some way before you buy them, sometimes with preservatives added to them
b. elements in food needed for good health
c. without a lot of fat
d. birds, such as chicken, turkey, and duck, raised for food
e. chemicals added to food to stop it from going bad quickly
f. foods made from the entire seed of grains such as wheat, rice, corn, and oats
g. a nutrient that your body needs to stay strong and healthy
h. part of plants that, when eaten, is not digested and helps food to move through your body

B **Find out how much you know about nutrition. Read the sentences. Then circle *T* for *True* or *F* for *False*. If you don't know an answer, you can guess.**

How much do you know about nutrition?
Take this quiz and find out.

1. Every color in vegetables and fruits represents different nutrients. (T) F
2. Fruit juice is as good for you as fresh fruit. T F
3. Whole grain foods contain fiber. T F
4. Whole wheat bread is better for you than white bread. T F
5. Fish, poultry, and meat are sources of protein. T F
6. You can get protein from foods like milk and cheese. T F
7. Eating a lot of red meat is the best way to get protein. T F
8. Processed meats often have chemicals that are bad for your body. T F
9. All kinds of oil are bad for you. T F
10. Diabetes can result from eating too much sugar. T F
11. You shouldn't eat the same foods every day. T F
12. You can get protein from some vegetables. T F

C **Read the article. Then check your answers to the quiz on page 154.**

Eating Well for a Healthy Life

Eating well is one of the best things you can do to protect yourself against many diseases and to live a long and healthy life. Here is some basic, but important, information.

Vegetables and fruits build your health and reduce the risk of many diseases, including heart disease and some kinds of cancer. Try to eat 1 1/2 pounds of vegetables a day. Put something of every color on your plate every day to get a variety of nutrients. Limit fruit juice, which is high in sugar. Eat whole fruit instead—two or more pieces a day.

Whole grains are high in nutrients and fiber. Some common whole grain foods include brown rice, oatmeal, whole wheat bread, and whole wheat pasta. Eating whole grains may help reduce the risk of many diseases such as diabetes and cancer. Products made from refined grains, such as white bread, don't offer these benefits.

Protein is essential for the growth and health of our bodies. The most healthful protein sources are vegetable proteins (such as soybeans, tofu, and avocados), fish (such as salmon, sardines, flounder, and cod), low-fat dairy products (especially yogurt), and poultry (without the skin). Dried beans, raw nuts, and seeds are sources of protein, too, when combined with whole grains. Red meat provides protein, but it can contribute to diabetes, heart disease, and cancer. If you eat red meat, limit the amount and make sure it's lean. Also limit processed meats such as bacon, ham, hot dogs, and sliced deli meat, as these often contain harmful preservatives.

There are good fats and bad fats. Good (unsaturated) fats are important for the brain and heart. Good fats can be found in walnuts, certain vegetable oils (such as olive and canola oils), certain fish (such as salmon and sardines), and some vegetables (such as kidney beans and avocados). At the same time, it's important to limit bad (saturated) fat—avoid fatty meat, choose low-fat dairy products, and limit butter to one teaspoon per day. And avoid trans fats, also called hydrogenated fats, which are used in most margarines, many packaged and snack foods, and French fries. These fats can lead to cancer and heart disease.

Eating too much sugar can lead to serious diseases, including cancer, diabetes, heart disease, and depression. Avoid foods that have added sugar, such as many breakfast cereals, soda, fruit drinks, ketchup, and desserts. Read ingredients labels, but be careful because there are many different names for different kinds of sugar. *Cane syrup*, *corn syrup*, *fructose*, and *dextrose* are just a few of the different names.

Vary the kinds of foods you eat to get all the different vitamins and minerals you need. Eat fresh foods as much as possible and avoid processed foods, which frequently contain harmful preservatives and usually have a lot of sugar as well as salt. If you do buy processed foods, read the ingredients labels to help you know what you're eating.

D *CLASS.* **Talk about the questions below.**

1. After reading the information about healthy food, would you answer the questions in the quiz on page 156 the same way? Which answers would you change?
2. Did you read anything that surprised you? Tell your classmates.

Practice

A **Look at the article on page 155 again. Answer the question.**

Imagine that you need to make a complete vegetarian protein (soy products, dry beans, nuts, or seeds + a whole grain food) for three meals. Which items would you combine with the foods already listed at each meal? Choose one per meal. (Note: There is more than one possible answer for each meal.)

bean dip	broccoli	cream cheese	onions
black bean soup	carrots	maple syrup	soy milk

Breakfast	**Lunch**	**Dinner**
oatmeal	whole wheat bread	brown rice
+ __________	+ __________	+ __________

B *PAIRS.* **Plan menus for a day. Circle the four foods that would make the healthiest meals and snacks.**

1. **Breakfast** eggs pancakes whole wheat toast jelly orange juice white toast 1/2 teaspoon butter maple syrup orange
2. **Snacks** apple potato chips donut celery candy bar pretzels raw almonds yogurt candied almonds cookies
3. **Lunch** hot dog white bread spinach salad French fries turkey soda carrot sticks strawberries
4. **Dinner** steak baked fish broccoli brown rice white rice canned corn chocolate cake fruit salad

C *CLASS.* **Check your answers. Discuss the reason why each food is or isn't a healthy choice.**

Learn

A *CLASS.* **Which words about food preparation do you know? Talk about the meanings of these words.**

bake	broil	grill	steam
boil	fry	peel	stir-fry

B **Read the article.**

How to Prepare Healthy Food

Choosing nutritious foods is a very important part of staying healthy. But another important consideration is how to prepare food. Some methods of food preparation decrease a food's nutritional value. Some methods can even cause health problems.

Always wash fruits and vegetables before eating them. If they are hard, clean them with a brush. Soft fruits and vegetables like strawberries or lettuce can be washed two or three times. If possible, peel fruits and vegetables, especially if you're eating them raw.

When you cook vegetables, it's best to lightly steam or boil them quickly. This way they keep most of their nutrients. (And you can use the cooking water later for soup.) You can also lightly stir-fry them in a little olive, canola, or other vegetable oil for a few minutes and then add some liquid to the pan to finish the cooking if longer cooking is needed.

One healthful way to cook fish, meat, and poultry is to cook it in liquid, such as water or broth. Baking and broiling are also good.

Don't grill too often, and avoid frying any food. These cooking methods cause a brown layer to form on the outside of the food. This layer is delicious, but it's also dangerous—it's made up of chemicals that can cause cancer and other diseases. Frying is the worst method of cooking. When you heat oil to high temperatures, not only are the benefits of oil destroyed, but dangerous chemicals are formed.

Practice

Look at the article again. Answer these questions on a separate piece of paper.

1. What should you always do to fruits and vegetables before you eat them?
2. What are three good ways to cook vegetables?
3. What are three good ways to cook fish, meat, and poultry?
4. What happens when you heat oil to very high temperatures?
5. What is the least healthful way to cook food?

BONUS **Keep a food journal for a week. Write down everything you eat for snacks and meals. At the end of the week, look at your journal. Which kinds of foods do you eat too much of? Which kinds of foods should you eat more?**

Lesson 3 Food Safety

Learn

A **Match the sentence beginnings and endings.**

1. Bacteria are very small living things that
2. Something that is raw isn't
3. You have leftovers when there's
4. You use a cutting board to
5. When you defrost food, you
6. When you chill something,

cooked.

cut food on when you're cooking.

let it get warmer so it isn't frozen anymore.

you make it cold.

can cause illness and disease.

extra food at the end of a meal that you keep to eat later.

B **Find out how much you know about food safety. Read the sentences. Then circle *T* for *True* or *F* for *False*. If you don't know an answer, you can guess.**

You probably don't think of food as dangerous.
But if you're not careful, the bacteria in it can make you very sick.
How much do you know about food safety?
Take this quiz and find out.

1.	You should wash your hands for 10 seconds before you touch food.	T	(F)
2.	It's better to use wooden cutting boards than plastic ones.	T	F
3.	You shouldn't let raw fish touch other food in your refrigerator.	T	F
4.	It's OK to use the same cutting board for raw meat and raw vegetables.	T	F
5.	You can get sick from eating meat or poultry that is still pink inside.	T	F
6.	Raw eggs are good for you.	T	F
7.	You should cook chicken until it's 145°F.	T	F
8.	The temperature of your refrigerator should be 40°F.	T	F
9.	Any food that normally requires refrigeration should be thrown away after it has been at room temperature for half an hour.	T	F
10.	You should defrost frozen food in the refrigerator, not at room temperature.	T	F

C **Read the article on page 159 and check your answers. Underline the information in the article that gives the correct answers to the quiz.**

D ***GROUPS OF 3.*** **Look at the quiz again. Which of these things do you do? Do you think you will change any of your habits after reading the article? Why or why not?**

Here are four easy ways to help prevent bacteria from making your family sick.

Clean

- Always wash your hands with soap and warm water for 20 seconds before touching food. Wash them after touching raw meat, poultry, or fish, blowing your nose, touching pets, going to the bathroom, or changing a baby's diaper.
- Use hot, soapy water to wash anything (such as knives, cutting boards, or plates) that has touched raw meat, poultry, fish, or eggs.
- Wash towels, dishcloths, and sponges in hot water daily. Let sponges dry between uses. Frequently disinfect sponges by boiling them in hot water or by putting them in the dishwasher and then in the microwave on high for two minutes.
- Use wooden, not plastic, cutting boards. Bacteria can live on plastic for longer than they can live on wood.

Separate

- Make sure raw meat, poultry, and fish or liquid from these doesn't touch other foods in the refrigerator.
- Never put any food on a plate or cutting board that had raw meat, poultry, or fish on it without washing it first.
- Use one cutting board for raw meat, poultry, and fish. Use another for other foods.

Cook

- Don't eat meat, poultry, or fish that is still pink in the middle. Don't eat foods that contain raw eggs. Undercooked or raw proteins can contain dangerous bacteria.
- Use a food thermometer. Cook beef, veal, and lamb until the temperature reaches 145°F. Cook hamburger, pork, and egg dishes to 160°F and poultry to 165°F.

Chill

- Keep your refrigerator at 40°F or colder. Keep your freezer at 0°F or colder.
- Food that normally requires refrigeration should not be left out at room temperature for more than 2 hours (or 1 hour when it's 90°F or hotter). After this amount of time, throw the food away. This includes leftovers after a meal as well as food at a party.
- Defrost frozen food in the refrigerator, not at room temperature.

Source: http://www.fsis.usda.gov/factsheets/

Practice

Look at the article again. Answer the questions on a separate sheet of paper.

1. What should you always do before you begin to cook?
2. A plate had raw meat on it. Before using it again, what should you do?
3. What are two ways to know when meat, poultry, or fish is cooked enough to eat?
4. What should you do with food that hasn't been refrigerated for 3 hours?

Lesson 4 Finding Health Care Providers

Learn

A *PAIRS.* **Which words do you know? Match the words with their meanings.**

__g__ 1. treatment
_____ 2. health insurance
_____ 3. pediatrics
_____ 4. immunization
_____ 5. depression
_____ 6. substance abuse
_____ 7. gynecology
_____ 8. family planning

a. a condition in which you are so unhappy that you cannot live a normal life
b. the area of medicine that deals with conditions that affect only women, especially their ability to have babies
c. receiving a very small amount of a disease that causes the body to build up immunity, or protection, to the disease
d. the habit of taking too much of a drug (including alcohol), in a way that harms your health
e. controlling the number of children that are born by using contraception (birth control)
f. the area of medicine that deals with children and their illnesses
g. something that is done to make a sick person better
h. arrangement with a company in which you pay a certain amount of money in return for the company paying all or part of the costs when you see a doctor or go to the hospital.

B **Read the article.**

Low-Cost Health Care Solutions

Prevention (stopping an illness from happening) and early diagnosis (identifying a medical condition) are the best treatments for any medical problem. But doctors' visits can be expensive, and many people without health insurance may not know how to get inexpensive medical care.

One common solution is to go to a hospital emergency room for any medical problem, even if it is not an emergency. It's true that you can get care at an emergency room, but for non-emergencies, it's not the best place to go. One reason is that you can't receive treatment at an emergency room for long-term conditions, such as high blood pressure or high cholesterol. You can't get specialty care either, such as dental or prenatal care (care for babies before they are born). Lastly, emergency rooms can't provide preventative care, which may help you avoid medical problems before they start.

A good solution is clinics. Clinics are places where medical treatment is given at a low (or sometimes no) cost. Some clinics charge on a sliding scale—the amount you pay depends on how much you can afford. Others offer student discounts or "hardship" discounts for people who have a difficult time paying.

At a clinic you can receive preventative care and treatment for non-emergencies. There are clinics for general medical care as well as for specialized care. To find a clinic in your area, you can use the Yellow Pages (look under *clinics*). Or visit the following website: http://ask.hrsa.gov/pc/. (Type in your state and county to get a list of health care centers that provide low-cost or free health care.)

C Write your answers to this question on a separate sheet of paper: What are three reasons you *shouldn't* go to the emergency room for medical problems that aren't emergencies?

Practice

A Look at the information about three clinics. Answer the questions.

Community Health Clinic

Adults and pediatrics services include general health care, as well as immunizations, dental care, and medical specialties. By appointment only. Services at low cost.

Center for Mental Health

Complete mental health care, including
- treatment of depression
- substance abuse treatment

No appointment necessary.

Student and hardship discounts available.

Women's Care Clinic

- Complete gynecological care
- Family planning services
- Prenatal care

Sliding scale fees

1. For which clinic do you need an appointment? ____________
2. Which clinic would you take a sick child to? ____________

B Look at the information about clinics again. Then read the situations. Which is the best place for each person? Write *CHC* (Community Health Clinic), *CMH* (Center for Mental Health), *WCC* (Women's Care Clinic), or *ER* (an emergency room).

1. Deepak has been losing weight, and he doesn't know why. CHC
2. Lin's daughter needs immunizations for school. ________
3. Jenny is pregnant. ________
4. Sarah's five-year-old son has been coughing for a few days. ________
5. Sandra and Omar are married. They want to wait a few years before they have children. ________
6. Victor has been feeling really sad for the past few months, and he can't explain why. ________
7. Emel found a lump (something hard) in her breast. ________
8. Mohammed fell and hurt his ankle very badly. He thinks it might be broken. ________
9. Kasha thinks she has a problem with drinking too much alcohol. ________
10. Mark doesn't feel sick, but he would like a checkup (a visit with a doctor) to make sure he is healthy. ________

C *PAIRS.* Check your answers. Explain why you chose each place for the person. Talk about the service each person needs.

BONUS Create a list of low-cost medical care providers in your community. (Look under *clinics* in the Yellow Pages or go to http://ask.hrsa.gov/pc/.)

Lesson 5 Communicating with Your Doctor

Learn

A *PAIRS.* **Which words do you know? Write each word from the box next to its meaning.**

abdominal cramps	chills	food poisoning	joint pain	nausea	weakness
(no) appetite	~~diarrhea~~	fever	muscle aches	vomiting	

____diarrhea____ 1. watery waste from the bowels

__________ 2. sharp, severe (strong) pains in the stomach area

__________ 3. throwing up (when food or drink comes up from your stomach and out through your mouth)

__________ 4. feeling you have when you think you're going to vomit

__________ 5. pain in the muscles, especially behind the eyes and in the neck, that often comes with illness

__________ 6. pain in a part of the body where two bones meet

__________ 7. feeling of not being strong, not having energy

__________ 8. feeling of being cold, caused by an illness

__________ 9. illness in which you have a high temperature

__________ 10. (no) desire for food

__________ 11. illness caused by food containing harmful bacteria

B CD2 TRACK 18 **Look at the words in the box in Exercise A again. Listen to the conversation between a doctor and patient. Check each symptom above that the patient has.**

C **Listen again and read. Check your answers to Exercise B.**

A: Hello, Mrs. Ivanov. You don't look good. What's the problem?
B: I feel terrible. I have diarrhea and abdominal cramps.
A: How bad are the cramps?
B: They're severe.
A: Have you had any vomiting or nausea?
B: Yes.
A: How long has this been going on?
B: Since yesterday.
A: Have you had any muscle aches, joint pain, weakness, chills, or fever?
B: Well, I feel weak, and my muscles ache. I don't have any appetite, either.
A: OK. This sounds like food poisoning. Have you eaten anything that might have made you sick?
B: I'm not sure. I went to a picnic yesterday. Maybe the food sat out in the heat too long.

D **Look at the conversation again. Complete the sentences. Circle *a, b,* or *c.***

1. Mrs. Ivanov's abdominal cramps are ____.

   a. severe **b.** not bad **c.** weak

2. Mrs. Ivanov has been sick ____.

   a. for a week **b.** for three days **c.** since yesterday

3. Mrs. Ivanov says that she doesn't have ____.

   a. diarrhea **b.** food poisoning **c.** an appetite

Listen

Listen to the question. What's the correct answer? Circle *a* or *b*.

1. **a.** I'm nauseous, and I have diarrhea. **b.** Yes, I have other symptoms.
2. **a.** The cramps are severe. **b.** Yes, I have cramps.
3. **a.** Yes, the pain is severe. **b.** Yes, and I've been vomiting.
4. **a.** Since yesterday morning. **b.** Tomorrow morning.

Practice

Listen to the conversation and read.

Doctor: So, Mr. Dee. What's the matter?
Mr. Dee: I feel terrible. I have diarrhea and abdominal cramps.
Doctor: How bad are the cramps?
Mr. Dee: They're severe.
Doctor: When did it begin?
Mr. Dee: Yesterday.
Doctor: Do you have any other symptoms?
Mr. Dee: Yes. I have chills, and I don't have any appetite.
Doctor: OK, let me examine you.

***PAIRS.* Practice the conversation.**

Make It Yours

***PAIRS. ROLE PLAY.* Practice the conversation in Exercise A. Use the information below. Use your own names. Switch roles.**

First patient: You have severe joint pain, a fever, and chills. It started last night.
Second patient: You've been vomiting. You also have abdominal cramps and diarrhea. It started this morning.

Lesson 6 Medical History Forms

Learn

A *PAIRS.* **Which words do you know? Complete the sentences. Use the words in the box.**

at present	physician	surgery

1. A ____________________ is a doctor.
2. Another way to say *now* is ____________________.
3. When you have ____________________, a doctor cuts open your body to repair something inside.

B **Read the medical history form.**

Medical History ***Please record all information clearly and completely.***

First name: Arturo Last name: Montes
Date of birth (mm/dd/yy) 07/06/55

Do you have health insurance? ☐ yes ☒ no
Insurance company name ____________ Policy number ____________

Are you under the care of a physician for any condition at present? ☒ yes ☐ no
If yes, please explain. I have high blood pressure. I see my doctor every 6 months.

Are you taking any medication at present? ☒ yes ☐ no Which? metolazone

Are you allergic to any medications? ☒ yes ☐ no Which? amoxicillin

Do you have any other allergies? ☒ yes ☐ no
If yes, please explain. I'm allergic to wheat and peanuts.

Have you been hospitalized or had surgery in the past year? ☒ yes ☐ no
If yes, please explain. I was in the hospital for four days for pneumonia.

Have you ever received treatment for a mental condition? ☒ yes ☐ no
If yes, please explain. I received treatment for depression from May 2008 to May 2010.

Please use an X to record any medical conditions that you or any family members currently have or have had.

	You	Family Member		You	Family Member
asthma	☐	☐	heart disease	☐	☒
cancer	☐	☐	high cholesterol	☒	☒

Practice

Look at the medical history form again. Complete the sentences. Circle the correct word or phrase.

1. Arturo's birthday is in **June / July.**
2. Arturo is receiving treatment for **high blood pressure / pneumonia**.
3. Arturo takes **metolazone / amoxicillin.**
4. Arturo was in the hospital for **pneumonia / depression**.
5. Arturo has **heart disease / high cholesterol**.

Make It Yours

Fill out the medical history form. Use real or made-up information.

Medical History *Please record all information clearly and completely.*

First name: ______________________ Last name: ______________________
Date of birth (mm/dd/yy) ______________

Do you have health insurance? ☐ yes ☐ no
Insurance company name ______________________ Policy number ______________

Are you under the care of a physician for any condition at present? ☐ yes ☐ no
If yes, please explain. ____

Are you taking any medication at present? ☐ yes ☐ no Which? ______________

Are you allergic to any medications? ☐ yes ☐ no Which? ______________

Do you have any other allergies? ☐ yes ☐ no
If yes, please explain. ____

Have you been hospitalized or had surgery in the past year? ☐ yes ☐ no
If yes, please explain. ____

Have you ever received treatment for a mental condition? ☐ yes ☐ no
If yes, please explain. ____

Lesson 7 Drug Labels

Learn

Note >>>>> *For some drugs, you need a prescription, or a written order, from a doctor. Other drugs, called over-the-counter (OTC) medications, can be bought without a prescription.*

PAIRS. **Which words do you know? Write each word from the box next to its meaning.**

consult	discard	dosage	out of reach	refill	use caution
despite	dizziness	drowsiness	persist	~~Rx~~	warning

Rx ____ 1. abbreviation for the word *prescription*

____ 2. amount of medication that you should take at one time

____ 3. statement that tells you something is bad or dangerous

____ 4. feeling that you are losing your balance and are about to fall

____ 5. be careful

____ 6. in a place where someone can't get something

____ 7. getting another container of prescription medicine when the one you have is finished

____ 8. throw away

____ 9. ask for advice or information

____ 10. continue

____ 11. without being affected by something

____ 12. feeling of extreme tiredness, like you're almost asleep

Practice

A **Read the drug label. Answer the questions on page 167.**

Great Life Pharmacy

Rx#41040100 Patient: Yoon Kwock

FEXOFENADINE 60 mg. tablet

Dosage: Take one tablet with water two times daily.

Warning: May cause dizziness. Use caution when operating vehicles or machinery until you know how this medication will affect you.

1 refill before 5/20/10 Discard after: 10/20/10

Prescribing physician: Dr. Doris A. Sonoda

1. Is this a prescription drug or an OTC drug? How do you know?
   It's a prescriptiion drug. It has an Rx number.
2. How many tablets should Yoon take at one time? ____
3. How many times each day should Yoon take the medication? ____
4. How many tablets should Yoon take in total each day? ____
5. Why should Yoon be careful driving when taking this medication?
   ____
6. Can Yoon get more of this medication? How do you know?
   ____
7. If Yoon still has the medication on November 20, 2010, what should he do with it?
   ____

B **Read the drug label. Answer the questions.**

Loratadine tablets, 10 mg.
Uses: For relief of sneezing, runny nose; itchy, watery eyes; itchy throat or nose.
Directions: Adults and children six years and older, take 1 tablet daily.
Consult a physician before giving this medication to children under six years of age.
Warnings:
- If you are pregnant or breastfeeding, consult a physician before using.
- If symptoms persist despite treatment, consult a physician.
- Do not take more than directed. May cause dizziness or drowsiness.
- Keep out of reach of children.

1. What is the dosage of this medication for an adult? ____________
2. What might happen if you take more than the correct dosage of this drug?
   ____
3. What do you need to do before you give this medication to a five-year-old child?
   ____

Make It Yours

PAIRS. **Look at the drug label in Exercise B again. Read the situations. Discuss the answers to each question.**

1. Rachel is pregnant. What does she need to do before she takes this drug?
2. Elena has a four-year-old son. Is it OK for her to keep this drug in a cabinet under her bathroom sink? Why or why not?
3. Kashev drives to work every morning. Is it OK for him to take two tablets before he drives? Why or why not?
4. Rick has been taking the drug for two weeks, but his symptoms aren't getting any better. What should he do?

Unit 10 Test

Before you take the test

ⒶⒷⒸⒹ Use the answer sheet for Unit 10 on page 223.

1. Print your name.
2. Print your teacher's name.
3. Write your student identification number, and bubble in the information below the boxes.
4. Write the test date and bubble in the information.
5. Write your class number and bubble in the information.

CD2 Listening I [Track 21]

Listen to the sentence. Which of the following means the same as the sentence you heard: A, B, or C?

1. A. Take this medicine before you go to sleep.
B. This medicine can make you sleepy.
C. Take this medicine if you feel sleepy.

2. A. She's taking her to a pediatric clinic.
B. She's taking her to a women's health clinic.
C. She's taking her to the emergency room at a children's hospital.

3. A. You should get a prescription.
B. You should talk to a doctor.
C. You should get a refill of the medication.

4. A. You need to cook this fish.
B. You need to chill this fish.
C. You need to defrost this fish.

CD2 Listening II [Track 22]

Listen. Test items 5, 6, and 7 are on the audio CD.

Reading

Read. What is the correct answer: A, B, C, or D?

Medical History Form

Please write all information clearly.

Last name: Gomez First name: Alicia

Date of birth 07/05/65

Health insurance company: ITT Health Group number: 777-888-0303

At present, are you under the care of a physician for any condition? ☑ yes ☐ no

Name of doctor: Dr. L H. Randall Reason: high cholesterol

List all medications you are taking at present. fluvastatin

List all allergies to medications. penicillin

List all other allergies. wheat and dairy

Have you ever received treatment for a mental condition? ☑ yes ☐ no

Please explain. Last year I was treated for depression. I took escitalopram.

---

8. Which medicine does Alicia take now?

A. fluvastatin

B. penicillin

C. escitalopram

D. none

9. Why is Alicia receiving medical treatment now?

A. She has high cholesterol.

B. She has allergies.

C. She is depressed.

D. She isn't receiving medical treatment now.

Lan works a lot. A few weeks ago, she started to feel sick. She felt extremely tired and nauseous, and she didn't have any appetite. So she decided to see a doctor.

She went to a local health clinic, and she told the doctor there about her symptoms. The doctor asked Lan about her lifestyle, including her job, her diet, her sleep habits, and things she did for fun.

The doctor didn't give Lan any medicine, but he gave her some instructions. He said the stress in Lan's life was making her sick. The doctor said Lan needed to exercise more, relax, and make time for fun activities. He said these things would help reduce Lan's stress and make her feel better.

The doctor also gave Lan some information on healthy eating. He said that the ingredients in the processed foods she was eating could be making her symptoms worse. He said that she should eat more fresh fruit and vegetables and avoid processed foods.

10. What is one of the reasons that Lan went to the doctor?

A. She was vomiting.

B. She didn't feel hungry or want to eat anything.

C. She wanted to relax.

D. She needed a refill of her prescription.

11. What did the doctor tell Lan to do?

A. sleep more

B. set personal goals

C. take medicine

D. exercise

12. What was one of the doctor's recommendations?

A. making more time for work

B. going to a health clinic

C. not working for a few weeks

D. eating more vegetables

Many kinds of bacteria can live in raw meat and poultry. These bacteria can cause food poisoning and other illnesses. Because of this, you should be sure that no raw meat or poultry touches any other foods in your refrigerator or during food preparation. Always wash well any knives, cutting boards, or plates that have touched raw meat or poultry before using them again with other foods.

High temperatures can destroy most of the bacteria in raw foods. Whether you bake, broil, or use any other cooking method, make sure that the food gets hot enough to kill the bacteria. You can use the temperature guide below.

beef (except hamburger) veal lamb	Cook to at least 145°F.
hamburger pork food that contains eggs	Cook to at least 160°F.
all poultry	Cook to at least 165°F.

13. What is the purpose of this information?

A. to explain why bacteria in food can make people sick

B. to teach how to cut raw meat and poultry

C. to give some information about safe food preparation

D. to compare different cooking methods for meat and poultry

14. Which of the following is true?

A. You shouldn't keep raw meat or poultry in your refrigerator.

B. You can make meat safe to eat by cooking it to specific temperatures.

C. You can only be sure that meat is safe to eat if you bake it.

D. You should cook chicken to 160° F to kill any bacteria in it.

Public Health Clinic

Services include:

- general and preventative health care
- immunizations
- gynecological care
- family planning and prenatal care
- pediatric services
- dental care
- mental health care, including substance abuse treatment

By appointment only.
Sliding scale fees.
Student and hardship discounts available.

Women and Children's Clinic

• gynecological care •
• family planning and prenatal care •
• pediatric care •

Quality health care at a low cost.
No appointment necessary.

15. Which clinic can help couples plan and control the number of children they have?

A. only the Public Health Clinic

B. only the Women and Children's Clinic

C. both clinics

D. neither clinic

16. Which clinic offers services to people with a drug or alcohol problem?

A. only the Public Health Clinic

B. only the Women and Children's Clinic

C. both clinics

D. neither clinic

Unit 11 Housing and Utilities

Lesson 1 **Rental Leases**
- Understand a lease
- Identify some rights and responsibilities of tenants and landlords

Lesson 2 **Fair Housing Laws**
- Understand tenants' rights against discrimination

Lesson 3 **Utility Bills**
- Interpret a utility bill

Lesson 4 **Communicating with Utility Companies**
- Use an automated phone system
- Ask about a mistake on a bill

Lesson 1 Rental Leases

Learn

A **Alonzo has found a beautiful two-bedroom apartment that he's going to rent. Read the conditions of his lease.**

a. This lease agreement made on Sept. 30, 2010 between George King as landlord and Alonzo Garza as tenant.

b. Location and Description: The landlord agrees to lease to the tenant the premises described as follows: 4351 SE 164th St., Renton, WA 98058.

c. Term: The lease will begin Oct. 1, 2010 and terminate in one year on Sept. 30, 2011.

d. Rent: The tenant agrees to pay the landlord, George King, $875.00 due on the first of each month for the leased premises.

e. Security Deposit: At the signing of this lease agreement, the tenant will pay a security deposit of $875.00. The landlord will return this deposit to the tenant upon termination of the lease provided the premises are in good condition and the tenant does not owe rent.

f. Utilities and Services:

1. The landlord will pay for trash collection.
2. The tenant will pay for all other utilities and services to the leased premises, which will include, but not be limited to, water, electricity, and heat.

g. Additional Conditions:

1. The tenant will not have pets without prior authorization from the landlord.
2. The tenant agrees that only those people listed on the lease agreement will live on the premises. Overnight guests are allowed but may not stay more than four nights in any one month.
3. The tenant will not do anything that creates a nuisance to neighbors or that is hazardous to the property or other persons.
4. The landlord is responsible for keeping the common areas clean and in good repair. The tenant is responsible for reporting any problems in common areas to the landlord.
5. The tenant is responsible for keeping the premises clean and in good and safe condition. The tenant will be held responsible for any damage caused to the premises that is not normal wear and tear.
6. The landlord must give 24 hours advance notice before entering the leased premises.

B **PAIRS. Look at the lease on page 174 again. Which words do you know? Match the words with their meanings.**

__i__ 1. premises	a. a person, thing, or situation that is annoying
____ 2. term	b. before
____ 3. terminate	c. official permission to do something
____ 4. prior	d. information or warning that something will happen
____ 5. authorization	e. places that are used by all tenants
____ 6. nuisance	f. make something, such as a job or contract, end
____ 7. common areas	g. damage that happens with ordinary use
____ 8. normal wear and tear	h. an officially agreed period of time
____ 9. advance notice	i. land or building that someone uses or lives in

Practice

A **Under which section of the lease can you find the answer to each of the questions below? Write the letter of the section next to the question. If a section is numbered, use both the letter and the number.**

__b__ 1. What is the address of the leased premises?
____ 2. What does the tenant need to do before he buys a pet?
____ 3. Will the landlord return the tenant's security deposit?
____ 4. What is the tenant not allowed to do on the leased premises?
____ 5. When is the rent due every month?
____ 6. Will the tenant pay for heat and electricity?
____ 7. Can the tenant allow a friend to live in the leased premises for several weeks?
____ 8. Which service will the landlord pay for?
____ 9. Who is responsible for making repairs in the common areas?
____ 10. What is the term of the lease?

B ***PAIRS.*** **Look at the lease again. Ask and answer the questions above. Take turns.**

C ***PAIRS.*** **In section f2 of the lease, *will include* means that the tenant is responsible for paying for the utilities listed: water, electricity, and heat. *But not be limited to* means there could be other utilities not listed that the tenant would also be responsible for, such as cable TV. What other utilities might a tenant use and need to pay for? Discuss.**

Make It Yours

GROUPS OF 3. **Discuss: The tenant is responsible for not creating a nuisance for neighbors. What are some examples of things that could be nuisances for neighbors?**

Lesson 2 Fair Housing Laws

Learn

A *PAIRS.* **Which words do you know? Match the words with their meanings.**

__i__ 1. discrimination
_____ 2. race
_____ 3. disability
_____ 4. refuse
_____ 5. availability
_____ 6. facility
_____ 7. reasonable
_____ 8. accommodation
_____ 9. policy

a. one of the groups that people are divided into, based on skin color and other physical features
b. a way of doing something that is officially agreed on
c. a place or building used for a particular activity
d. fair and sensible
e. a change in the way things are done, in order to solve a problem
f. say or show that you will not do something that someone has asked you to do
g. ability for something to be used by someone
h. a physical or mental condition that makes it difficult for someone to do the things most people are able to do
i. treat a person or group unfairly and differently from others

B **Read this notice about housing discrimination. Then answer the question.**

Have You Been a Victim of Housing Discrimination?

The Fair Housing Act protects tenants from discrimination. It says it is illegal for landlords to discriminate on the basis of race or color, national origin, religion, sex, familial status (families with children), or disability. If you believe that you have been discriminated against when looking for housing, contact a local Fair Housing office in your area.

Know Your Rights!

1. It is illegal to refuse to rent housing based on race or national origin, religion, sex, familial status (families with children), or disability.
2. It is illegal to base availability of different housing services or facilities on race or national origin, religion, sex, familial status (families with children), or disability.
3. If you have a disability, it is illegal for a landlord to refuse to make reasonable and necessary accommodations in rules and policies to enable you to use the housing.

What does the community notice explain?

☐ laws about landlords' rights

☐ laws against discrimination in housing

☐ laws about accommodations at work for people with disabilities

Practice

Read about the situations of the people below. Decide which of the Fair Housing laws on page 176 is being violated. Write the number (1, 2, or 3) next to each situation.

_____ 1. Evelyne uses a wheelchair. She asked the apartment manager if she could park her car in the parking space near her front door. The manager said that each parking space was assigned to a specific apartment unit and could not be changed. The manager told Evelyne that she was lucky because her parking space was not very far away from her apartment unit.

_____ 2. Masa and Miki have a three-year-old toddler and an infant. They found a condominium in the city that they were interested in renting. When the couple met the landlord, he told them that he wouldn't be able to rent the unit to them because the building was not for families with young children. The landlord explained that people living in that condominium were active young singles or couples without children. He suggested that they look at other apartment buildings where there were families with children.

_____ 3. Minh and Doan recently came to the U.S. from Vietnam. They found a house in the suburbs they wanted to rent. The landlord met with the couple and told them that no one in the neighborhood spoke Vietnamese and that there were no Asian restaurants or stores nearby. The landlord predicted that their children would not be comfortable at the public schools in the district. When Minh and Doan said they were still interested in renting the house, the landlord refused and recommended that they rent a house closer to the city where there was more diversity.

_____ 4. Raul and Aurora are living in a nice apartment complex. They asked the apartment manager if they could use the community center for a family party. She told them that they would need to give her a $250 deposit, and they wouldn't be able to play "their kind of music" too loud since it would bother the other tenants. Raul and Aurora had never heard about a deposit for the community center before. They asked their neighbor Ron about the time he rented the community center. He said that he hadn't paid a deposit.

Make It Yours

GROUPS OF 3. **Talk about experiences you have had with rentals in the past. Have you experienced or do you know anyone who has experienced housing discrimination? What did you or the person do?**

BONUS **Go to www.hud.gov (the website for the U.S. Department of Housing and Urban Development), and find the phone number for a local Fair Housing office in your area.**

Utility Bills

Learn

Note

Some cities provide gas, electricity, water, garbage collection, wastewater removal, and other utilities. In other areas, these are provided by private companies. In some places, each service is handled by a different provider. In others, the same provider delivers two or more of these services.

Learn

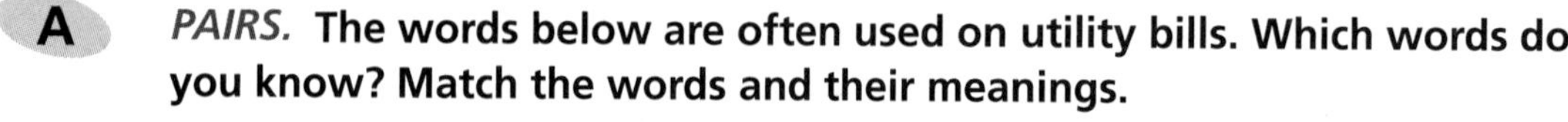

A *PAIRS.* **The words below are often used on utility bills. Which words do you know? Match the words and their meanings.**

c	1. previous balance	a. money charged when a bill is not paid on time
____	2. current charges	b. the period of time a customer is charged for a service
____	3. balance forward	c. the amount on the bill that you owed last month
____	4. meter	d. the amount on the bill that is due now
____	5. kWh	e. an amount owed from a previous bill
____	6. billing period	f. kilowatt hour, a unit for measuring electrical power
____	7. late fee	g. equipment that measures gas, water, or electricity

B **Leonid Sidorov lives in Ridgefield, where electricity is provided by the city. Read his bill for this month and the note and story on the next page.**

City of Ridgefield Electric Utility		**Account Information**	
Statement Date:	AUG 15, 2010	Account Number:	0000999
Due Date:	SEPT 5, 2010	Customer:	Leonid Sidorov

Billing Information			**Amount to pay**		
	Previous Balance:	$82.37		Current Charges:	$92.00
	Payment (7/25/10)	–$82.37		Balance forward:	$.00
	Balance	$.00	**Amount due this statement:**		**$92.00**

Electric Detail 123 Pine St, Ridgefield, WA 98058

Meter Number	Present Read	Previous Read	KWH Usage	Billing Period
U11111111	85152	84501	651	06/29/10 to 07/30/10

Service Charge		$6.02	A late fee of 1% will be applied to unpaid balances if bill is received after due date of SEPT 5, 2010.
Electric Charge	600 kWh @ $.074684 per kWh	$44.81	
Electric Charge	51 kWh @ $.092492 per kWh	$4.72	
Delivery Charge	651 kWh @ $.054200 per kWh	$35.28	
		$90.83	

A late fee of 1% will be applied to unpaid balances if bill is received after due date. Mail your payment in the enclosed envelope to Ridgefield Electric Utility, Box 11005, Ridgefield, WA 98058. Or call 1-888-000-1111 to pay by phone or with a credit card.

For information, emergencies, loss of electrical power (due to an outage), or for changes in your account call 1-800-555-9999.

Note

Utility bills can be hard to understand. Because of this, utility companies provide explanations of services and charges on the back of their bills and often on their websites as well.

Leonid looked at the back of his bill to find out why there were two charges for electricity. He learned that the first 600 kWh were charged at the base rate and that the electricity he used after that was charged at a higher rate. He also learned that there were additional charges: a delivery charge for bringing the electricity into his home, and a service charge for having the city read and maintain his electric meter.

Practice

Look at the electric bill again. Answer the questions.

1. How much does Leonid have to pay this month for electricity? $92
2. What is the statement date? ______
3. When is payment of his bill due? ______
4. How much did Leonid pay last month? ______
5. When did the billing period start and end? ______
6. What is the cost of Leonid's first 600 kWhs? ______
7. How many kWh did Leonid use in addition to the 600 that were charged at the base rate? ______
8. What is the total charge for those additional kWh? ______
9. What two charges does Leonid have to pay in addition to the electric charges? ______
10. How much is each of these fees? ______
11. What will happen if Leonid doesn't pay the bill on time? ______
12. To report an electrical outage, what number should Leonid call? ______
13. What are the two ways that Leonid can pay his bill? ______

BONUS

GROUPS OF 4. **Utility bills all look a little different. Bring one of your utility bills to class. (You can make a copy of the bill and darken any personal information.) Look at the charges with your group. Talk about what each charge is for.**

Lesson 4 Communicating with Utility Companies

Learn

A *PAIRS.* **Which words do you know? Match the words and their meanings.**

_____ 1. options a. stop something

_____ 2. discontinue b. a person who works for a company or other organization

_____ 3. representative c. choices

B CD2 TRACK 23 **This is the recording callers hear when they call Palm Cable Company. Listen and read.**

Thank you for calling Palm Cable Company. Please listen carefully to the following options: To add a new service, press 1. To report trouble with your service, press 2. For billing and payment questions, press 3. To discontinue your service, press 4. To request information about our services, press 5. To speak with a representative, press 0.

C **Read what callers hear again. Then read the situations of some Palm Cable Company customers, and write the number each person should press.**

1. Ting already has cable service for her TV through Palm Cable Company. Now she'd also like to get Internet service through the company. Press __1__.
2. Kiyomi has a question about getting international channels. She looked at the company's website, but she couldn't find the answer to her question. She'd like to talk to someone at the company. Press _____.
3. Dani heard about another company offering a special deal on cable service. He wants to cancel his services with Palm Cable Company. Press _____.
4. Nikolay turned on the TV and couldn't get a clear picture. Press _____.
5. Rosalyn ordered the basic cable package, but she is being charged for the premium cable package, which is more expensive. Press _____.

Practice

CD2 TRACK 24 **Ana, Jim, Ron, and Elena are customers of Sunrise Cable Company who need to call the company. Read about each person's situation. Then listen to the recording and circle the number each person should press.**

1. Ana is moving.	1	2	3	4	5	0
2. Jim has a question about his bill.	1	2	3	4	5	0
3. Ron wants to talk with a representative.	1	2	3	4	5	0
4. Elena is having problems with her cable service.	1	2	3	4	5	0

Learn

Note

It is important to find out about the policies of your utility companies. For example, sometimes when you start or end service in the middle of a month, you can pay a prorated fee for services, that is, you pay only for the days you received service. But sometimes you have to pay for the whole month.

CD2 TRACK 25 **Jin moved out of her apartment on June 25. She received a bill from her cable company and found that they charged her for the whole month of June. She called about the bill. Listen to the conversation and read.**

Representative: Hello, this is Shanika in Customer Service. What's your account number?
Jin: 123-45-6789.
Representative: Who am I speaking to?
Jin: Jin Wang.
Representative: How can I help you, Ms. Wang?
Jin: I think there's a mistake on my last bill. I was charged for the whole month of June, but I canceled my service as of June 25.
Representative: Let me check your record. Yes, I see. The last date you received service was June 25. However, we don't prorate your charges if you've received more than 20 days of cable service for the month.
Jin: So even though I didn't have cable from June 25 to June 30, I still have to pay for it?
Representative: Yes. That's our policy. It's written on the back of each month's bill.
Jin: Oh, I wish I had known that. Well, thanks for your help.

Practice

Read the conversation again. Answer the questions.

1. Why did Jin think there was a mistake on her last bill?

   ____

2. Why did Jin have to pay for the whole month of June?

   ____

3. Where is the policy written?

   ____

Make It Yours

PAIRS. **Have you ever called a utility company? What was the problem or reason for calling? Did you use an automated system with a recording or did you speak with someone? Was the problem resolved? Talk about your experiences.**

Unit 11 Test

Before you take the test

Ⓐ Ⓑ Ⓒ Ⓓ Use the answer sheet for Unit 11 on page 225.

1. Print your name.
2. Print your teacher's name.
3. Write your student identification number, and bubble in the information below the boxes.
4. Write the test date and bubble in the information.
5. Write your class number and bubble in the information.

Listening I [Track 26]

Listen to the question and three answers. What is the correct answer: A, B, or C?

1. A. one year
B. $800
C. 24 hours

2. A. from January 1 to January 31
B. February 1
C. $75.00

3. A. June 15
B. $100
C. one month

Listening II [Track 27]

Listen. Test items 4, 5, and 6 are on the audio CD.

Reading

Read. What is the correct answer: A, B, C, or D?

Tom and Lisa recently signed a lease for the new house they're renting. The term of the lease is one year. It began on November 1. By signing the lease, Tom and Lisa agreed to pay $1,175 for rent on the first day of each month. They have to pay a late fee of $25 if they are more than five days late in paying the rent. They paid a security deposit of $1,000. This will be returned to them at the end of the lease if the house is in good condition and they don't owe any rent.

Tom and Lisa also agreed to some other rules when they signed the lease. They have to keep the apartment in good condition, and they can't change anything in the house without the landlord's permission. Finally, they agreed not to make too much noise or bother their neighbors in any other way.

7. What is the term of the lease?

A. recently

B. one month

C. one year

D. since November 1

8. How much is the rent for the house?

A. $1,175 a month

B. $1,175 + $25 a month

C. $25 after five days

D. $1,000

9. What do Tom and Lisa need the landlord's permission to do?

A. sign the lease

B. keep the house in good condition

C. change anything in the house

D. bother their neighbors

Account Information			**Southeast Power and Light Company**	
Account Number:	1111778		Statement Date:	June 15, 2010
Customer:	Viviana Solero		Due Date:	July 5, 2010
Billing Information	Previous Balance:	$94.11	Current Charges:	$107.66
	Payment (6/5/10)	– $90.00	Balance forward:	$4.11
	Balance	$4.11	**Amount due:**	**$111.77**

Electric Detail

Meter Number	Present Read	Previous Read	KWH Usage	Billing Period
U11111111	85174	85928	754	05/1/10 to 05/31/10

Service Charge		$ 8.34
Electric Charge	700 kWh @ $.074684 per kWh	52.29
Electric Charge	54 kWh @ .092492 per kWh	4.99
Delivery Charge	754 kWh @ .054200 per kWh	40.87
Energy Conservation Charge	754 kWh @ .001801 per kWh	1.17
		$107.66

For information, emergencies, to report an outage, or for changes in your account call 1-800-555-9999.

10. By when must Viviana's payment be received?

A. 6/15/10

B. 7/5/10

C. 6/5/10

D. 5/31/10

11. What is the total amount that Viviana owes?

A. $90.00

B. $94.11

C. $107.66

D. $111.77

Sofia had been living in Los Angeles for several years when she got a good job opportunity in another city. She decided to take the job and move. She found a nice apartment that she was interested in renting. When Sofia spoke to the landlord about the apartment, he told her that no one in the neighborhood spoke Spanish and that there were no Hispanic restaurants or stores in the area. The landlord explained that Sofia probably wouldn't feel comfortable in a neighborhood with so few Hispanics. When Sofia said she was still interested in renting the apartment, the landlord said he really didn't think it was the right apartment for her and recommended that she look for a place in a Hispanic neighborhood.

12. Which of the following did Sofia experience?

A. fair housing

B. discrimination

C. reasonable accommodations

D. victims' rights

13. What did the landlord refuse to do?

A. help Sofia find an apartment in a Hispanic neighborhood

B. tell Sofia about Hispanic restaurants and stores in the area

C. help Sofia move

D. rent the apartment to Sofia

- The tenant agrees to pay the landlord $950.00, due on the first day of each month, for the leased premises.
- The landlord will pay for water, wastewater removal, and trash collection. The tenant will pay for all other utilities and services to the leased premises, which will include, but not be limited to, electricity and heat.
- The tenant agrees to keep the premises clean and in good and safe condition. The tenant will be responsible for any damage to the premises that is not normal wear and tear. The landlord agrees to keep the common areas clean and in good repair. The tenant will report any problems in common areas to the landlord.

14. What is the purpose of the information in the section of the lease above?

A. to explain the fair use of common areas

B. to explain when the lease will terminate

C. to explain the tenant's and landlord's responsibilities

D. to explain fair housing laws to the tenant

15. Which of the following does the tenant agree to do?

A. tell the landlord about wear and tear on the premises

B. keep the common areas clean and in good condition

C. give a security deposit of $950.00

D. pay for electricity

Unit 12 Getting Ahead at Work

Lesson 1 **Reporting Progress**
- Communicate with your supervisor about assigned tasks
- Learn to take initiative in providing updates

Lesson 2 **Job Evaluations**
- Understand the performance review process
- Recognize workplace values in a self-evaluation form
- Think about your own performance

Lesson 3 **Job Promotions**
- Recognize the requirements for promotion
- Identify ways to qualify for a promotion

Lesson 1 Reporting Progress

Learn

A **Read the information. Then answer the questions on a separate sheet of paper.**

In the American workplace, supervisors in many areas of work expect employees to regularly give them updates, or reports with recent information, on what's happing at their jobs. Often this is done informally in a quick conversation. It's not necessary to report every detail, but you should give complete information on important points. For example, tell your supervisor whether or not you're meeting your schedule and report any problems you're having. Briefly describe the problems, and then explain the steps you're taking to fix them. This way you'll show good communication skills, as well as your ability to solve problems. It's important to take the initiative when giving updates to your supervisor—it's generally better to give the information before the person asks for it.

1. When you give an update do you give old information or new information?
2. If you're having a problem at work, should you tell your supervisor or hide the problem?
3. If you take the initiative, do you take control of a situation or wait for instructions?

B CD2 TRACK 28 **Farisa is a customer service representative for Get Around, a company that makes wheelchairs. Listen and read as Farisa gives her supervisor an update on a customer order.**

Farisa: Excuse me, Mr. Jones. Do you have a moment? I'd like to give you an update on the order we got from Healthworks.

Mr. Jones: Right. How's everything going with that?

Farisa: Well, last week they ordered 50 wheelchairs, and they want them by next Tuesday.

Mr. Jones: Sounds good.

Farisa: Yeah, but there's a problem. We only have 10 chairs ready to send. We're expecting more by the end of the month, but we can't fill the order by next Tuesday.

Mr. Jones: So, what did you tell them?

Farisa: I said we could send 10 chairs next week and the other 40 as soon as they're ready. But they weren't satisfied with that solution. They wanted to cancel the order, but I asked them to wait until I could check with you. Do you think we could offer them a discount?

Mr. Jones: Well, we don't usually give discounts, but let's offer them free shipping. Try that and let me know what happens.

C **Read the conversation in Exercise B again. Answer the questions on a separate sheet of paper.**

1. Farisa takes the initiative to talk to her supervisor. What does she say to start the conversation? Excuse me, Mr. Jones. Do you have a moment? I'd like to give you an update on the order we got from Healthworks.
2. What's the problem with the Healthworks order?
3. What solution did Farisa offer to Healthworks?
4. What suggestion does Farisa make to her supervisor?
5. What does Farisa have to do next?
6. When does Farisa's supervisor want another update?

Listen

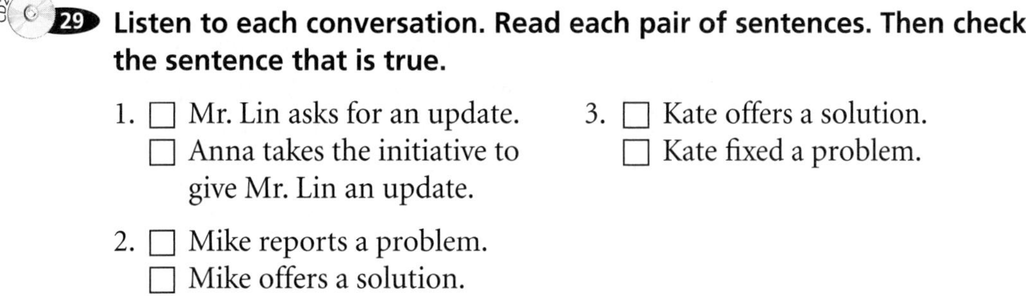

CD2 TRACK 29 **Listen to each conversation. Read each pair of sentences. Then check the sentence that is true.**

1. ☐ Mr. Lin asks for an update.
   ☐ Anna takes the initiative to give Mr. Lin an update.
2. ☐ Mike reports a problem.
   ☐ Mike offers a solution.
3. ☐ Kate offers a solution.
   ☐ Kate fixed a problem.

Practice

A CD2 TRACK 30 **Farisa is giving her supervisor an update. Listen and read.**

A: Excuse me. Do you have a moment? I'd like to give you an update on the order for Mercy Hospital.
B: Good. How are you doing with that?
A: I've prepared the new orders, but it took longer than planned.
B: The orders are due tomorrow.
A: I know. I'll come in early tomorrow morning and deliver the orders to the right departments.
B: Sounds good. Get back to me if you have any problems.

B ***PAIRS. ROLE PLAY.*** **Practice the conversation in Exercise A. Use the information below. Switch roles.**

1. • the report you asked for
   • prepared the report, and Elsie is making copies of it now
   • I need the report by 5:00.
   • I'm going to get the copies and check them over. I'll bring them to you by 4:00.
2. • the programs for tomorrow's conference
   • sent the programs to the print shop and I'm picking them up tomorrow
   • The conference starts at 1:00.
   • I made arrangements to get them at 9:00.

Lesson 2 Job Evaluations

Learn

A *PAIRS.* **Which words do you know? Write each word from the box next to its meaning. Then read the information below.**

evaluate	promotion	raise

________________ 1. Decide how good, useful, or successful something is

________________ 2. a move to a more important job or position in a company

________________ 3. an increase in the money you are paid for your job

Many American companies use annual (yearly) performance reviews to evaluate employees' performance during that year and to identify future goals and training needs for the next year. The evaluation is different at each company. But usually the employee completes a self-evaluation, and the supervisor writes a separate evaluation of the employee. After this, the employee and the supervisor meet to discuss the employee's performance. The supervisor then writes an official performance review. A positive evaluation, one in which the employee exceeds expectations, or performs better than the basic requirements, is important for achieving promotions and raises.

B *PAIRS.* **Which words do you know? Match the words and their meanings.**

_d_ 1. production line
____ 2. rating
____ 3. technical
____ 4. quality
____ 5. interpersonal skills
____ 6. set priorities
____ 7. flexibility
____ 8. challenge

a. ability to change in response to different situations
b. skills needed for building good relationships with others
c. level on a scale that shows how well someone does
d. a factory system in which a product is moved through several processes in order to make the final item
e. decide the order of importance of things
f. how good or bad something is
g. something that tests a person's strength, skill, or ability, especially in a way that is interesting
h. relating to skills and knowledge used in a particular area, often in science or industry

Practice

Laily, another employee at Get Around, is an assembler on the production line. She puts together part of the chairs. Before her annual performance review, she filled out a self-evaluation form. Read the form.

SELF-EVALUATION FORM

Complete this form before you meet with your supervisor for your annual performance review.

Name: Laily McKay Date: 5/21/2010 Position: assembler

Performance Ratings

3 = Excellent (performs above expectations most of the time)
1 = Developing (meets expectations some of the time)
2 = Good (meets expectations most of the time)
0 = Unsatisfactory (performs below expectations)

JOB KNOWLEDGE AND PERFORMANCE	
3	understands job procedures
3	demonstrates required technical skills
3	meets quality standards
3	pays attention to details
3	meets production goals
INTERPERSONAL AND COMMUNICATION SKILLS	
2	works effectively with others
3	provides necessary information to supervisors and co-workers
2	communicates clearly and effectively
WORK HABITS	
3	works scheduled hours
3	follows company rules, directions, and safety procedures
3	manages time effectively
3	organizes tasks and sets priorities
3	shows flexibility to meet new challenges
3	takes initiative to solve problems

How did you do this past year? I have done very well this year. I know how to do most of the jobs on the production line. I've met my production goals, and my work is always high quality. This year my English has improved, and I have gotten better at communicating with my co-workers and supervisor. I have very good work habits.

What could you have done better? One day a new worker on the line was not putting the wheels on the chairs correctly. Because of his mistake, I couldn't do my part right. I didn't want to stop the production line, but I wanted to tell him how to fix the mistake. The production line is noisy, so I shouted at him, and I told him what to do. I tried to solve the problem by myself, but I don't know if I did it in the best way.

PERFOMANCE / TRAINING GOALS FOR NEXT YEAR

What will you do to improve your performance next year? Discuss goals and plans.
Do you need further training or development?

Next year, I would like to be considered for a promotion to production line supervisor. To do this, I will continue to improve my communication skills by taking ESL classes and talking with my co-workers and with my supervisor regularly. I know I need leadership experience. I'm interested in any training the company offers on effective leadership skills. I also need to learn a few more jobs on the production line.

B **Read the self-evaluation form again. Answer the questions. Circle *a*, *b*, or *c*.**

1. Who completed the form?
   - (**a.**) Laily
   - **b.** Laily's supervisor
   - **c.** Laily's co-worker
2. What is the purpose of a self-evaluation?
   - **a.** to give yourself excellent ratings
   - **b.** to decide what the supervisor thinks about your work
   - **c.** to think about how well you are doing at work
3. In which area does Laily think her work is excellent?
   - **a.** meeting her production goals
   - **b.** working effectively with others
   - **c.** communicating clearly
4. How often does Laily think she takes the initiative to solve problems?
   - **a.** most of the time
   - **b.** some of the time
   - **c.** never
5. In which of these areas has Laily improved since last year?
   - **a.** She works more quickly.
   - **b.** She follows the rules more often.
   - **c.** She communicates with her co-workers better.
6. What does Laily want to do over the next year?
   - **a.** improve her work habits
   - **b.** improve her leadership skills
   - **c.** improve her goals

Make It Yours

PAIRS. **Think about your responsibilities at your job, at school, or at home. On a separate piece of paper answer these questions: What is one thing you think you do very well in one of those places? What is one thing you'd like to improve next year? Overall, do you think your performance is excellent, good, developing, or unsatisfactory? Why? Share your answers with your partner.**

Practice

A  **31 Laily and her supervisor, Samantha, are discussing Laily's job performance. Listen and read.**

Samantha: Laily, your work is excellent. I'm impressed with how your English has improved and how you're able to communicate more effectively.

Laily: Well, I've been going to English class twice a week. I think it's helping.

Samantha: I think so, too. I read your self-evaluation and was surprised that you gave yourself a 2 in some areas. Let's talk about that.

Laily: I gave myself a 2 in those areas because I had a problem with a new worker. He was doing something incorrectly, and instead of shutting down production and explaining it to him, I shouted at him, and told him what to do. I tried to handle the problem by myself, and I don't know if I did the right thing.

Samantha: Well, shouting is usually a bad way to communicate, but in this case I think it was the right thing to do. You were able to help him without stopping production, and you solved the problem.

Laily: I guess in that situation, it was the best way to communicate with him.

Samantha: Exactly. The problem had to be corrected, and if you had shut down production, we would have been behind schedule. You took the initiative to correct something that was going wrong. It was a difficult situation, but you made the right decision.

B **Read the conversation again. Complete the sentences. Write the letter of the correct answer in the blank.**

1. Samantha thinks that Laily has improved her ____ skills.

   a. communication **b.** organizational **c.** time-management

2. When Laily saw her co-worker doing something incorrectly, she ____.

   a. closed the production line **b.** told him what to do **c.** told the supervisor

3. Samantha thought Laily ____.

   a. didn't solve the problem **b.** communicated badly **c.** made a good decision

Make It Yours

GROUPS OF 3. **If you are working, tell others about your workplace. Are evaluations done at your job? Do you complete a self-evaluation form? Does your supervisor write a review for you? Do you meet with your supervisor to talk about your job performance for the year? Talk about your experiences.**

Lesson 3 Job Promotions

Learn

A *PAIRS.* **Which words do you know? Match the words with their meanings.**

__d__ 1. qualified
_____ 2. get ahead
_____ 3. reputation
_____ 4. punctuality
_____ 5. dependable
_____ 6. accurate
_____ 7. duties

a. being on time
b. things you have to do because they're part of your job
c. correct and true in every detail
d. having the knowledge, experience, or skills necessary for a particular job
e. gain skills and improve; make progress
f. able to be trusted to do what people need or expect you to do
g. the opinion that people have about someone because of past actions

B **Read the article. Then answer the question. Check the correct answer.**

Get That Promotion!

So, you've been at your job for a while now. You're good at it, and you enjoy it. But you're ready for a new challenge and the financial benefits that come with it. You're ready for a promotion! How do you do it? By showing that you're well qualified for the position. Follow these tips to get ahead!

- Build a reputation as a strong employee. Punctuality and attendance are important for any job. Be dependable. Take responsibility for doing accurate work, solving problems, and doing things on time. Take on additional work even if it takes extra time and effort.
- Communicate regularly with your supervisor. Give specific examples of progress you have made that are tied to company goals.
- Be an effective team member and leader. Work on your communication skills. Share information. Offer to train others. The relationships you build with co-workers, supervisors, and others in the organization can help you get ahead.
- Plan for your promotion. Identify the duties and responsibilities of the job that you want. Identify the technical knowledge and skills you need to gain or improve in order to do that job.
- Get the knowledge and skills you need. Find out if the company offers training or education, and sign up for it. If not, look for schools in your area where you can get the training you need. Sign up for classes and earn any necessary certificates or degrees.

What is the purpose of the information?

☐ to explain why promotions are important in your career
☐ to give advice on how to get a promotion
☐ to show some of the advantages of getting a promotion

C **Look at the article again. Read the sentences. Circle *T* for *True* or *F* for *False*.**

1. There's not much you can do to help yourself get a promotion. T (F)
2. Relationships with your co-workers can be important in getting a promotion. T F
3. Good daily work habits can help you get a promotion. T F
4. It's a good idea to do extra work if you want a promotion. T F
5. If you want a promotion, make sure you can work well with others. T F
6. It's the responsibility of your co-workers to tell your supervisor you deserve a promotion. T F

Practice

A **Laily wants to be promoted to production line supervisor next year. To qualify for this promotion, Laily needs to do the following five things. Write the letters of all the tips below that would help her achieve these goals. (You can use some of the tips in more than one answer.)**

__d, h__ 1. find out more about the duties and responsibilities of the job

______ 2. build a reputation as a strong employee

______ 3. build her technical skills

______ 4. gain some experience leading other assemblers

______ 5. develop the communication and leadership skills of a supervisor

a. Take the initiative to solve problems.
b. Teach new procedures and job skills to co-workers.
c. Work on different parts of the assembly line to learn all the jobs.
d. Interview someone who currently has the job she wants.
e. Continue to come to work on time and have good attendance.
f. Offer to train new workers.
g. Take technical training courses.
h. Research the job skills needed for the position.
i. Practice clear communication and active listening skills with her boss and co-workers.
j. Take courses to improve speaking and listening skills.

B **Compare your answers with a partner. Explain why you chose each tip.**

BONUS

Get more information on getting a promotion by going online, visiting your career center, or talking to someone at your workplace. Present the information to your classmates.

Unit 12 Test

Before you take the test

Ⓐ Ⓑ Ⓒ Ⓓ Use the answer sheet for Unit 12 on page 227.

1. Print your name.
2. Print your teacher's name.
3. Write your student identification number, and bubble in the information below the boxes.
4. Write the test date and bubble in the information.
5. Write your class number and bubble in the information.

CD2 Listening I [Track 32]

You will hear a conversation. Then you will hear a question about the conversation. What is the correct answer: A, B, or C?

1. A. her job performance over the past year

B. her plans for becoming eligible for a promotion

C. her job duties over the past year

2. A. report on something he's doing at work

B. ask for a promotion

C. talk about his performance review

3. A. the man

B. the woman

C. no one has a suggestion

CD2 Listening II [Track 33]

Listen. Test items 4, 5, and 6 are on the audio CD.

Reading

Read. What is the correct answer: A, B, C, or D?

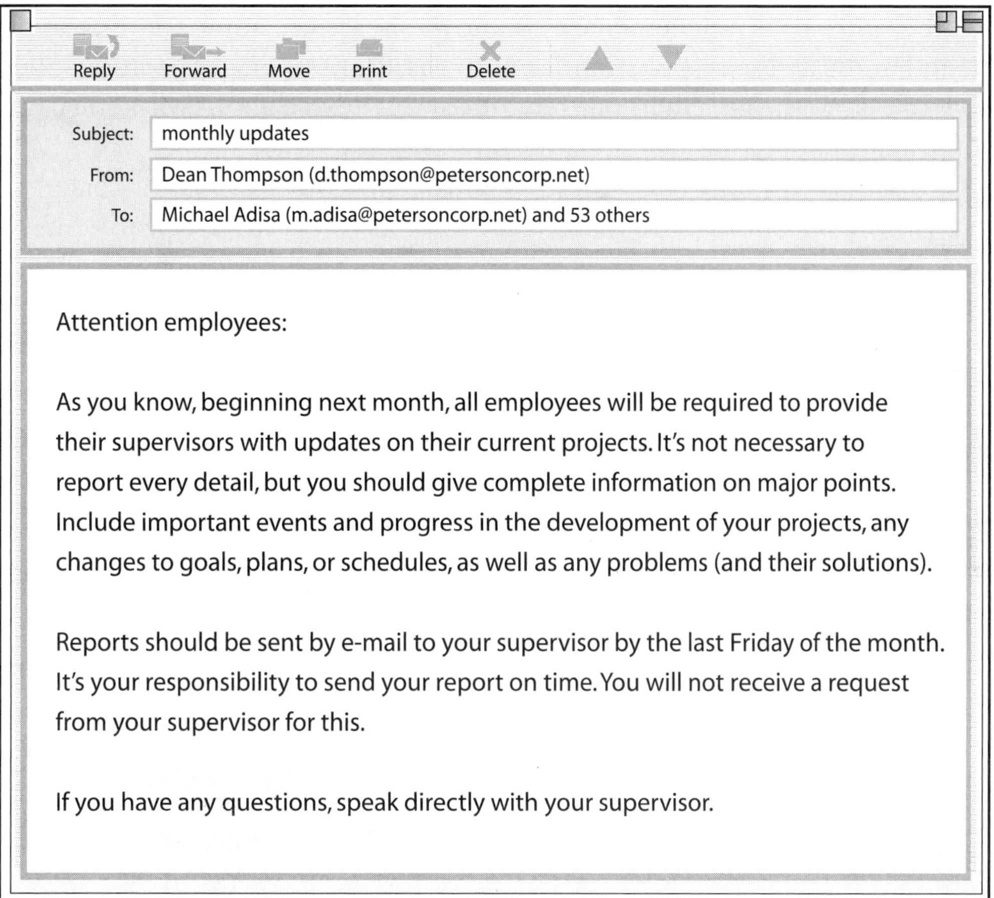

Reply Forward Move Print Delete

Subject: monthly updates

From: Dean Thompson (d.thompson@petersoncorp.net)

To: Michael Adisa (m.adisa@petersoncorp.net) and 53 others

Attention employees:

As you know, beginning next month, all employees will be required to provide their supervisors with updates on their current projects. It's not necessary to report every detail, but you should give complete information on major points. Include important events and progress in the development of your projects, any changes to goals, plans, or schedules, as well as any problems (and their solutions).

Reports should be sent by e-mail to your supervisor by the last Friday of the month. It's your responsibility to send your report on time. You will not receive a request from your supervisor for this.

If you have any questions, speak directly with your supervisor.

7. What is the purpose of this e-mail?

A. to give a supervisor an update

B. to explain a problem with an update

C. to request an update

D. to give instructions for providing updates

8. Which of the following is true?

A. You need an appointment to give an update.

B. All supervisors must give updates to employees.

C. You must give your update on or before the last Friday of the month.

D. You must wait to give your update until your supervisor asks for it.

Cho is an employee at a restaurant. She started out as a cook. Then she was promoted to a waitress. Now she's interested in having more responsibility, and she'd like to work toward becoming an assistant manager. Cho knows she's not ready for the position yet. She needs to learn some of the other jobs in the kitchen. She also knows she'll need some training to be able to handle all the responsibilities of the assistant manager position. She's going to talk to the general manager and ask his advice about ways she can get the skills and knowledge she'll need to reach her goal.

Cho is already doing a few things to show she would be a good person for the position. She makes sure that she always gets to work a little early. She cooperates with the other restaurant employees, and she provides excellent customer service. She's even offered to take on additional duties at the restaurant.

9. What does Cho need to do before she can become an assistant manager?

A. improve her customer service skills

B. get training

C. work on her communication skills

D. get a certificate

10. Which of the following is Cho doing now to build a reputation as a strong employee?

A. learning about jobs in the kitchen

B. training new employees

C. working well with others

D. receiving training

Your performance reviews provide you with valuable opportunities to present yourself as you want to be seen and to build your career. Prepare for your job evaluations carefully, and they will serve you well. This information lets you know what to expect and how to make the most of your next one.

Performance reviews are handled differently from company to company, but it's likely that you'll start by receiving a self-evaluation form. Take your time with the form, and fill it out honestly and completely.

Once you have completed the form, you'll probably discuss your self-evaluation and your job performance with your supervisor. Use this opportunity to talk about the progress you've made since you started your job or since your last review. Listen carefully to your supervisor's opinions and comments on your work, both about your strengths and the areas in which you could improve. This is also a good time to talk about your goals for the future. Whether you're interested in learning to do your job better, taking on more responsibility, or getting a promotion, you should discuss it with your supervisor. He or she can help you make a plan, including training needs if necessary, that can help you reach your goal.

After the interview, your supervisor will probably write an official performance review. Most companies look at performance reviews when they make decisions about raises and promotions.

11. What is the main idea of this information?

A. to explain how to fill out a self-evaluation

B. to give information on performance reviews

C. to suggest ways to reach your goals

D. to give suggestions on getting a promotion

12. According to the article, which of the following is true?

A. Your supervisor will complete your self-evaluation form.

B. You shouldn't talk about your skills with your supervisor.

C. Part of your review will probably include rating your own job performance.

D. Raises are based on self-evaluations.

SELF-EVALUATION FORM	
You must complete this form before meeting with your supervisor for your annual performance review.	
Name: Mauricio Santos Date: 7/7/2010 Position: warehouse associate	
Performance Ratings 3 = Excellent (performs above expectations most of the time) 2 = Good (meets expectations most of the time) 1 = Developing (meets expectations some of the time) 0 = Unsatisfactory (performs below expectations)	
JOB KNOWLEDGE AND PERFORMANCE	
2	understands job procedures
2	demonstrates required technical skills
2	meets quality standards
2	meets production goals
3	pays attention to details
WORK HABITS	
3	follows company rules, directions, and safety procedures
3	works scheduled hours
2	manages time effectively
2	organizes tasks and sets priorities
1	takes initiative to solve problems
2	shows flexibility to meet new challenges
INTERPERSONAL AND COMMUNICATION SKILLS	
1	communicates clearly and effectively
2	provides necessary information to supervisors and co-workers
2	works effectively with others

13. What did the employee report on this form?

A. progress on a project at work

B. the results of his annual performance review

C. a recommendation for a job promotion

D. how well he thinks he's doing at work

14. What does the employee think about his job performance?

A. He thinks he often doesn't follow the rules at work.

B. He thinks he almost always communicates clearly.

C. He thinks he usually meets his production goals.

D. He thinks he rarely pays attention to details.

Audioscript

UNIT 1 Lesson 1

Listen page 3

1. I graduated from high school in China, and I studied at a university there for one year.
2. Now I work in a supermarket. I'm a cashier.
3. Before my present job, I worked in a hospital. I was a maintenance worker.
4. I'm creative, and I'm good at working with other people on a team. I speak Chinese. I can use a computer.
5. At my job I'm responsible for the money in my cash register. I have to help customers, too.

Lesson 4

Listen page 13

1.

A: Tell me about your future goals.

B: Well, I want to be a teacher. But first I have to get accepted to college and get a bachelor's degree.

2.

A: I heard you finished high school. What are you going to do next?

B: First I'm going to find a part-time job. Then I'm going to apply to a community college. I want to get an associate degree.

3.

A: What are your goals for the future?

B: My long-term goal is to become a nurse. But first I have to get my degree.

4.

A: Do you go to school, James?

B: Yeah, I'm taking a course to prepare for the GED test.

A: What do you plan to do after that?

B: After I get my GED certificate, I want to study at a technical school.

UNIT 2 Lesson 1

Listen page 21

1.

A: How much are tickets?

B: They're $10 for adults and $5 for children.

2.

A: When is the game?

B: It's Saturday night. It starts at 7:30.

3.

A: Where is the yoga class?

B: It's at the community center.

4.

A: So, tell me about the arts festival.

B: Well, a lot of local artists are going to be there. And it's a fun event for the whole family.

Lesson 2

Listen page 24

1. Start at the Daytown Police Station. Head west on Bird Street, then make a right on Spring. Go two blocks and turn left. It's the building on your left.
2. Start at First Bank. Go south on Summer. At the third intersection, go east on Bird. Continue on Bird for one block until you get to a stop sign. Cross that intersection, and it's the building on your left.
3. Start at the Winter Avenue Apartments. Go north on Winter, then make a left on Bird. Go for two blocks, and then head north on Summer for one block. Make a left onto White, and it's on your left.
4. Start at the Daytown Bus Station. Head west on Dell Street until you get to Fall Avenue. Make a left and go south for two blocks. Then head west on Bird. It's the first building on your left.

UNIT 3 Lesson 1

Listen page 37

1.

A: I saw an ad for a job opening at The Hair Salon. Are you interested in the job?

B: Sure. How do I apply?

A: You have to call the manager.

2.

A: How's your job?

B: It's fine. It's busy now, and I have to work extra hours, but I get paid extra for them.

3.

A: Do I need experience to apply for the job?

B: No. Experience is preferred, but it's not required.

4.

A: I heard that they need workers at Bob's Bookstore.

B: Really? That's great. How do I apply?

A: You have to apply in person at the store.

UNIT 4 Lesson 2

Learn, Exercise B page 64

1. She needs an ambulance.
2. He's choking.
3. He's having a heart attack.
4. She's unconscious.
5. He's drowning.
6. She swallowed poison.
7. He got burned.
8. A house is on fire.
9. There's a downed power line.
10. There's a violent fight.
11. There was a hit-and-run.
12. Someone is breaking into a house.

Listen page 65

A: 9-1-1. What's your emergency?
B: My house is on fire!
A: OK. What's the location of the emergency?
B: The address is 184 National Street. It's a small white house.
A: OK. What's the closest cross street?
B: Front Avenue.
A: All right. Is anyone inside your home?
B: Yes, my son is!
A: How old is your son?
B: He's 10.
A: And what's your name?
B: Tania Perez.
A: What number are you calling from?
B: 202-555-9718.
A: All right, Tania. Help is on the way. Stay on the line until the fire department arrives.

UNIT 5 Lesson 2

Listen page 79

1.
A: We're having a great sale right now. You pay only $20 a month.
B: Are there any extra fees?

2.
A: Let's buy this cereal. It's healthy. See—it says *healthy* here on the box.
B: Yes, but you should look at the ingredients. That's how you'll know if it's really healthy.

3.
A: I think this chair is a good price. It's $35.00.
B: I think it's a good price too, but I want to look at other stores to make sure.

4.
A: This cell phone is a great price.
B: Sure, but is that the price just for the cell phone? Or does it include the battery, too?

UNIT 6 Lesson 1

Listen page 91

1. How much is your down payment?
2. What's the APR?
3. What percentage are you putting down on the car?
4. What's the interest rate?
5. What's the term of the loan?

UNIT 7 Lesson 1

Listen page 105

1. Student 1
A: Hello. This is Green Valley School District. May I help you?
B: Yes. I want to register my daughter in high school. She'll be a junior.
A: What's her last name?
B: Nguyen. N-G-U-Y-E-N
A: Nguyen. OK. She'll register on August 7. Are her immunizations up to date?
B: Yes.
A: Please bring that record.
B: OK. Does she need to have a physical exam by a doctor?
A: No, the school nurse can do a health screen within 90 days of registration. Just make sure she makes an appointment to get it done.
B: Is there anything else I need to bring?
A: Yes. Proof of residency and the transcript from her previous school.
B: Does it have to be the official transcript sent directly from her school?
A: No, you can just bring us a copy.

2. Student 2
A: Hello. Washington School District Registration Office.
B: Hello. I want to register my grandson for classes. He just moved here from North Park School District.
A: How old is he?
B: He's five.

A: Then you want to enroll him in kindergarten?

B: Yes.

A: What's his last name?

B: Petrov. His first name is Alexander.

A: Petrov. OK, you need to register him on August 7 between 9 A.M. and 3 P.M.

B: I'm sorry. I'm working then. Is there any other time I could come?

A: Yes. You can come on August 8 in the evening from 7 to 9 P.M.

B: Perfect. Thanks.

A: OK. We'll need to see his birth certificate. And you said he's your grandson?

B: Yes.

A: Are you his legal guardian?

B: Yes. I'll bring proof of guardianship.

A: Good. You'll need that. You'll also need to bring his immunization record. Has he had a physical examination by a doctor?

B: No, not yet.

A: Then please have the doctor give him an examination and fill out the form before registration.

Lesson 2

Listen, Exercise A page 107

1.

B: Hello, this is the attendance office. May I help you?

A: Hello. This is Mrs. Fu. My son will be late to school today. He has a dental appointment.

B: What's your son's name?

A: Ben Fu.

B: OK. What time do you think he'll get to school?

A: He should be back at school by noon. I guess he'll miss about half a day. Will I need to get a note from the dentist?

B: No, that's not necessary.

2.

A: Hello. This is Westside High School. May I help you?

B: Yes. Is this the attendance office?

A: Yes it is.

B: This is Layla Kashani. I'm calling to let you know that my daughter can't come to school today.

A: What's her name?

B: Zari Kashani.

A: Is she sick?

B: No. We're Muslim. Today is the Islamic New Year.

A: Will she be back tomorrow?

B: Yes.

A: OK, thank you for calling.

3.

A: Hello. This is the attendance office at High Park Middle School. Are you calling to report an absence or late arrival?

B: Yes. My daughter will be a little late to school today.

A: What's her name?

B: Elena Baranova.

A: Does she have a medical appointment?

B: No. It's my fault. We overslept, and now we're stuck in traffic.

A: When do you expect her to arrive?

B: The traffic is clearing up. We should be there in about 15 minutes. I guess she'll be about half an hour late.

A: OK. Make sure she reports to the attendance office immediately.

B: All right. Thank you.

UNIT 8 Lesson 1

Listen page 119

A: Hi. This is the computer help desk.

B: Hi. My computer isn't working.

A: What do you mean?

B: I was trying to log on. Now the mouse pointer won't move.

A: Hmm, it's probably frozen.

B: Frozen?

A: Doesn't work. Don't worry. Just hit Control, Alt, and Delete at the same time. Then . . .

B: Wait. Wait. You're going too fast. What are Control, Alt, Delete?

A: They're three keys on the keyboard. Once you find them, press them at the same time.

B: I can't.

A: Just use three fingers.

B: I'm trying. But I don't know which keys you mean.

A: OK, let's start again. First look for Control. On the keyboard it says C-T-R-L.

B: C-T-R-L. OK, I found it.

A: The next key says Alt.

B: Can you repeat that?

A: Alt. A-L-T.

B: OK, A-L-T. Got it.

A: The last key is Delete. D-E-L.

B: OK.

A: Now hold them all down together. Then, on the computer screen, click *Shut down*. Your computer should be shutting down now.

B: OK. It's turned off now.

A: Good. Now you can turn it on again. It should reboot.

B: Great, it's booting up! It's working again.

A: Good. Just remember that you can try this next time before calling the computer help desk. Many computer problems can be solved by pressing Control, Alt, Delete and then rebooting.

B: Thanks so much.

A: Don't mention it.

Lesson 3

Listen page 124

All employees of this company need specialized training with hazardous materials. You will see many signs in this workplace that say "authorized personnel only." That means you must complete this training successfully to enter these areas. In our business we work with many flammable materials. If you do not follow directions when you use flammable materials or store them properly, you can cause a fire. We will discuss what kind of protective gear you need to wear and when you will need to wear it. We will cover how to properly wipe up spills of liquid flammables such as gasoline to prevent fire. And remember, you will see signs all over this worksite that prohibit you from smoking. Be sure to obey them, or you could be responsible for starting a fire.

UNIT 9 Lesson 3

Listen page 141

Conversation 1

A: Good morning. How can I help you?

B: I'd like to open a checking account.

A: What kind of account are you interested in?

B: Well, I only have $75 to open an account. What is the minimum opening balance?

A: We have one you can open for $25.

B: That sounds good. . . .

Conversation 2

A: Hello. What can I do for you?

B: I'd like to open a checking account.

A: Of course, I'd be glad to help you. What kind of account are you interested in?

B: I'm looking for an account where I don't have to pay a monthly service charge.

A: We have one with no monthly service charge if your minimum balance is $200.

B: Hmm . . .

UNIT 10 Lesson 5

Listen page 163

1. What's the matter?
2. How bad are the cramps?
3. Have you had any nausea?
4. How long has this been going on?

UNIT 11 Lesson 4

Practice page 180

Thank you for calling Sunrise Cable Company. Please listen carefully to the following options.

If you are having trouble with your cable service, press 1.
If you have questions about your bill, press 2.
If you are moving or need to discontinue service, press 3.
To request information about our services, press 4.
To speak with a representative, press 0.

UNIT 12 Lesson 1

Listen page 189

1. A: Excuse me, Mr. Lin. Can I give you an update?
B: Sure, Anna. How's everything going?

2. A: Hey, Mike. How's everything going with the project?
B: Well, we're not going to meet our schedule.

3. A: Ms. Snow, I have an update for you on the project.
B: Good, Kate. How's that going?
A: Well, there was a problem with the schedule, but I was able to fix it.

Life Skills and Test Prep 4

Unit 1 Test Answer Sheet

① ______________________________

Last Name First Name Middle

② ______________________________

Teacher's Name

TEST

1 (A) (B) (C) (D)
2 (A) (B) (C) (D)
3 (A) (B) (C) (D)
4 (A) (B) (C) (D)
5 (A) (B) (C) (D)
6 (A) (B) (C) (D)
7 (A) (B) (C) (D)
8 (A) (B) (C) (D)
9 (A) (B) (C) (D)
10 (A) (B) (C) (D)
11 (A) (B) (C) (D)
12 (A) (B) (C) (D)
13 (A) (B) (C) (D)
14 (A) (B) (C) (D)
15 (A) (B) (C) (D)
16 (A) (B) (C) (D)
17 (A) (B) (C) (D)
18 (A) (B) (C) (D)
19 (A) (B) (C) (D)
20 (A) (B) (C) (D)

Directions for marking answers

- Use a No. 2 pencil. Do NOT use ink.
- Make dark marks and bubble in your answers completely.
- If you change an answer, erase your first mark completely.

Right

(A) (B) (C) (D)

Wrong

(A) (B) (C) (D)
(A) (B) (C) (D)

③ **STUDENT IDENTIFICATION**

0	0	0	0	0	0	0	0	0
1	1	1	1	1	1	1	1	1
2	2	2	2	2	2	2	2	2
3	3	3	3	3	3	3	3	3
4	4	4	4	4	4	4	4	4
5	5	5	5	5	5	5	5	5
6	6	6	6	6	6	6	6	6
7	7	7	7	7	7	7	7	7
8	8	8	8	8	8	8	8	8
9	9	9	9	9	9	9	9	9

Is this your Social Security number?
Yes ◯ **No** ◯

④ **TEST DATE**

MM		D	D	Y	Y
Jan	◯	0	0	20	09
Feb	◯	1	1	20	10
Mar	◯	2	2	20	11
Apr	◯	3	3	20	12
May	◯		4	20	13
Jun	◯		5	20	14
Jul	◯		6	20	15
Aug	◯		7	20	16
Sep	◯		8	20	17
Oct	◯		9	20	18
Nov	◯				
Dec	◯				

⑤ **CLASS NUMBER**

0	0	0	0	0	0	0	0
1	1	1	1	1	1	1	1
2	2	2	2	2	2	2	2
3	3	3	3	3	3	3	3
4	4	4	4	4	4	4	4
5	5	5	5	5	5	5	5
6	6	6	6	6	6	6	6
7	7	7	7	7	7	7	7
8	8	8	8	8	8	8	8
9	9	9	9	9	9	9	9

⑥ **RAW SCORE**

0	0
1	1
2	2
3	3
4	4
5	5
6	6
7	7
8	8
9	9

Life Skills and Test Prep 4

Unit 1 Test Answer Sheet

① ____

Last Name First Name Middle

② ____

Teacher's Name

TEST

1 Ⓐ Ⓑ Ⓒ Ⓓ
2 Ⓐ Ⓑ Ⓒ Ⓓ
3 Ⓐ Ⓑ Ⓒ Ⓓ
4 Ⓐ Ⓑ Ⓒ Ⓓ
5 Ⓐ Ⓑ Ⓒ Ⓓ
6 Ⓐ Ⓑ Ⓒ Ⓓ
7 Ⓐ Ⓑ Ⓒ Ⓓ
8 Ⓐ Ⓑ Ⓒ Ⓓ
9 Ⓐ Ⓑ Ⓒ Ⓓ
10 Ⓐ Ⓑ Ⓒ Ⓓ
11 Ⓐ Ⓑ Ⓒ Ⓓ
12 Ⓐ Ⓑ Ⓒ Ⓓ
13 Ⓐ Ⓑ Ⓒ Ⓓ
14 Ⓐ Ⓑ Ⓒ Ⓓ
15 Ⓐ Ⓑ Ⓒ Ⓓ
16 Ⓐ Ⓑ Ⓒ Ⓓ
17 Ⓐ Ⓑ Ⓒ Ⓓ
18 Ⓐ Ⓑ Ⓒ Ⓓ
19 Ⓐ Ⓑ Ⓒ Ⓓ
20 Ⓐ Ⓑ Ⓒ Ⓓ

Directions for marking answers

- Use a No. 2 pencil. Do NOT use ink.
- Make dark marks and bubble in your answers completely.
- If you change an answer, erase your first mark completely.

Right

Ⓐ Ⓑ Ⓒ Ⓓ

Wrong

Ⓐ Ⓑ Ⓒ Ⓓ
Ⓐ Ⓑ Ⓒ Ⓓ

③ **STUDENT IDENTIFICATION**

0	0	0	0	0	0	0	0	0
1	1	1	1	1	1	1	1	1
2	2	2	2	2	2	2	2	2
3	3	3	3	3	3	3	3	3
4	4	4	4	4	4	4	4	4
5	5	5	5	5	5	5	5	5
6	6	6	6	6	6	6	6	6
7	7	7	7	7	7	7	7	7
8	8	8	8	8	8	8	8	8
9	9	9	9	9	9	9	9	9

Is this your Social Security number?

Yes ◯ **No** ◯

④ **TEST DATE**

MM		D	D	Y	Y
Jan	◯	0	0	20	09
Feb	◯	1	1	20	10
Mar	◯	2	2	20	11
Apr	◯	3	3	20	12
May	◯		4	20	13
Jun	◯		5	20	14
Jul	◯		6	20	15
Aug	◯		7	20	16
Sep	◯		8	20	17
Oct	◯		9	20	18
Nov	◯				
Dec	◯				

⑤ **CLASS NUMBER**

0	0	0	0	0	0	0	0
1	1	1	1	1	1	1	1
2	2	2	2	2	2	2	2
3	3	3	3	3	3	3	3
4	4	4	4	4	4	4	4
5	5	5	5	5	5	5	5
6	6	6	6	6	6	6	6
7	7	7	7	7	7	7	7
8	8	8	8	8	8	8	8
9	9	9	9	9	9	9	9

⑥ **RAW SCORE**

0	0
1	1
2	2
3	3
4	4
5	5
6	6
7	7
8	8
9	9

Life Skills and Test Prep 4

Unit 2 Test Answer Sheet

① ____________________
Last Name   First Name   Middle

② ____________________
Teacher's Name

TEST

1 Ⓐ Ⓑ Ⓒ Ⓓ
2 Ⓐ Ⓑ Ⓒ Ⓓ
3 Ⓐ Ⓑ Ⓒ Ⓓ
4 Ⓐ Ⓑ Ⓒ Ⓓ
5 Ⓐ Ⓑ Ⓒ Ⓓ
6 Ⓐ Ⓑ Ⓒ Ⓓ
7 Ⓐ Ⓑ Ⓒ Ⓓ
8 Ⓐ Ⓑ Ⓒ Ⓓ
9 Ⓐ Ⓑ Ⓒ Ⓓ
10 Ⓐ Ⓑ Ⓒ Ⓓ
11 Ⓐ Ⓑ Ⓒ Ⓓ
12 Ⓐ Ⓑ Ⓒ Ⓓ
13 Ⓐ Ⓑ Ⓒ Ⓓ
14 Ⓐ Ⓑ Ⓒ Ⓓ
15 Ⓐ Ⓑ Ⓒ Ⓓ
16 Ⓐ Ⓑ Ⓒ Ⓓ
17 Ⓐ Ⓑ Ⓒ Ⓓ
18 Ⓐ Ⓑ Ⓒ Ⓓ
19 Ⓐ Ⓑ Ⓒ Ⓓ
20 Ⓐ Ⓑ Ⓒ Ⓓ

Directions for marking answers

- Use a No. 2 pencil. Do NOT use ink.
- Make dark marks and bubble in your answers completely.
- If you change an answer, erase your first mark completely.

Right
Ⓐ Ⓑ Ⓒ Ⓓ

Wrong
Ⓐ Ⓑ Ⓒ Ⓓ
Ⓐ Ⓑ Ⓒ Ⓓ

③ **STUDENT IDENTIFICATION**

0	0	0	0	0	0	0	0	0
1	1	1	1	1	1	1	1	1
2	2	2	2	2	2	2	2	2
3	3	3	3	3	3	3	3	3
4	4	4	4	4	4	4	4	4
5	5	5	5	5	5	5	5	5
6	6	6	6	6	6	6	6	6
7	7	7	7	7	7	7	7	7
8	8	8	8	8	8	8	8	8
9	9	9	9	9	9	9	9	9

Is this your Social Security number?
Yes ◯ **No** ◯

④ **TEST DATE**

MM		D	D	Y	Y
Jan	◯	0	0	20	09
Feb	◯	1	1	20	10
Mar	◯	2	2	20	11
Apr	◯	3	3	20	12
May	◯		4	20	13
Jun	◯		5	20	14
Jul	◯		6	20	15
Aug	◯		7	20	16
Sep	◯		8	20	17
Oct	◯		9	20	18
Nov	◯				
Dec	◯				

⑤ **CLASS NUMBER**

0	0	0	0	0	0	0	0
1	1	1	1	1	1	1	1
2	2	2	2	2	2	2	2
3	3	3	3	3	3	3	3
4	4	4	4	4	4	4	4
5	5	5	5	5	5	5	5
6	6	6	6	6	6	6	6
7	7	7	7	7	7	7	7
8	8	8	8	8	8	8	8
9	9	9	9	9	9	9	9

⑥ **RAW SCORE**

0	0
1	1
2	2
3	3
4	4
5	5
6	6
7	7
8	8
9	9

Life Skills and Test Prep 4
Unit 2 Test Answer Sheet

① ______________________________
Last Name First Name Middle

② ______________________________
Teacher's Name

TEST

1 (A)(B)(C)(D)
2 (A)(B)(C)(D)
3 (A)(B)(C)(D)
4 (A)(B)(C)(D)
5 (A)(B)(C)(D)
6 (A)(B)(C)(D)
7 (A)(B)(C)(D)
8 (A)(B)(C)(D)
9 (A)(B)(C)(D)
10 (A)(B)(C)(D)
11 (A)(B)(C)(D)
12 (A)(B)(C)(D)
13 (A)(B)(C)(D)
14 (A)(B)(C)(D)
15 (A)(B)(C)(D)
16 (A)(B)(C)(D)
17 (A)(B)(C)(D)
18 (A)(B)(C)(D)
19 (A)(B)(C)(D)
20 (A)(B)(C)(D)

Directions for marking answers

- Use a No. 2 pencil. Do NOT use ink.
- Make dark marks and bubble in your answers completely.
- If you change an answer, erase your first mark completely.

Right
(A)(B)(C)(D)

Wrong
(A)(B)(C)(D)
(A)(B)(C)(D)

③ **STUDENT IDENTIFICATION**

0	0	0	0	0	0	0	0	0
1	1	1	1	1	1	1	1	1
2	2	2	2	2	2	2	2	2
3	3	3	3	3	3	3	3	3
4	4	4	4	4	4	4	4	4
5	5	5	5	5	5	5	5	5
6	6	6	6	6	6	6	6	6
7	7	7	7	7	7	7	7	7
8	8	8	8	8	8	8	8	8
9	9	9	9	9	9	9	9	9

Is this your Social Security number?
Yes ( ) **No** ( )

④ **TEST DATE**

MM		D	D	Y	Y
Jan	( )	0	0	20	09
Feb	( )	1	1	20	10
Mar	( )	2	2	20	11
Apr	( )	3	3	20	12
May	( )		4	20	13
Jun	( )		5	20	14
Jul	( )		6	20	15
Aug	( )		7	20	16
Sep	( )		8	20	17
Oct	( )		9	20	18
Nov	( )				
Dec	( )				

⑤ **CLASS NUMBER**

0	0	0	0	0	0	0	0
1	1	1	1	1	1	1	1
2	2	2	2	2	2	2	2
3	3	3	3	3	3	3	3
4	4	4	4	4	4	4	4
5	5	5	5	5	5	5	5
6	6	6	6	6	6	6	6
7	7	7	7	7	7	7	7
8	8	8	8	8	8	8	8
9	9	9	9	9	9	9	9

⑥ **RAW SCORE**

0	0
1	1
2	2
3	3
4	4
5	5
6	6
7	7
8	8
9	9

Life Skills and Test Prep 4

Unit 3 Test Answer Sheet

① ______________________________
Last Name First Name Middle

② ______________________________
Teacher's Name

TEST

1 Ⓐ Ⓑ Ⓒ Ⓓ
2 Ⓐ Ⓑ Ⓒ Ⓓ
3 Ⓐ Ⓑ Ⓒ Ⓓ
4 Ⓐ Ⓑ Ⓒ Ⓓ
5 Ⓐ Ⓑ Ⓒ Ⓓ
6 Ⓐ Ⓑ Ⓒ Ⓓ
7 Ⓐ Ⓑ Ⓒ Ⓓ
8 Ⓐ Ⓑ Ⓒ Ⓓ
9 Ⓐ Ⓑ Ⓒ Ⓓ
10 Ⓐ Ⓑ Ⓒ Ⓓ
11 Ⓐ Ⓑ Ⓒ Ⓓ
12 Ⓐ Ⓑ Ⓒ Ⓓ
13 Ⓐ Ⓑ Ⓒ Ⓓ
14 Ⓐ Ⓑ Ⓒ Ⓓ
15 Ⓐ Ⓑ Ⓒ Ⓓ
16 Ⓐ Ⓑ Ⓒ Ⓓ
17 Ⓐ Ⓑ Ⓒ Ⓓ
18 Ⓐ Ⓑ Ⓒ Ⓓ
19 Ⓐ Ⓑ Ⓒ Ⓓ
20 Ⓐ Ⓑ Ⓒ Ⓓ

Directions for marking answers

- Use a No. 2 pencil. Do NOT use ink.
- Make dark marks and bubble in your answers completely.
- If you change an answer, erase your first mark completely.

Right
Ⓐ Ⓑ Ⓒ Ⓓ

Wrong
Ⓐ Ⓑ Ⓒ Ⓓ
Ⓐ Ⓑ Ⓒ Ⓓ

③ **STUDENT IDENTIFICATION**

0	0	0	0	0	0	0	0	0
1	1	1	1	1	1	1	1	1
2	2	2	2	2	2	2	2	2
3	3	3	3	3	3	3	3	3
4	4	4	4	4	4	4	4	4
5	5	5	5	5	5	5	5	5
6	6	6	6	6	6	6	6	6
7	7	7	7	7	7	7	7	7
8	8	8	8	8	8	8	8	8
9	9	9	9	9	9	9	9	9

Is this your Social Security number?
Yes ◯ **No** ◯

④ **TEST DATE**

MM	D	D	Y	Y
Jan	0	0	20	09
Feb	1	1	20	10
Mar	2	2	20	11
Apr	3	3	20	12
May		4	20	13
Jun		5	20	14
Jul		6	20	15
Aug		7	20	16
Sep		8	20	17
Oct		9	20	18
Nov				
Dec				

⑤ **CLASS NUMBER**

0	0	0	0	0	0	0	0
1	1	1	1	1	1	1	1
2	2	2	2	2	2	2	2
3	3	3	3	3	3	3	3
4	4	4	4	4	4	4	4
5	5	5	5	5	5	5	5
6	6	6	6	6	6	6	6
7	7	7	7	7	7	7	7
8	8	8	8	8	8	8	8
9	9	9	9	9	9	9	9

⑥ **RAW SCORE**

0	0
1	1
2	2
3	3
4	4
5	5
6	6
7	7
8	8
9	9

Life Skills and Test Prep 4
Unit 3 Test Answer Sheet

① ______________________________
Last Name First Name Middle

② ______________________________
Teacher's Name

TEST

1 A B C D
2 A B C D
3 A B C D
4 A B C D
5 A B C D
6 A B C D
7 A B C D
8 A B C D
9 A B C D
10 A B C D
11 A B C D
12 A B C D
13 A B C D
14 A B C D
15 A B C D
16 A B C D
17 A B C D
18 A B C D
19 A B C D
20 A B C D

Directions for marking answers

- Use a No. 2 pencil. Do NOT use ink.
- Make dark marks and bubble in your answers completely.
- If you change an answer, erase your first mark completely.

Right
A B C D

Wrong
A B C D
A B C D

③ **STUDENT IDENTIFICATION**

0	0	0	0	0	0	0	0	0
1	1	1	1	1	1	1	1	1
2	2	2	2	2	2	2	2	2
3	3	3	3	3	3	3	3	3
4	4	4	4	4	4	4	4	4
5	5	5	5	5	5	5	5	5
6	6	6	6	6	6	6	6	6
7	7	7	7	7	7	7	7	7
8	8	8	8	8	8	8	8	8
9	9	9	9	9	9	9	9	9

Is this your Social Security number?
Yes ◯ **No** ◯

④ **TEST DATE**

MM	D	D	Y	Y
Jan	0	0	20	09
Feb	1	1	20	10
Mar	2	2	20	11
Apr	3	3	20	12
May		4	20	13
Jun		5	20	14
Jul		6	20	15
Aug		7	20	16
Sep		8	20	17
Oct		9	20	18
Nov				
Dec				

⑤ **CLASS NUMBER**

0	0	0	0	0	0	0	0
1	1	1	1	1	1	1	1
2	2	2	2	2	2	2	2
3	3	3	3	3	3	3	3
4	4	4	4	4	4	4	4
5	5	5	5	5	5	5	5
6	6	6	6	6	6	6	6
7	7	7	7	7	7	7	7
8	8	8	8	8	8	8	8
9	9	9	9	9	9	9	9

⑥ **RAW SCORE**

0	0
1	1
2	2
3	3
4	4
5	5
6	6
7	7
8	8
9	9

Life Skills and Test Prep 4

Unit 4 Test Answer Sheet

① ______________________________________
Last Name   First Name   Middle

② ______________________________________
Teacher's Name

TEST

1 (A) (B) (C) (D)
2 (A) (B) (C) (D)
3 (A) (B) (C) (D)
4 (A) (B) (C) (D)
5 (A) (B) (C) (D)
6 (A) (B) (C) (D)
7 (A) (B) (C) (D)
8 (A) (B) (C) (D)
9 (A) (B) (C) (D)
10 (A) (B) (C) (D)
11 (A) (B) (C) (D)
12 (A) (B) (C) (D)
13 (A) (B) (C) (D)
14 (A) (B) (C) (D)
15 (A) (B) (C) (D)
16 (A) (B) (C) (D)
17 (A) (B) (C) (D)
18 (A) (B) (C) (D)
19 (A) (B) (C) (D)
20 (A) (B) (C) (D)

Directions for marking answers

- Use a No. 2 pencil. Do NOT use ink.
- Make dark marks and bubble in your answers completely.
- If you change an answer, erase your first mark completely.

Right
(A) (B) (C) (D)

Wrong
(A) (B) (C) (D)
(A) (B) (C) (D)

③ **STUDENT IDENTIFICATION**

0	0	0	0	0	0	0	0	0
1	1	1	1	1	1	1	1	1
2	2	2	2	2	2	2	2	2
3	3	3	3	3	3	3	3	3
4	4	4	4	4	4	4	4	4
5	5	5	5	5	5	5	5	5
6	6	6	6	6	6	6	6	6
7	7	7	7	7	7	7	7	7
8	8	8	8	8	8	8	8	8
9	9	9	9	9	9	9	9	9

Is this your Social Security number?
Yes ◯ **No** ◯

④ **TEST DATE**

MM	D	D	Y	Y
Jan	0	0	20	09
Feb	1	1	20	10
Mar	2	2	20	11
Apr	3	3	20	12
May		4	20	13
Jun		5	20	14
Jul		6	20	15
Aug		7	20	16
Sep		8	20	17
Oct		9	20	18
Nov				
Dec				

⑤ **CLASS NUMBER**

0	0	0	0	0	0	0	0
1	1	1	1	1	1	1	1
2	2	2	2	2	2	2	2
3	3	3	3	3	3	3	3
4	4	4	4	4	4	4	4
5	5	5	5	5	5	5	5
6	6	6	6	6	6	6	6
7	7	7	7	7	7	7	7
8	8	8	8	8	8	8	8
9	9	9	9	9	9	9	9

⑥ **RAW SCORE**

0	0
1	1
2	2
3	3
4	4
5	5
6	6
7	7
8	8
9	9

Life Skills and Test Prep 4

Unit 4 Test Answer Sheet

① ______________________________

Last Name First Name Middle

② ______________________________

Teacher's Name

TEST

1 (A) (B) (C) (D)
2 (A) (B) (C) (D)
3 (A) (B) (C) (D)
4 (A) (B) (C) (D)
5 (A) (B) (C) (D)
6 (A) (B) (C) (D)
7 (A) (B) (C) (D)
8 (A) (B) (C) (D)
9 (A) (B) (C) (D)
10 (A) (B) (C) (D)
11 (A) (B) (C) (D)
12 (A) (B) (C) (D)
13 (A) (B) (C) (D)
14 (A) (B) (C) (D)
15 (A) (B) (C) (D)
16 (A) (B) (C) (D)
17 (A) (B) (C) (D)
18 (A) (B) (C) (D)
19 (A) (B) (C) (D)
20 (A) (B) (C) (D)

Directions for marking answers

- Use a No. 2 pencil. Do NOT use ink.
- Make dark marks and bubble in your answers completely.
- If you change an answer, erase your first mark completely.

Right

(A) (B) (C) (D)

Wrong

(A) (B) (C) (D)
(A) (B) (C) (D)

③ **STUDENT IDENTIFICATION**

0	0	0	0	0	0	0	0	0
1	1	1	1	1	1	1	1	1
2	2	2	2	2	2	2	2	2
3	3	3	3	3	3	3	3	3
4	4	4	4	4	4	4	4	4
5	5	5	5	5	5	5	5	5
6	6	6	6	6	6	6	6	6
7	7	7	7	7	7	7	7	7
8	8	8	8	8	8	8	8	8
9	9	9	9	9	9	9	9	9

Is this your Social Security number?

Yes ( ) **No** ( )

④ **TEST DATE**

MM		D	D	Y	Y
Jan	( )	0	0	20	09
Feb	( )	1	1	20	10
Mar	( )	2	2	20	11
Apr	( )	3	3	20	12
May	( )		4	20	13
Jun	( )		5	20	14
Jul	( )		6	20	15
Aug	( )		7	20	16
Sep	( )		8	20	17
Oct	( )		9	20	18
Nov	( )				
Dec	( )				

⑤ **CLASS NUMBER**

0	0	0	0	0	0	0	0
1	1	1	1	1	1	1	1
2	2	2	2	2	2	2	2
3	3	3	3	3	3	3	3
4	4	4	4	4	4	4	4
5	5	5	5	5	5	5	5
6	6	6	6	6	6	6	6
7	7	7	7	7	7	7	7
8	8	8	8	8	8	8	8
9	9	9	9	9	9	9	9

⑥ **RAW SCORE**

0	0
1	1
2	2
3	3
4	4
5	5
6	6
7	7
8	8
9	9

Life Skills and Test Prep 4
Unit 5 Test Answer Sheet

① ____

Last Name First Name Middle

② ____

Teacher's Name

TEST

1 Ⓐ Ⓑ Ⓒ Ⓓ
2 Ⓐ Ⓑ Ⓒ Ⓓ
3 Ⓐ Ⓑ Ⓒ Ⓓ
4 Ⓐ Ⓑ Ⓒ Ⓓ
5 Ⓐ Ⓑ Ⓒ Ⓓ
6 Ⓐ Ⓑ Ⓒ Ⓓ
7 Ⓐ Ⓑ Ⓒ Ⓓ
8 Ⓐ Ⓑ Ⓒ Ⓓ
9 Ⓐ Ⓑ Ⓒ Ⓓ
10 Ⓐ Ⓑ Ⓒ Ⓓ
11 Ⓐ Ⓑ Ⓒ Ⓓ
12 Ⓐ Ⓑ Ⓒ Ⓓ
13 Ⓐ Ⓑ Ⓒ Ⓓ
14 Ⓐ Ⓑ Ⓒ Ⓓ
15 Ⓐ Ⓑ Ⓒ Ⓓ
16 Ⓐ Ⓑ Ⓒ Ⓓ
17 Ⓐ Ⓑ Ⓒ Ⓓ
18 Ⓐ Ⓑ Ⓒ Ⓓ
19 Ⓐ Ⓑ Ⓒ Ⓓ
20 Ⓐ Ⓑ Ⓒ Ⓓ

Directions for marking answers

- Use a No. 2 pencil. Do NOT use ink.
- Make dark marks and bubble in your answers completely.
- If you change an answer, erase your first mark completely.

Right

Ⓐ Ⓑ Ⓒ Ⓓ

Wrong

Ⓐ Ⓑ Ⓒ Ⓓ
Ⓐ Ⓑ Ⓒ Ⓓ

③ **STUDENT IDENTIFICATION**

0	0	0	0	0	0	0	0	0
1	1	1	1	1	1	1	1	1
2	2	2	2	2	2	2	2	2
3	3	3	3	3	3	3	3	3
4	4	4	4	4	4	4	4	4
5	5	5	5	5	5	5	5	5
6	6	6	6	6	6	6	6	6
7	7	7	7	7	7	7	7	7
8	8	8	8	8	8	8	8	8
9	9	9	9	9	9	9	9	9

Is this your Social Security number?
Yes ◯ **No** ◯

④ **TEST DATE**

MM	D	D	Y	Y
Jan	0	0	20	09
Feb	1	1	20	10
Mar	2	2	20	11
Apr	3	3	20	12
May		4	20	13
Jun		5	20	14
Jul		6	20	15
Aug		7	20	16
Sep		8	20	17
Oct		9	20	18
Nov				
Dec				

⑤ **CLASS NUMBER**

0	0	0	0	0	0	0	0
1	1	1	1	1	1	1	1
2	2	2	2	2	2	2	2
3	3	3	3	3	3	3	3
4	4	4	4	4	4	4	4
5	5	5	5	5	5	5	5
6	6	6	6	6	6	6	6
7	7	7	7	7	7	7	7
8	8	8	8	8	8	8	8
9	9	9	9	9	9	9	9

⑥ **RAW SCORE**

0	0
1	1
2	2
3	3
4	4
5	5
6	6
7	7
8	8
9	9

Life Skills and Test Prep 4

Unit 5 Test Answer Sheet

① ____

Last Name First Name Middle

② ____

Teacher's Name

TEST

1 (A) (B) (C) (D)
2 (A) (B) (C) (D)
3 (A) (B) (C) (D)
4 (A) (B) (C) (D)
5 (A) (B) (C) (D)
6 (A) (B) (C) (D)
7 (A) (B) (C) (D)
8 (A) (B) (C) (D)
9 (A) (B) (C) (D)
10 (A) (B) (C) (D)
11 (A) (B) (C) (D)
12 (A) (B) (C) (D)
13 (A) (B) (C) (D)
14 (A) (B) (C) (D)
15 (A) (B) (C) (D)
16 (A) (B) (C) (D)
17 (A) (B) (C) (D)
18 (A) (B) (C) (D)
19 (A) (B) (C) (D)
20 (A) (B) (C) (D)

Directions for marking answers

- Use a No. 2 pencil. Do NOT use ink.
- Make dark marks and bubble in your answers completely.
- If you change an answer, erase your first mark completely.

Right

(A) (B) (C) (D)

Wrong

(A) (B) (C) (D)
(A) (B) (C) (D)

③ **STUDENT IDENTIFICATION**

0	0	0	0	0	0	0	0	0
1	1	1	1	1	1	1	1	1
2	2	2	2	2	2	2	2	2
3	3	3	3	3	3	3	3	3
4	4	4	4	4	4	4	4	4
5	5	5	5	5	5	5	5	5
6	6	6	6	6	6	6	6	6
7	7	7	7	7	7	7	7	7
8	8	8	8	8	8	8	8	8
9	9	9	9	9	9	9	9	9

Is this your Social Security number?

Yes ( ) **No** ( )

④ **TEST DATE**

MM		D	D	Y	Y
Jan	( )	0	0	20	09
Feb	( )	1	1	20	10
Mar	( )	2	2	20	11
Apr	( )	3	3	20	12
May	( )		4	20	13
Jun	( )		5	20	14
Jul	( )		6	20	15
Aug	( )		7	20	16
Sep	( )		8	20	17
Oct	( )		9	20	18
Nov	( )				
Dec	( )				

⑤ **CLASS NUMBER**

0	0	0	0	0	0	0	0
1	1	1	1	1	1	1	1
2	2	2	2	2	2	2	2
3	3	3	3	3	3	3	3
4	4	4	4	4	4	4	4
5	5	5	5	5	5	5	5
6	6	6	6	6	6	6	6
7	7	7	7	7	7	7	7
8	8	8	8	8	8	8	8
9	9	9	9	9	9	9	9

⑥ **RAW SCORE**

0	0
1	1
2	2
3	3
4	4
5	5
6	6
7	7
8	8
9	9

Life Skills and Test Prep 4

Unit 6 Test Answer Sheet

① ______________________________

Last Name First Name Middle

② ______________________________

Teacher's Name

TEST

1 (A) (B) (C) (D)
2 (A) (B) (C) (D)
3 (A) (B) (C) (D)
4 (A) (B) (C) (D)
5 (A) (B) (C) (D)
6 (A) (B) (C) (D)
7 (A) (B) (C) (D)
8 (A) (B) (C) (D)
9 (A) (B) (C) (D)
10 (A) (B) (C) (D)
11 (A) (B) (C) (D)
12 (A) (B) (C) (D)
13 (A) (B) (C) (D)
14 (A) (B) (C) (D)
15 (A) (B) (C) (D)
16 (A) (B) (C) (D)
17 (A) (B) (C) (D)
18 (A) (B) (C) (D)
19 (A) (B) (C) (D)
20 (A) (B) (C) (D)

Directions for marking answers

- Use a No. 2 pencil. Do NOT use ink.
- Make dark marks and bubble in your answers completely.
- If you change an answer, erase your first mark completely.

Right
(A) (B) (C) (D)

Wrong
(A) (B) (C) (D)
(A) (B) (C) (D)

③ **STUDENT IDENTIFICATION**

0	0	0	0	0	0	0	0	0
1	1	1	1	1	1	1	1	1
2	2	2	2	2	2	2	2	2
3	3	3	3	3	3	3	3	3
4	4	4	4	4	4	4	4	4
5	5	5	5	5	5	5	5	5
6	6	6	6	6	6	6	6	6
7	7	7	7	7	7	7	7	7
8	8	8	8	8	8	8	8	8
9	9	9	9	9	9	9	9	9

Is this your Social Security number?
Yes ☐ **No** ☐

④ **TEST DATE**

MM		D	D	Y	Y
Jan	☐	0	0	20	09
Feb	☐	1	1	20	10
Mar	☐	2	2	20	11
Apr	☐	3	3	20	12
May	☐		4	20	13
Jun	☐		5	20	14
Jul	☐		6	20	15
Aug	☐		7	20	16
Sep	☐		8	20	17
Oct	☐		9	20	18
Nov	☐				
Dec	☐				

⑤ **CLASS NUMBER**

0	0	0	0	0	0	0	0
1	1	1	1	1	1	1	1
2	2	2	2	2	2	2	2
3	3	3	3	3	3	3	3
4	4	4	4	4	4	4	4
5	5	5	5	5	5	5	5
6	6	6	6	6	6	6	6
7	7	7	7	7	7	7	7
8	8	8	8	8	8	8	8
9	9	9	9	9	9	9	9

⑥ **RAW SCORE**

0	0
1	1
2	2
3	3
4	4
5	5
6	6
7	7
8	8
9	9

Life Skills and Test Prep 4

Unit 6 Test Answer Sheet

① ______________________________

Last Name First Name Middle

② ______________________________

Teacher's Name

TEST

1 Ⓐ Ⓑ Ⓒ Ⓓ
2 Ⓐ Ⓑ Ⓒ Ⓓ
3 Ⓐ Ⓑ Ⓒ Ⓓ
4 Ⓐ Ⓑ Ⓒ Ⓓ
5 Ⓐ Ⓑ Ⓒ Ⓓ
6 Ⓐ Ⓑ Ⓒ Ⓓ
7 Ⓐ Ⓑ Ⓒ Ⓓ
8 Ⓐ Ⓑ Ⓒ Ⓓ
9 Ⓐ Ⓑ Ⓒ Ⓓ
10 Ⓐ Ⓑ Ⓒ Ⓓ
11 Ⓐ Ⓑ Ⓒ Ⓓ
12 Ⓐ Ⓑ Ⓒ Ⓓ
13 Ⓐ Ⓑ Ⓒ Ⓓ
14 Ⓐ Ⓑ Ⓒ Ⓓ
15 Ⓐ Ⓑ Ⓒ Ⓓ
16 Ⓐ Ⓑ Ⓒ Ⓓ
17 Ⓐ Ⓑ Ⓒ Ⓓ
18 Ⓐ Ⓑ Ⓒ Ⓓ
19 Ⓐ Ⓑ Ⓒ Ⓓ
20 Ⓐ Ⓑ Ⓒ Ⓓ

Directions for marking answers

- Use a No. 2 pencil. Do NOT use ink.
- Make dark marks and bubble in your answers completely.
- If you change an answer, erase your first mark completely.

Right

Ⓐ ● Ⓒ Ⓓ

Wrong

Ⓐ ⊗ Ⓒ Ⓓ

Ⓐ Ⓑ Ⓒ Ⓓ

③ **STUDENT IDENTIFICATION**

0	0	0	0	0	0	0	0	0
1	1	1	1	1	1	1	1	1
2	2	2	2	2	2	2	2	2
3	3	3	3	3	3	3	3	3
4	4	4	4	4	4	4	4	4
5	5	5	5	5	5	5	5	5
6	6	6	6	6	6	6	6	6
7	7	7	7	7	7	7	7	7
8	8	8	8	8	8	8	8	8
9	9	9	9	9	9	9	9	9

Is this your Social Security number?
Yes ◯ **No** ◯

④ **TEST DATE**

MM	D	D	Y	Y
Jan ◯	0	0	20	09
Feb ◯	1	1	20	10
Mar ◯	2	2	20	11
Apr ◯	3	3	20	12
May ◯		4	20	13
Jun ◯		5	20	14
Jul ◯		6	20	15
Aug ◯		7	20	16
Sep ◯		8	20	17
Oct ◯		9	20	18
Nov ◯				
Dec ◯				

⑤ **CLASS NUMBER**

0	0	0	0	0	0	0	0
1	1	1	1	1	1	1	1
2	2	2	2	2	2	2	2
3	3	3	3	3	3	3	3
4	4	4	4	4	4	4	4
5	5	5	5	5	5	5	5
6	6	6	6	6	6	6	6
7	7	7	7	7	7	7	7
8	8	8	8	8	8	8	8
9	9	9	9	9	9	9	9

⑥ **RAW SCORE**

0	0
1	1
2	2
3	3
4	4
5	5
6	6
7	7
8	8
9	9

Unit 7 Test Answer Sheet

① ______________________________
Last Name First Name Middle

② ______________________________
Teacher's Name

TEST

1 (A) (B) (C) (D)
2 (A) (B) (C) (D)
3 (A) (B) (C) (D)
4 (A) (B) (C) (D)
5 (A) (B) (C) (D)
6 (A) (B) (C) (D)
7 (A) (B) (C) (D)
8 (A) (B) (C) (D)
9 (A) (B) (C) (D)
10 (A) (B) (C) (D)
11 (A) (B) (C) (D)
12 (A) (B) (C) (D)
13 (A) (B) (C) (D)
14 (A) (B) (C) (D)
15 (A) (B) (C) (D)
16 (A) (B) (C) (D)
17 (A) (B) (C) (D)
18 (A) (B) (C) (D)
19 (A) (B) (C) (D)
20 (A) (B) (C) (D)

Directions for marking answers

- Use a No. 2 pencil. Do NOT use ink.
- Make dark marks and bubble in your answers completely.
- If you change an answer, erase your first mark completely.

Right
(A) (B) (C) (D)

Wrong
(A) (B) (C) (D)
(A) (B) (C) (D)

③ **STUDENT IDENTIFICATION**

0	0	0	0	0	0	0	0	0
1	1	1	1	1	1	1	1	1
2	2	2	2	2	2	2	2	2
3	3	3	3	3	3	3	3	3
4	4	4	4	4	4	4	4	4
5	5	5	5	5	5	5	5	5
6	6	6	6	6	6	6	6	6
7	7	7	7	7	7	7	7	7
8	8	8	8	8	8	8	8	8
9	9	9	9	9	9	9	9	9

Is this your Social Security number?
Yes ( ) **No** ( )

④ **TEST DATE**

MM		D	D	Y	Y
Jan	( )	0	0	20	09
Feb	( )	1	1	20	10
Mar	( )	2	2	20	11
Apr	( )	3	3	20	12
May	( )		4	20	13
Jun	( )		5	20	14
Jul	( )		6	20	15
Aug	( )		7	20	16
Sep	( )		8	20	17
Oct	( )		9	20	18
Nov	( )				
Dec	( )				

⑤ **CLASS NUMBER**

0	0	0	0	0	0	0	0
1	1	1	1	1	1	1	1
2	2	2	2	2	2	2	2
3	3	3	3	3	3	3	3
4	4	4	4	4	4	4	4
5	5	5	5	5	5	5	5
6	6	6	6	6	6	6	6
7	7	7	7	7	7	7	7
8	8	8	8	8	8	8	8
9	9	9	9	9	9	9	9

⑥ **RAW SCORE**

0	0
1	1
2	2
3	3
4	4
5	5
6	6
7	7
8	8
9	9

Life Skills and Test Prep 4
Unit 7 Test Answer Sheet

① ______________________________
Last Name First Name Middle

② ______________________________
Teacher's Name

TEST

1 Ⓐ Ⓑ Ⓒ Ⓓ
2 Ⓐ Ⓑ Ⓒ Ⓓ
3 Ⓐ Ⓑ Ⓒ Ⓓ
4 Ⓐ Ⓑ Ⓒ Ⓓ
5 Ⓐ Ⓑ Ⓒ Ⓓ
6 Ⓐ Ⓑ Ⓒ Ⓓ
7 Ⓐ Ⓑ Ⓒ Ⓓ
8 Ⓐ Ⓑ Ⓒ Ⓓ
9 Ⓐ Ⓑ Ⓒ Ⓓ
10 Ⓐ Ⓑ Ⓒ Ⓓ
11 Ⓐ Ⓑ Ⓒ Ⓓ
12 Ⓐ Ⓑ Ⓒ Ⓓ
13 Ⓐ Ⓑ Ⓒ Ⓓ
14 Ⓐ Ⓑ Ⓒ Ⓓ
15 Ⓐ Ⓑ Ⓒ Ⓓ
16 Ⓐ Ⓑ Ⓒ Ⓓ
17 Ⓐ Ⓑ Ⓒ Ⓓ
18 Ⓐ Ⓑ Ⓒ Ⓓ
19 Ⓐ Ⓑ Ⓒ Ⓓ
20 Ⓐ Ⓑ Ⓒ Ⓓ

Directions for marking answers

- Use a No. 2 pencil. Do NOT use ink.
- Make dark marks and bubble in your answers completely.
- If you change an answer, erase your first mark completely.

Right
Ⓐ Ⓑ Ⓒ Ⓓ

Wrong
Ⓐ Ⓑ Ⓒ Ⓓ
Ⓐ Ⓑ Ⓒ Ⓓ

③ **STUDENT IDENTIFICATION**

0	0	0	0	0	0	0	0	0
1	1	1	1	1	1	1	1	1
2	2	2	2	2	2	2	2	2
3	3	3	3	3	3	3	3	3
4	4	4	4	4	4	4	4	4
5	5	5	5	5	5	5	5	5
6	6	6	6	6	6	6	6	6
7	7	7	7	7	7	7	7	7
8	8	8	8	8	8	8	8	8
9	9	9	9	9	9	9	9	9

Is this your Social Security number?
Yes ◯ **No** ◯

④ **TEST DATE**

MM	D	D	Y	Y
Jan	0	0	20	09
Feb	1	1	20	10
Mar	2	2	20	11
Apr	3	3	20	12
May		4	20	13
Jun		5	20	14
Jul		6	20	15
Aug		7	20	16
Sep		8	20	17
Oct		9	20	18
Nov				
Dec				

⑤ **CLASS NUMBER**

0	0	0	0	0	0	0	0
1	1	1	1	1	1	1	1
2	2	2	2	2	2	2	2
3	3	3	3	3	3	3	3
4	4	4	4	4	4	4	4
5	5	5	5	5	5	5	5
6	6	6	6	6	6	6	6
7	7	7	7	7	7	7	7
8	8	8	8	8	8	8	8
9	9	9	9	9	9	9	9

⑥ **RAW SCORE**

0	0
1	1
2	2
3	3
4	4
5	5
6	6
7	7
8	8
9	9

Life Skills and Test Prep 4
Unit 8 Test Answer Sheet

① ____
Last Name First Name Middle

② ____
Teacher's Name

TEST

1 (A) (B) (C) (D)
2 (A) (B) (C) (D)
3 (A) (B) (C) (D)
4 (A) (B) (C) (D)
5 (A) (B) (C) (D)
6 (A) (B) (C) (D)
7 (A) (B) (C) (D)
8 (A) (B) (C) (D)
9 (A) (B) (C) (D)
10 (A) (B) (C) (D)
11 (A) (B) (C) (D)
12 (A) (B) (C) (D)
13 (A) (B) (C) (D)
14 (A) (B) (C) (D)
15 (A) (B) (C) (D)
16 (A) (B) (C) (D)
17 (A) (B) (C) (D)
18 (A) (B) (C) (D)
19 (A) (B) (C) (D)
20 (A) (B) (C) (D)

Directions for marking answers

- Use a No. 2 pencil. Do NOT use ink.
- Make dark marks and bubble in your answers completely.
- If you change an answer, erase your first mark completely.

Right
(A) (B) (C) (D)

Wrong
(A) (B) (C) (D)
(A) (B) (C) (D)

③ **STUDENT IDENTIFICATION**

0	0	0	0	0	0	0	0	0
1	1	1	1	1	1	1	1	1
2	2	2	2	2	2	2	2	2
3	3	3	3	3	3	3	3	3
4	4	4	4	4	4	4	4	4
5	5	5	5	5	5	5	5	5
6	6	6	6	6	6	6	6	6
7	7	7	7	7	7	7	7	7
8	8	8	8	8	8	8	8	8
9	9	9	9	9	9	9	9	9

Is this your Social Security number?
Yes ( ) **No** ( )

④ **TEST DATE**

MM	D	D	Y	Y
Jan	0	0	20	09
Feb	1	1	20	10
Mar	2	2	20	11
Apr	3	3	20	12
May		4	20	13
Jun		5	20	14
Jul		6	20	15
Aug		7	20	16
Sep		8	20	17
Oct		9	20	18
Nov				
Dec				

⑤ **CLASS NUMBER**

0	0	0	0	0	0	0	0
1	1	1	1	1	1	1	1
2	2	2	2	2	2	2	2
3	3	3	3	3	3	3	3
4	4	4	4	4	4	4	4
5	5	5	5	5	5	5	5
6	6	6	6	6	6	6	6
7	7	7	7	7	7	7	7
8	8	8	8	8	8	8	8
9	9	9	9	9	9	9	9

⑥ **RAW SCORE**

0	0
1	1
2	2
3	3
4	4
5	5
6	6
7	7
8	8
9	9

Life Skills and Test Prep 4

Unit 8 Test Answer Sheet

① ______________________________

Last Name First Name Middle

② ______________________________

Teacher's Name

TEST

1 Ⓐ Ⓑ Ⓒ Ⓓ
2 Ⓐ Ⓑ Ⓒ Ⓓ
3 Ⓐ Ⓑ Ⓒ Ⓓ
4 Ⓐ Ⓑ Ⓒ Ⓓ
5 Ⓐ Ⓑ Ⓒ Ⓓ
6 Ⓐ Ⓑ Ⓒ Ⓓ
7 Ⓐ Ⓑ Ⓒ Ⓓ
8 Ⓐ Ⓑ Ⓒ Ⓓ
9 Ⓐ Ⓑ Ⓒ Ⓓ
10 Ⓐ Ⓑ Ⓒ Ⓓ
11 Ⓐ Ⓑ Ⓒ Ⓓ
12 Ⓐ Ⓑ Ⓒ Ⓓ
13 Ⓐ Ⓑ Ⓒ Ⓓ
14 Ⓐ Ⓑ Ⓒ Ⓓ
15 Ⓐ Ⓑ Ⓒ Ⓓ
16 Ⓐ Ⓑ Ⓒ Ⓓ
17 Ⓐ Ⓑ Ⓒ Ⓓ
18 Ⓐ Ⓑ Ⓒ Ⓓ
19 Ⓐ Ⓑ Ⓒ Ⓓ
20 Ⓐ Ⓑ Ⓒ Ⓓ

Directions for marking answers

- Use a No. 2 pencil. Do NOT use ink.
- Make dark marks and bubble in your answers completely.
- If you change an answer, erase your first mark completely.

Right

Ⓐ Ⓑ Ⓒ Ⓓ

Wrong

Ⓐ Ⓑ Ⓒ Ⓓ

Ⓐ Ⓑ Ⓒ Ⓓ

③ **STUDENT IDENTIFICATION**

0	0	0	0	0	0	0	0	0
1	1	1	1	1	1	1	1	1
2	2	2	2	2	2	2	2	2
3	3	3	3	3	3	3	3	3
4	4	4	4	4	4	4	4	4
5	5	5	5	5	5	5	5	5
6	6	6	6	6	6	6	6	6
7	7	7	7	7	7	7	7	7
8	8	8	8	8	8	8	8	8
9	9	9	9	9	9	9	9	9

Is this your Social Security number?

Yes ◯ **No** ◯

④ **TEST DATE**

MM		D	D	Y	Y
Jan	◯	0	0	20	09
Feb	◯	1	1	20	10
Mar	◯	2	2	20	11
Apr	◯	3	3	20	12
May	◯		4	20	13
Jun	◯		5	20	14
Jul	◯		6	20	15
Aug	◯		7	20	16
Sep	◯		8	20	17
Oct	◯		9	20	18
Nov	◯				
Dec	◯				

⑤ **CLASS NUMBER**

0	0	0	0	0	0	0	0
1	1	1	1	1	1	1	1
2	2	2	2	2	2	2	2
3	3	3	3	3	3	3	3
4	4	4	4	4	4	4	4
5	5	5	5	5	5	5	5
6	6	6	6	6	6	6	6
7	7	7	7	7	7	7	7
8	8	8	8	8	8	8	8
9	9	9	9	9	9	9	9

⑥ **RAW SCORE**

0	0
1	1
2	2
3	3
4	4
5	5
6	6
7	7
8	8
9	9

Unit 9 Test Answer Sheet

① ______________________________

Last Name First Name Middle

② ______________________________

Teacher's Name

TEST

1 (A) (B) (C) (D)
2 (A) (B) (C) (D)
3 (A) (B) (C) (D)
4 (A) (B) (C) (D)
5 (A) (B) (C) (D)
6 (A) (B) (C) (D)
7 (A) (B) (C) (D)
8 (A) (B) (C) (D)
9 (A) (B) (C) (D)
10 (A) (B) (C) (D)
11 (A) (B) (C) (D)
12 (A) (B) (C) (D)
13 (A) (B) (C) (D)
14 (A) (B) (C) (D)
15 (A) (B) (C) (D)
16 (A) (B) (C) (D)
17 (A) (B) (C) (D)
18 (A) (B) (C) (D)
19 (A) (B) (C) (D)
20 (A) (B) (C) (D)

Directions for marking answers

- Use a No. 2 pencil. Do NOT use ink.
- Make dark marks and bubble in your answers completely.
- If you change an answer, erase your first mark completely.

Right

(A) (B) (C) (D)

Wrong

(A) (B) (C) (D)
(A) (B) (C) (D)

③ **STUDENT IDENTIFICATION**

0	0	0	0	0	0	0	0	0
1	1	1	1	1	1	1	1	1
2	2	2	2	2	2	2	2	2
3	3	3	3	3	3	3	3	3
4	4	4	4	4	4	4	4	4
5	5	5	5	5	5	5	5	5
6	6	6	6	6	6	6	6	6
7	7	7	7	7	7	7	7	7
8	8	8	8	8	8	8	8	8
9	9	9	9	9	9	9	9	9

Is this your Social Security number?

Yes ( ) **No** ( )

④ **TEST DATE**

MM		D	D	Y	Y
Jan	( )	0	0	20	09
Feb	( )	1	1	20	10
Mar	( )	2	2	20	11
Apr	( )	3	3	20	12
May	( )		4	20	13
Jun	( )		5	20	14
Jul	( )		6	20	15
Aug	( )		7	20	16
Sep	( )		8	20	17
Oct	( )		9	20	18
Nov	( )				
Dec	( )				

⑤ **CLASS NUMBER**

0	0	0	0	0	0	0	0
1	1	1	1	1	1	1	1
2	2	2	2	2	2	2	2
3	3	3	3	3	3	3	3
4	4	4	4	4	4	4	4
5	5	5	5	5	5	5	5
6	6	6	6	6	6	6	6
7	7	7	7	7	7	7	7
8	8	8	8	8	8	8	8
9	9	9	9	9	9	9	9

⑥ **RAW SCORE**

0	0
1	1
2	2
3	3
4	4
5	5
6	6
7	7
8	8
9	9

Life Skills and Test Prep 4
Unit 9 Test Answer Sheet

① ______________________________

Last Name First Name Middle

② ______________________________

Teacher's Name

TEST

1 Ⓐ Ⓑ Ⓒ Ⓓ
2 Ⓐ Ⓑ Ⓒ Ⓓ
3 Ⓐ Ⓑ Ⓒ Ⓓ
4 Ⓐ Ⓑ Ⓒ Ⓓ
5 Ⓐ Ⓑ Ⓒ Ⓓ
6 Ⓐ Ⓑ Ⓒ Ⓓ
7 Ⓐ Ⓑ Ⓒ Ⓓ
8 Ⓐ Ⓑ Ⓒ Ⓓ
9 Ⓐ Ⓑ Ⓒ Ⓓ
10 Ⓐ Ⓑ Ⓒ Ⓓ
11 Ⓐ Ⓑ Ⓒ Ⓓ
12 Ⓐ Ⓑ Ⓒ Ⓓ
13 Ⓐ Ⓑ Ⓒ Ⓓ
14 Ⓐ Ⓑ Ⓒ Ⓓ
15 Ⓐ Ⓑ Ⓒ Ⓓ
16 Ⓐ Ⓑ Ⓒ Ⓓ
17 Ⓐ Ⓑ Ⓒ Ⓓ
18 Ⓐ Ⓑ Ⓒ Ⓓ
19 Ⓐ Ⓑ Ⓒ Ⓓ
20 Ⓐ Ⓑ Ⓒ Ⓓ

Directions for marking answers

- Use a No. 2 pencil. Do NOT use ink.
- Make dark marks and bubble in your answers completely.
- If you change an answer, erase your first mark completely.

Right

Ⓐ Ⓑ Ⓒ Ⓓ

Wrong

Ⓐ Ⓑ Ⓒ Ⓓ

Ⓐ Ⓑ Ⓒ Ⓓ

③ **STUDENT IDENTIFICATION**

0	0	0	0	0	0	0	0	0
1	1	1	1	1	1	1	1	1
2	2	2	2	2	2	2	2	2
3	3	3	3	3	3	3	3	3
4	4	4	4	4	4	4	4	4
5	5	5	5	5	5	5	5	5
6	6	6	6	6	6	6	6	6
7	7	7	7	7	7	7	7	7
8	8	8	8	8	8	8	8	8
9	9	9	9	9	9	9	9	9

Is this your Social Security number?
Yes ◯ **No** ◯

④ **TEST DATE**

MM		D	D	Y	Y
Jan	◯	0	0	20	09
Feb	◯	1	1	20	10
Mar	◯	2	2	20	11
Apr	◯	3	3	20	12
May	◯		4	20	13
Jun	◯		5	20	14
Jul	◯		6	20	15
Aug	◯		7	20	16
Sep	◯		8	20	17
Oct	◯		9	20	18
Nov	◯				
Dec	◯				

⑤ **CLASS NUMBER**

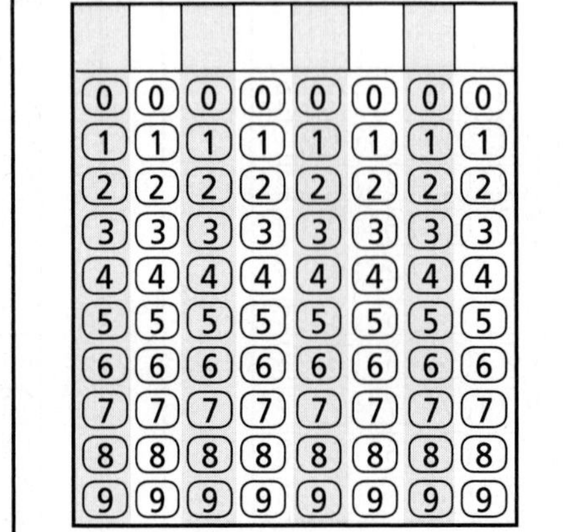

0	0	0	0	0	0	0	0
1	1	1	1	1	1	1	1
2	2	2	2	2	2	2	2
3	3	3	3	3	3	3	3
4	4	4	4	4	4	4	4
5	5	5	5	5	5	5	5
6	6	6	6	6	6	6	6
7	7	7	7	7	7	7	7
8	8	8	8	8	8	8	8
9	9	9	9	9	9	9	9

⑥ **RAW SCORE**

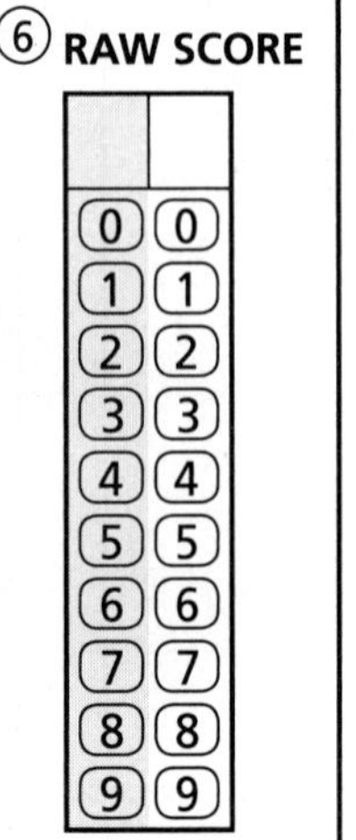

0	0
1	1
2	2
3	3
4	4
5	5
6	6
7	7
8	8
9	9

Life Skills and Test Prep 4

Unit 10 Test Answer Sheet

① ____

Last Name First Name Middle

② ____

Teacher's Name

TEST

1 (A) (B) (C) (D)
2 (A) (B) (C) (D)
3 (A) (B) (C) (D)
4 (A) (B) (C) (D)
5 (A) (B) (C) (D)
6 (A) (B) (C) (D)
7 (A) (B) (C) (D)
8 (A) (B) (C) (D)
9 (A) (B) (C) (D)
10 (A) (B) (C) (D)
11 (A) (B) (C) (D)
12 (A) (B) (C) (D)
13 (A) (B) (C) (D)
14 (A) (B) (C) (D)
15 (A) (B) (C) (D)
16 (A) (B) (C) (D)
17 (A) (B) (C) (D)
18 (A) (B) (C) (D)
19 (A) (B) (C) (D)
20 (A) (B) (C) (D)

Directions for marking answers

- Use a No. 2 pencil. Do NOT use ink.
- Make dark marks and bubble in your answers completely.
- If you change an answer, erase your first mark completely.

Right

(A) (B) (C) (D)

Wrong

(A) (B) (C) (D)

(A) (B) (C) (D)

③ **STUDENT IDENTIFICATION**

0	0	0	0	0	0	0	0	0
1	1	1	1	1	1	1	1	1
2	2	2	2	2	2	2	2	2
3	3	3	3	3	3	3	3	3
4	4	4	4	4	4	4	4	4
5	5	5	5	5	5	5	5	5
6	6	6	6	6	6	6	6	6
7	7	7	7	7	7	7	7	7
8	8	8	8	8	8	8	8	8
9	9	9	9	9	9	9	9	9

Is this your Social Security number?
Yes ( ) **No** ( )

④ **TEST DATE**

MM	D	D	Y	Y
Jan	0	0	20	09
Feb	1	1	20	10
Mar	2	2	20	11
Apr	3	3	20	12
May		4	20	13
Jun		5	20	14
Jul		6	20	15
Aug		7	20	16
Sep		8	20	17
Oct		9	20	18
Nov				
Dec				

⑤ **CLASS NUMBER**

0	0	0	0	0	0	0	0
1	1	1	1	1	1	1	1
2	2	2	2	2	2	2	2
3	3	3	3	3	3	3	3
4	4	4	4	4	4	4	4
5	5	5	5	5	5	5	5
6	6	6	6	6	6	6	6
7	7	7	7	7	7	7	7
8	8	8	8	8	8	8	8
9	9	9	9	9	9	9	9

⑥ **RAW SCORE**

0	0
1	1
2	2
3	3
4	4
5	5
6	6
7	7
8	8
9	9

Life Skills and Test Prep 4

Unit 10 Test Answer Sheet

① ______________________________________

Last Name First Name Middle

② ______________________________________

Teacher's Name

TEST

1 (A) (B) (C) (D)
2 (A) (B) (C) (D)
3 (A) (B) (C) (D)
4 (A) (B) (C) (D)
5 (A) (B) (C) (D)
6 (A) (B) (C) (D)
7 (A) (B) (C) (D)
8 (A) (B) (C) (D)
9 (A) (B) (C) (D)
10 (A) (B) (C) (D)
11 (A) (B) (C) (D)
12 (A) (B) (C) (D)
13 (A) (B) (C) (D)
14 (A) (B) (C) (D)
15 (A) (B) (C) (D)
16 (A) (B) (C) (D)
17 (A) (B) (C) (D)
18 (A) (B) (C) (D)
19 (A) (B) (C) (D)
20 (A) (B) (C) (D)

Directions for marking answers

- Use a No. 2 pencil. Do NOT use ink.
- Make dark marks and bubble in your answers completely.
- If you change an answer, erase your first mark completely.

Right

(A) (B) (C) (D)

Wrong

(A) (B) (C) (D)
(A) (B) (C) (D)

③ **STUDENT IDENTIFICATION**

0	0	0	0	0	0	0	0	0
1	1	1	1	1	1	1	1	1
2	2	2	2	2	2	2	2	2
3	3	3	3	3	3	3	3	3
4	4	4	4	4	4	4	4	4
5	5	5	5	5	5	5	5	5
6	6	6	6	6	6	6	6	6
7	7	7	7	7	7	7	7	7
8	8	8	8	8	8	8	8	8
9	9	9	9	9	9	9	9	9

Is this your Social Security number?

Yes ◯ **No** ◯

④ **TEST DATE**

MM		D	D	Y	Y
Jan	◯	0	0	20	09
Feb	◯	1	1	20	10
Mar	◯	2	2	20	11
Apr	◯	3	3	20	12
May	◯		4	20	13
Jun	◯		5	20	14
Jul	◯		6	20	15
Aug	◯		7	20	16
Sep	◯		8	20	17
Oct	◯		9	20	18
Nov	◯				
Dec	◯				

⑤ **CLASS NUMBER**

0	0	0	0	0	0	0	0
1	1	1	1	1	1	1	1
2	2	2	2	2	2	2	2
3	3	3	3	3	3	3	3
4	4	4	4	4	4	4	4
5	5	5	5	5	5	5	5
6	6	6	6	6	6	6	6
7	7	7	7	7	7	7	7
8	8	8	8	8	8	8	8
9	9	9	9	9	9	9	9

⑥ **RAW SCORE**

0	0
1	1
2	2
3	3
4	4
5	5
6	6
7	7
8	8
9	9

Life Skills and Test Prep 4

Unit 11 Test Answer Sheet

① ______________________________

Last Name First Name Middle

② ______________________________

Teacher's Name

TEST

1 Ⓐ Ⓑ Ⓒ Ⓓ
2 Ⓐ Ⓑ Ⓒ Ⓓ
3 Ⓐ Ⓑ Ⓒ Ⓓ
4 Ⓐ Ⓑ Ⓒ Ⓓ
5 Ⓐ Ⓑ Ⓒ Ⓓ
6 Ⓐ Ⓑ Ⓒ Ⓓ
7 Ⓐ Ⓑ Ⓒ Ⓓ
8 Ⓐ Ⓑ Ⓒ Ⓓ
9 Ⓐ Ⓑ Ⓒ Ⓓ
10 Ⓐ Ⓑ Ⓒ Ⓓ
11 Ⓐ Ⓑ Ⓒ Ⓓ
12 Ⓐ Ⓑ Ⓒ Ⓓ
13 Ⓐ Ⓑ Ⓒ Ⓓ
14 Ⓐ Ⓑ Ⓒ Ⓓ
15 Ⓐ Ⓑ Ⓒ Ⓓ
16 Ⓐ Ⓑ Ⓒ Ⓓ
17 Ⓐ Ⓑ Ⓒ Ⓓ
18 Ⓐ Ⓑ Ⓒ Ⓓ
19 Ⓐ Ⓑ Ⓒ Ⓓ
20 Ⓐ Ⓑ Ⓒ Ⓓ

Directions for marking answers

- Use a No. 2 pencil. Do NOT use ink.
- Make dark marks and bubble in your answers completely.
- If you change an answer, erase your first mark completely.

Right

Ⓐ ● Ⓒ Ⓓ

Wrong

Ⓐ ⊗ Ⓒ Ⓓ

Ⓐ Ⓑ Ⓒ Ⓓ

③ **STUDENT IDENTIFICATION**

0	0	0	0	0	0	0	0	0
1	1	1	1	1	1	1	1	1
2	2	2	2	2	2	2	2	2
3	3	3	3	3	3	3	3	3
4	4	4	4	4	4	4	4	4
5	5	5	5	5	5	5	5	5
6	6	6	6	6	6	6	6	6
7	7	7	7	7	7	7	7	7
8	8	8	8	8	8	8	8	8
9	9	9	9	9	9	9	9	9

Is this your Social Security number?
Yes ◯ **No** ◯

④ **TEST DATE**

MM	D	D	Y	Y
Jan ◯	0	0	20	09
Feb ◯	1	1	20	10
Mar ◯	2	2	20	11
Apr ◯	3	3	20	12
May ◯		4	20	13
Jun ◯		5	20	14
Jul ◯		6	20	15
Aug ◯		7	20	16
Sep ◯		8	20	17
Oct ◯		9	20	18
Nov ◯				
Dec ◯				

⑤ **CLASS NUMBER**

0	0	0	0	0	0	0	0
1	1	1	1	1	1	1	1
2	2	2	2	2	2	2	2
3	3	3	3	3	3	3	3
4	4	4	4	4	4	4	4
5	5	5	5	5	5	5	5
6	6	6	6	6	6	6	6
7	7	7	7	7	7	7	7
8	8	8	8	8	8	8	8
9	9	9	9	9	9	9	9

⑥ **RAW SCORE**

0	0
1	1
2	2
3	3
4	4
5	5
6	6
7	7
8	8
9	9

Unit 11 Test Answer Sheet

① ______________________________

Last Name First Name Middle

② ______________________________

Teacher's Name

TEST

1 (A) (B) (C) (D)
2 (A) (B) (C) (D)
3 (A) (B) (C) (D)
4 (A) (B) (C) (D)
5 (A) (B) (C) (D)
6 (A) (B) (C) (D)
7 (A) (B) (C) (D)
8 (A) (B) (C) (D)
9 (A) (B) (C) (D)
10 (A) (B) (C) (D)
11 (A) (B) (C) (D)
12 (A) (B) (C) (D)
13 (A) (B) (C) (D)
14 (A) (B) (C) (D)
15 (A) (B) (C) (D)
16 (A) (B) (C) (D)
17 (A) (B) (C) (D)
18 (A) (B) (C) (D)
19 (A) (B) (C) (D)
20 (A) (B) (C) (D)

Directions for marking answers

- Use a No. 2 pencil. Do NOT use ink.
- Make dark marks and bubble in your answers completely.
- If you change an answer, erase your first mark completely.

Right

(A) (B) (C) (D)

Wrong

(A) (B) (C) (D)

(A) (B) (C) (D)

③ **STUDENT IDENTIFICATION**

0	0	0	0	0	0	0	0	0
1	1	1	1	1	1	1	1	1
2	2	2	2	2	2	2	2	2
3	3	3	3	3	3	3	3	3
4	4	4	4	4	4	4	4	4
5	5	5	5	5	5	5	5	5
6	6	6	6	6	6	6	6	6
7	7	7	7	7	7	7	7	7
8	8	8	8	8	8	8	8	8
9	9	9	9	9	9	9	9	9

Is this your Social Security number?

Yes ( ) **No** ( )

④ **TEST DATE**

MM		D	D	Y	Y
Jan	( )	0	0	20	09
Feb	( )	1	1	20	10
Mar	( )	2	2	20	11
Apr	( )	3	3	20	12
May	( )		4	20	13
Jun	( )		5	20	14
Jul	( )		6	20	15
Aug	( )		7	20	16
Sep	( )		8	20	17
Oct	( )		9	20	18
Nov	( )				
Dec	( )				

⑤ **CLASS NUMBER**

0	0	0	0	0	0	0	0
1	1	1	1	1	1	1	1
2	2	2	2	2	2	2	2
3	3	3	3	3	3	3	3
4	4	4	4	4	4	4	4
5	5	5	5	5	5	5	5
6	6	6	6	6	6	6	6
7	7	7	7	7	7	7	7
8	8	8	8	8	8	8	8
9	9	9	9	9	9	9	9

⑥ **RAW SCORE**

0	0
1	1
2	2
3	3
4	4
5	5
6	6
7	7
8	8
9	9

Life Skills and Test Prep 4

Unit 12 Test Answer Sheet

① ______________________________________

Last Name First Name Middle

② ______________________________________

Teacher's Name

TEST

1 (A) (B) (C) (D)
2 (A) (B) (C) (D)
3 (A) (B) (C) (D)
4 (A) (B) (C) (D)
5 (A) (B) (C) (D)
6 (A) (B) (C) (D)
7 (A) (B) (C) (D)
8 (A) (B) (C) (D)
9 (A) (B) (C) (D)
10 (A) (B) (C) (D)
11 (A) (B) (C) (D)
12 (A) (B) (C) (D)
13 (A) (B) (C) (D)
14 (A) (B) (C) (D)
15 (A) (B) (C) (D)
16 (A) (B) (C) (D)
17 (A) (B) (C) (D)
18 (A) (B) (C) (D)
19 (A) (B) (C) (D)
20 (A) (B) (C) (D)

Directions for marking answers

- Use a No. 2 pencil. Do NOT use ink.
- Make dark marks and bubble in your answers completely.
- If you change an answer, erase your first mark completely.

Right

(A) (B) (C) (D)

Wrong

(A) (B) (C) (D)
(A) (B) (C) (D)

③ **STUDENT IDENTIFICATION**

0	0	0	0	0	0	0	0	0
1	1	1	1	1	1	1	1	1
2	2	2	2	2	2	2	2	2
3	3	3	3	3	3	3	3	3
4	4	4	4	4	4	4	4	4
5	5	5	5	5	5	5	5	5
6	6	6	6	6	6	6	6	6
7	7	7	7	7	7	7	7	7
8	8	8	8	8	8	8	8	8
9	9	9	9	9	9	9	9	9

Is this your Social Security number?

Yes ◯ **No** ◯

④ **TEST DATE**

MM	D	D	Y	Y
Jan	0	0	20	09
Feb	1	1	20	10
Mar	2	2	20	11
Apr	3	3	20	12
May		4	20	13
Jun		5	20	14
Jul		6	20	15
Aug		7	20	16
Sep		8	20	17
Oct		9	20	18
Nov				
Dec				

⑤ **CLASS NUMBER**

0	0	0	0	0	0	0	0
1	1	1	1	1	1	1	1
2	2	2	2	2	2	2	2
3	3	3	3	3	3	3	3
4	4	4	4	4	4	4	4
5	5	5	5	5	5	5	5
6	6	6	6	6	6	6	6
7	7	7	7	7	7	7	7
8	8	8	8	8	8	8	8
9	9	9	9	9	9	9	9

⑥ **RAW SCORE**

0	0
1	1
2	2
3	3
4	4
5	5
6	6
7	7
8	8
9	9

Life Skills and Test Prep 4

Unit 12 Test Answer Sheet

① ______________________________

Last Name First Name Middle

② ______________________________

Teacher's Name

TEST

1	A	B	C	D
2	A	B	C	D
3	A	B	C	D
4	A	B	C	D
5	A	B	C	D
6	A	B	C	D
7	A	B	C	D
8	A	B	C	D
9	A	B	C	D
10	A	B	C	D
11	A	B	C	D
12	A	B	C	D
13	A	B	C	D
14	A	B	C	D
15	A	B	C	D
16	A	B	C	D
17	A	B	C	D
18	A	B	C	D
19	A	B	C	D
20	A	B	C	D

Directions for marking answers

- Use a No. 2 pencil. Do NOT use ink.
- Make dark marks and bubble in your answers completely.
- If you change an answer, erase your first mark completely.

Right

A B C D

Wrong

A B C D

A B C D

③ **STUDENT IDENTIFICATION**

0	0	0	0	0	0	0	0	0
1	1	1	1	1	1	1	1	1
2	2	2	2	2	2	2	2	2
3	3	3	3	3	3	3	3	3
4	4	4	4	4	4	4	4	4
5	5	5	5	5	5	5	5	5
6	6	6	6	6	6	6	6	6
7	7	7	7	7	7	7	7	7
8	8	8	8	8	8	8	8	8
9	9	9	9	9	9	9	9	9

Is this your Social Security number?

Yes ☐ **No** ☐

④ **TEST DATE**

MM		D	D	Y	Y
Jan	☐	0	0	20	09
Feb	☐	1	1	20	10
Mar	☐	2	2	20	11
Apr	☐	3	3	20	12
May	☐		4	20	13
Jun	☐		5	20	14
Jul	☐		6	20	15
Aug	☐		7	20	16
Sep	☐		8	20	17
Oct	☐		9	20	18
Nov	☐				
Dec	☐				

⑤ **CLASS NUMBER**

0	0	0	0	0	0	0	0
1	1	1	1	1	1	1	1
2	2	2	2	2	2	2	2
3	3	3	3	3	3	3	3
4	4	4	4	4	4	4	4
5	5	5	5	5	5	5	5
6	6	6	6	6	6	6	6
7	7	7	7	7	7	7	7
8	8	8	8	8	8	8	8
9	9	9	9	9	9	9	9

⑥ **RAW SCORE**

0	0
1	1
2	2
3	3
4	4
5	5
6	6
7	7
8	8
9	9